Heroin's Puppet

– Amy (and her disease)

**The Rehab Journals of
Amelia F. W. Caruso
(1989–2009)**

**Story by
Melissa M. Weiksnar**

Amelibro Press

Published by Amelibro Press,
P.O. Box 251
Carlisle, MA 01741

www.amelibro.com

www.heroinspuppet.com

Library of Congress Control Number: 2012912095
ISBN: 978-0-9854787-0-4

Printed in the United States of America
The Troy Book Makers • www.thetroybookmakers.com

Cover photo by Gallery Portraits

Book design by Laurel Lloyd

To Amy

And to my husband, son, and first daughter

And everyone else who has been touched by addiction

"If we can keep at least one kid from going down the wrong path, one kid from not pursuing their dreams, then Amy's death will not be in vain."

Melissa
January 23, 2010

*Words that were in my head upon waking, **not** part of a dream*

Last Journal Entry

12-21-09

Moved to the "Circle Center" today with my roomie Claire. Lots of cool people here, but I was getting so anxious and depressed worrying about making friends.

I'm starting to realize just how sick I am. I read a pamphlet about self-acceptance from NA that read "Because we could not accept ourselves, we expected to be rejected by others. We would not allow anyone to get close to us for fear that if they really knew us, they would also hate us".

I'm terrified of rejection because I despise myself so much. My whole life I've been trying to be or act like someone else, anyone else. Why can't I just be?

My disease is controlling 90% of the thoughts that are going through my head. It tells me that I shouldn't be here. I won't fit in. Everyone hates me. I'll never beat the cravings.

It tells me that I can't recover without reaching a rock bottom. That jail might be the turning point that sets me straight. It has me scheming about ways to make money like selling my body, dating my drug dealer, stripping, robbing houses, selling back my textbooks and other belongings. It tells me I have a whole new world of drug addiction to experience before I can really make an effort to get clean. It assures me that relapses are part of recovery.

My disease pounds self loathing and insecurity into my mind. It perpetually reminds me that I have a big nose, I'm getting fat, I'm awkward and weird, I'm never going to make it in the world.

Worst of all, it tries to convince me that I don't have a disease but am simply going through a phase. It tells me that anyone who tries heroin will become addicted, so how can I be singled out as one of these addicts. It tells me I managed to handle all my drug use before, so why can't it work with heroin?

COME ON AMY, JUST INDULGE AND PICK UP ONE MORE TIME.

No! I've noticed my thoughts are very negative lately. I've been fantasizing about overdosing for a quick, painless death and telling myself I'd be doing everyone a favor (including myself).

I'm sick.

I'm weak.

Need Help.

But do I really want it?

— Amy (and her disease)

Partial List of People in this Story

Professional Help (key players, in order of appearance)

Ms. Firther, Licensed Clinical Social Worker (LICSW), Amy's therapist, ninth through tenth grade

Mrs. Guicona, LICSW, Amy's high school guidance counselor

Dr. Sporsy, Ph.D., Melissa's psychologist, February 2004 through May 2007

Dr. Loftad, M.D., Amy's psychiatrist, ninth through tenth grade

Dr. Hischolor, Ph.D., our first daughter's high school counselor

Dr. Pedreia, M.D., Amy's pediatrician

Dr. Erchild, M.D., Amy's Emergency Room psychiatrist at City Pediatrics Hospital, November 2004

Dr. Notting, M.D., Amy's psychiatrist at the holding hospital, November 2004

Ms. Sparrow, LICSW, social worker at the holding hospital, November 2004

Dr. Boyd, M.D., psychiatrist neighbor

Dr. Adderoth, M.D., Amy's psychopharmacologist, tenth grade through college

Dr. DeSantos, Ph.D., Amy's psychologist, tenth grade through college

Mrs. Ladaco, Licensed Alcohol and Drug Abuse Counselor, January 2005 through January 2006

Dr. Herowitz, M.D., consulting psychiatrist to family, August 2006 through April 2007

Mr. Coolwater, psychotherapist and substance abuse counselor

Mr. Longwood, Clinical Social Worker/Therapist, LICSW, leader of "didactic" group

Dr. Subone, M.D., Amy's Suboxone-prescribing psychiatrist near St. Louis University (SLU)

Dr. Buprine, M.D., Amy's local Suboxone-prescribing psychiatrist

Mr. Goodruco, Amy's substance abuse counselor near Boston College (BC)

Ms. Decelle, Amy's counselor in Triangle Center Detox

Mr. Robichaud, Amy's counselor in Rhombus rehab

Ms. Underwood, Amy's counselor in Circle Center transitional housing

Amy's Friends

Byron, close friend from middle school and pallbearer

Lily, best friend late middle school and ninth grade

Audrey, best friend ninth through eleventh grade at Blessed Virgin Mary Preparatory (BVMP)

Nancy, BVMP classmate tenth through twelfth grade

Liam, slightly older boyfriend, end of tenth grade

Chauncey, older boyfriend, late eleventh grade

Calvin, older boyfriend, end of eleventh grade

Liza, younger friend during eleventh grade

Maurann, close friend, twelfth grade at BVMP

Lonny, younger boyfriend, twelfth grade

Sherryl, close friend from ninth grade on

Tanisha, first year roommate at SLU

Oliver, older boyfriend, second semester college through mid-December 2009

Patrick, SLU friend whom Amy convinced to change his major to nursing

Ramona and Sandra, apartment mates at BC

Melissa's Friends

Corinne, friend present at our first two children's births, and her husband Frank, our son's godfather

Trina, a neighbor, mom, and school nurse

Meyer, former boss, and Giuliana, his wife, who lost their son in a traffic accident

Gail, nursing professor and her nurse husband George

Tara, best friend since childhood

Isabel, a friend living in Britain

Lois, former colleague

Brett, former colleague, and his wife, Risa

Gino, former colleague

Contents

Introduction

On Monday, November 16th, 2009, my twenty-year-old daughter, Amy, admitted to me—in the presence of her drug counselor—that she was a heroin addict and wanted to go into treatment. I was shocked. While I was expecting a difficult meeting, I never imagined I would hear these words from my daughter.

Amid our myriad conversations in the days that followed, Amy and I talked about how perhaps one positive outcome of the journey ahead could be a book to complement the two books that her pediatrician had recommended—*Beautiful Boy* by father David Sheff, and *Tweak* by son Nic Sheff, who struggled with multiple addictions. We thought we could tell a mother/daughter story, with heroin as the main drug of choice, in a family where the parents never used illegal drugs and had been married almost thirty years. I looked forward in hope to this collaboration.

On Saturday, December 26th, 2009, my husband, daughter (age twenty-four), and I were driving to visit my folks for the Christmas holiday. We had finished the audio recording of *Beautiful Boy* and were listening to a particularly graphic passage in *Tweak* about injecting when our son (age twenty-five) called my cell phone at 4:36 p.m. Amy's residential treatment house had called him as her designated emergency contact: She had been rushed, unconscious, to the hospital by ambulance. She would be pronounced dead at 6:00 p.m.

I hope many audiences can learn from this story. Adolescents, especially girls, may relate to the raw, agonizing feelings in Amy's journals and pursue safer ways to deal with peer pressure and stress. Clinicians have a six-year "case study" to analyze for effective and ineffective actions, in hopes of increasing their clinical proficiency. Parents and educators may learn new warning signs that will encourage them to point someone in trouble toward finding the help they need, and to ask hard questions about the caliber of care. Those with loved ones going through detoxification (detox), rehabilitation (rehab), or subsequent programs may now be prompted to ask the questions I never knew to ask. And those who have lost their addict may be comforted by common threads from our grief journey. Please pick and choose the sections most relevant to you.

Some mention is also made of the larger context of addiction. To adapt a well-known saying, it takes a village to enable a child, and I've learned how clueless I was in so many areas. The day-to-day stress of raising an adolescent is formidable. Add the specter of substance abuse and/or co-occurring mental health issues (including anxiety, depression, trauma, and low self-esteem) and the challenges can feel overwhelming, even when receiving help. Sadly, enough of the right resources are sorely lacking or inaccessible. Perhaps that gap will inspire some readers to "plug in" along the substance abuse prevention and treatment spectrum.

The intent of this book is to learn from Amy's complex tragedy, and not to "beat up" anyone. But to use a plane crash parallel—and I lost a close relative to one in 1992—could the outcome have been prevented? With aviation, you'd ask: How much was due to aircraft design, weather, maintenance issues, pilot judgment, air traffic control directives, or terrorism? Here I question how much was due to my daughter's DNA, her environments, her choices, the care she received, the company she kept, and the geopolitical terror of plentiful, cheap heroin? Using the analogy of a plane crash, Amy's rehab journals are the closest thing we have to a "black box" that explain what she was saying to herself in the cockpit, and her medical records are the "flight data recorder."

In writing this book, I used source material from the daily diary I've kept since age ten, thematic journals since my teens, and the copious notes I tend to take; I did not have to "recreate" memories. I've organized the story primarily by academic year, reflecting the rhythm of Amy's high school and college life, and my work as a teacher. I've tried to be as comprehensive as possible, referencing my notes, contemporaneous diaries, letters, texts, and documents. Except for public figures or published authors, and my family members, I've changed the names of all people (and, in some cases, identifying details) and most places. While Amy did keep extensive journals throughout middle and high school, the scope of this book does not include those entries. I feel that the sooner this book is available, imperfect as it may be, the sooner it can potentially help others.

Also, I write as a mother. My training is in economics, engineering, and business, and I have no professional education in psychology or substance abuse treatment. I share experience and offer opinions, but I am providing neither advice nor recommendations.

Amy had a delightful side and a huge, good heart that endeared her to almost everyone, even when she was "pushing your buttons." Very few people knew her darker side. She was a thrill seeker, risk taker, and manipulator, in the best and worst ways. She struggled to own up to her positive potential, as if it scared her. The best of Amy escalated with the worst of Amy until her double life came crashing down, as is often the case with addiction.

Finally, everyone grieves differently, and writing helps me. Telling Amy's story is a sacred and solemn task, as I'm sure she never imagined her rehab journals would be read by others, much less published. Amy and I should have written this book together, and I take very seriously what one of the priests at Boston College told me: "You are Amy's voice now." I hope I have done her justice. And while my husband, son, and first daughter have patiently supported this work, they respectfully preferred to remain in the periphery of the story.

Melissa Weiksnar
August 2010

In the second term I think I have improved in many ways I [met] all the goals I set for myself in November so I am proud of myself I decided that I really wanted to show some improvement from the first to the 2nd term and I worked hard, so I did. I did the absolute hardest I could do, worked the hardest I could work,

One
The Early Years:
school = the rules aren't for me

My husband and I never touched illegal drugs, not even one joint. We are very moderate consumers of alcohol. When a doctor asks me how much I drink, I usually quip "not enough." When we decided to have children, we thought we'd be dealing them a pretty decent gene pool. Addiction had not been an issue in our immediate families of origin, though you could find some among extended family. We assumed that as good role models and caring, involved parents, our children wouldn't have trouble with substances, either.

After a miscarriage in 1983, we had our son in 1984, our first daughter fourteen months later, and Amy in January of 1989. Before she was born, I heard the song "Amie" by Pure Prairie League while driving home from work. I suddenly decided that we would call a girl Amy, though her formal name would be Amelia. We'd already settled on John for a boy's name, so I kept talking to my child in utero as Amy-John.

It's almost as if Amy gave us a preview of her personality during labor, holding the home birth team hostage as my early evening contractions stopped in the middle of the night, necessitating that my waters be broken in the morning. I was delighted to have a second daughter, and within minutes of birth I was calling her "barracuda" because of how gleefully and voraciously she devoured her food.

Two months before Amy's birth our family had moved to a larger, contemporary colonial house in a picturesque town. With a large wooded yard on a quiet street, the children could safely go outside to play. We enjoyed the quiet of this bedroom community, where education was highly valued and it was not uncommon to read in the town newspaper's police blotter about a horse running loose. Our family took walks to the local farms, enjoyed weekend "bike runs" around our two-mile block, and spent hours at the town playground and library. A downside was that the nearest grocery store was a six-mile drive away, with no public transportation. We read and cooked together as a family, and our vacations were almost always to visit relatives or friends in other cities. In 1995, we bought a small condominium (condo) two hours away where we could more centrally meet up with family and friends, the children could swim and play tennis, and we all could enjoy the region's summer cultural offerings.

My day job was as a co-founder of a high-technology start-up company, so as an infant Amy joined her brother and sister at a home-based family daycare. After a few months, I moved her to the childcare center on the first floor of the office building where I worked. I loved commuting with her while we sang, recited poems, and watched the seasons change. I loved having her downstairs and being able to nurse her during lunch. In fact, she nursed in the evening until she was almost three years old, a special bonding time until I finally decided I wanted my body back.

Starting School

In the summer of 1991, we changed our primary childcare arrangement to having live-in au pairs from Europe. Amy began private preschool in September of 1992. Her acceptance was fortuitous, as the incoming class was low on girls. She enjoyed the half-day program, became a powerful presence amid a classroom full of boys, and she remained friends with the two other girls for many years.

Amy was already showing her strong will, and we would joke about the "four-year-old ruler of the world." One fifteen-degree day in the city, she refused to put on her light purple cloud jacket because of a chocolate candy stain. Crossing the windy city streets, strangers were looking at us as if we were child abusers. Amy threw a tantrum at a department store because we wouldn't buy her a "teeny tiny" food machine to make "teeny tiny" cookies. When grocery shopping she and I would sing "Twinkle Twinkle" in the aisle with backlit star cutouts above the breads. The manager once carried her out under his arm during one of her tantrums. Around age five, a former friend made a curious observation: "That child has way too much power in the family."

Upon entering kindergarten in the private school, Amy seemed hungry for academic challenge, asking for homework like her older siblings had. However, the school's approach emphasized social skills, and when Amy completed a task and needed more challenge, the teacher's response was, "She can help the other children." So at an early age, she received the rein-forcing message that school was primarily a social scene. In retrospect, we wish we had transferred her to our local public kindergarten, which we knew from our first daughter's experiences was more demanding of the students.

Right before Amy turned five years old, my start-up company was acquired and I began traveling occasionally for business, though never more than a few nights a month. Throughout my career, I was adamant about having nightly family dinners, even if that meant returning to the office after I put the children to bed. Fortunately, my husband's career as a senior level software architect also was conducive to a family life. The children loved when dad could answer their dinner table questions on topics ranging from the latest political scandal to the software "bugs" he caught that day. Their father was a true Renaissance man: Ph.D. mathematician, fluent in Russian, well-read in numerous disciplines, and a competitive chess player.

England and Repatriation

During first grade, Amy's challenges seemed like no match for her teacher's easygoing style. But the decision about what to do for second grade was dictated by other circumstances. The company that acquired my start-up transferred me to their $750 million division just outside of London to be the finance director, so my family moved to England for two years. I was thrilled to realize my career dream of an international assignment. Amy had been a bit reluctant until we reassured her that the queen was not going to chop off her head. We rented a home on a quiet street that had a yard cared for by a grandfatherly gentleman who helped Amy create "Amy's Garden" during her gardening lessons. My husband enjoyed being a home-based parent, and I began my tradition of writing a monthly letter to share our adventures with friends and family, providing a vicarious experience to appreciative readers.

Amy's private British school was a half-mile walk from our house. She was excited to be learning more content, especially in history, but her teacher remarked, "Amy's work habits are so laid back, she is almost horizontal." She easily made friends, but her academic performance wavered. Social interactions tended to be amplified in the small class of ten girls. Among activities outside of school, Amy was an altar server at church, and made her first communion. She wore the dress and veil that I had worn for mine, which felt very special to me.

Amy's signature story was when she was on a walk with her dad, and decided she needed potato chips, known in England as "crisps." My husband refused, stating it was too close to dinnertime. Amy used every ounce of drama as she fell limp in the crosswalk, bleating, "I feel weak...I need crisps...." I can't help but note that "I'm weak" appeared near the end of her last journal entry.

Upon repatriating in 1998, Amy seemed to transition socially with ease into fourth grade at the local public school, which enrolled kindergarten through eighth grade on the same campus. Her teacher appreciated our family's value of travel, and was most supportive when I took Amy for a week to visit cousins and former au pairs in Europe. During that trip, we often used a little code phrase about our hatred of cigarette smoking, "You know what I mean...." I was feeling joyfully confident that Amy's passionate stance against smoking at a young age had extinguished the lure of tobacco

or marijuana (also known as weed or pot) in her future. Another outcome from the trip was her frustration with being unable to communicate in our hosts' native language, so upon returning she began private German lessons.

Her first-term report card read, "Amy had a difficult time making the adjustment to class procedures. She has difficulty working in a group, as she tends to lose focus and use the time to socialize." The teacher requested a conference in late October, where she mentioned how Amy was refusing to "toe the line," needed to be different and defiant, and seemed to have a chip on her shoulder. She questioned what was keeping Amy back from being part of the class. A later conference echoed that Amy didn't want to own that she was a great kid. She had a real struggle for social connections ("be my friend exclusively"), and she had chosen to work with social kids instead of her academic equals. She became particularly attached to one girl and they were often in trouble together. But outside of school she had plenty of playovers and other extracurricular activities.

A June conference recapped that Amy was very disruptive and very sociable, even during work times. For example, she had mouthed off to the librarian, though later wrote a note of apology:

> I'm sorry for talking when the lights were out [in the library]. I'm not trying to make excuses but I do think that some other people (not mentioning names) were somewhat causing me to get into trouble. Talking is one of my main hobbies and I sometimes just talk without thinking. I apologize completely for talking and I will try not to talk when the lights are off again.

She seemed to be lacking interest, and not taking responsibility for learning. Yet the teacher also recognized, "She has so much to offer she doesn't know where to begin." At that point, nobody raised the prospect of having Amy tested or seeing a counselor. We all believed that in the right environment, Amy's intellect would blossom and the behavioral issues would take care of themselves.

We transferred Amy to an academically rigorous, all-girls Catholic school with smaller classes for fifth grade. Her fourth-grade teacher had commented, "Amy is a very capable student. I feel she would benefit from a challenging learning environment which might motivate her to realize her potential. . . . She is a complex, inquisitive, and intellectually delightful child." Part of the decision was my desire to have Amy educated by the same order of nuns who had taught me. Our first daughter was boarding for a second year at her performing arts school in England, and our son began ninth grade as a boarder at a prep school thirty minutes away, leaving Amy as our only child.

History repeated itself as Amy's social skills prevailed while the academic languished. In January a teacher commented, ". . . [she] has the potential to be a confident leader in the fifth grade. I would encourage her, however, to reach out to other members of the class and be more concerned with her own actions rather than with those of her peers." Recurring comments included "capable," "not working to potential," "loses focus," "easily distracted," "late," "disorganized," and "not handing in assignments."

A March conference included an observing psychologist. The teachers admitted that Amy was an enigma to them. They even saw her as wearing a victim filter, whining, "Nobody likes me," when in fact she and her inseparable friend went from adult to adult seeking advocates. The two girls isolated themselves from their classmates by manipulating what the teachers said. We moved Amy back to public school for sixth grade, largely due to the commute. Even with car pooling, the unpredictable driving times in commuting twenty-three miles to school and another thirty miles to work created too much stress. My husband and I also felt that despite its many strengths, the school seemed unable to provide an environment that Amy could not manipulate.

Looking back, Amy's pattern was already entrenched. She had changed schools, but the underlying behavior persisted. She had spent four years at one school for preschool through first grade, two years in England, one year in public school, one year in private school, and would now be returning to the public school for her last three elementary years. I do not recall having any discussions with our pediatrician about Amy's behavioral health. It just didn't cross my mind to raise such issues with the doctor, but neither do I recall being asked.

Middle School

Amy was glad to return to her friends at the local public elementary school, a mile and a half from our house. Now an emerging adolescent at eleven and a half, she soon earned a reputation among teachers for being boy crazy. At one teacher conference, family therapy was recommended to address Amy's behavioral issues. She refused, and we did not pursue treatment. We probably were hoping she was going through a phase, and knew we could not succeed without her buy-in. In retrospect, that was giving her too much control over the situation, and as parents we may have benefited even without her attending. However, the limited family therapy we had previously done, for issues not centered around Amy, hadn't left us feeling it would be worth our time. None of the practitioners had impressed us with their insights or expertise, raising our reluctance to try again. For example, one psychologist tried to reassure us that our son's yelling at me was age appropriate; yet I felt it was verbal abuse that should be stopped.

Throughout middle school, Amy's report cards were lackluster. Her only spike in performance came at the end of seventh grade, when she said she realized that it was possible to have friends *and* do well academically. In math especially, an area where she possessed high natural ability, teachers were frustrated that her attitude kept her out of honors classes. She claimed that, although drugs were available in middle school, she did not start experimenting at that time, and I believe that was true.

A pattern developed whereby Amy would get into trouble, and then try to argue herself out of it based on an altruistic motive. For example, when she was late for one class, she'd claim, "I stayed to help X clean up the art room." When late for another class, "I was with my friend Y who was crying in the bathroom and really needed a friend." This connection with others and lack of seeing her individual accountability thus evolved further. She formed a particularly intense dyad with another classmate, Lily, which extended to them calling each other the same androgynous nickname.

In May of 2002, a school counselor discussed with me a concern from the teaching team and other staff about Amy's "relentlessness in making poor choices." While the choices weren't destructive, the concern was that if they were not addressed before ninth grade we might see dangerous behaviors in high school. The counselor mentioned the general issues of lying, avoiding, and denial that were not easy to pinpoint or address. He sent me a list of counseling referrals a few weeks later. I suspect we did not pursue them then due to lack of Amy's buy-in. We were probably hoping that she would outgrow some of the middle school behaviors once in high school.

The comment by the former friend that Amy had "way too much power in the family" rings loudly in retrospect, but I didn't really hear it then.

Ironically, Amy referred to herself as the "class psychiatrist" because she mediated the tribulations of her fellow middle schoolers. But the question remained: Why did she focus so much on others and not on herself? Given how deftly Amy navigated issues among so many peers, she projected social acumen that I believed must have reflected some level of self-insight. Amy was already popular with her younger cousins and the children she babysat. Siblings of her friends adored her. One friend's younger sister insisted that Amy attend her birthday party.

She also showed her warm heart. One year, she insisted that we make eighty-four cupcakes to celebrate her birthday: one for each classmate and every teacher and staff member. Toward the end of fifth grade, Amy, our son, and I went to adopt two kittens in time for our first daughter's return from England. We chose the one remaining female, and one male chose our son. But then Amy saw "the shy one" huddled in the back of the cage. She was afraid no one would adopt him; that's how our family ended up with a third cat. For Christmas in 2002, she bought me the ASPCA *Complete Guide to Dogs*, inscribing in red marker:

Hey Mom! We've been trying for-ever to look at dogs but we've been putting it off so I got you this book. Hopefully we can find the kind of dog we want! Love,

Amy

xoxoxoxo

Athletically, Amy was comfortable playing basketball with the boys, skateboarding, and running. She was also a passionate Red Sox fan, especially of player No. 33. Her middle school buddies claimed that by sitting next to her in English, they didn't learn a whole lot about the subject, but everything about Jason Varitek. One day, her eighth-grade track coach called to ask, "I take it you do not want Amy Varitek monogrammed on her team jacket?"

....

After Amy died, one boy remembered being a wallflower in sixth grade when Amy asked him to dance. A girl praised Amy's strength in befriending everyone from the "cool kids" to the disenfranchised and all those in between, and how special that made her feel as one of the "not popular" girls.

The theme of missing assignments, losing focus, and not working to potential prevailed in the eighth grade. Approaching graduation, "It's the end of the year" became Amy's excuse. I was increasingly concerned about the next four years. I had felt that I would not survive our son's intensity if he lived at home during high school. Fortunately, he was accepted at boarding school, and we had become comfortable with this concept while living in England. Amy and her brother had very similar personalities, and I was starting to feel that Amy might also prove to be too big a parenting challenge and would benefit from the structure of boarding as her brother had. We applied to several schools for Amy, hoping again that she might be placed into an environment where she would be "pulled up" academically and work to her potential. She was blasé in the process and was not admitted to either school.

Reflections

So what did we learn? From an early age, Amy manipulated. The behavior exhibited itself in various school settings, yet seasoned educators and professionals were unable to stop it. I do not recall anyone recommending testing. We kept hoping she would outgrow some of the patterns and encouraged her to put her strengths toward positive pursuits, like community service and music lessons.

It might be an interesting screening question at annual physicals for a clinician to ask about family dynamics, perhaps even a variation on my friend's observation: How much power does the child have in the family? But realistically, pediatricians are so overwhelmed, and they need resources to whom they could refer a family if they sensed a problem. Research supports that successfully implementing even brief screening tools is easier said than done.

Should we have expected more expressions of concern from friends and relatives? I was grateful when my mother called Amy out one Christmas when she was mouthing off to me. Cultural norms dictate whether someone will voice something they see in a relative's family, and to whom. In retrospect, I could have tapped so many more of my relatives and friends, but I wasn't accustomed to doing that. I had vowed that as a mother I would provide explanations to my children, rather than being a "because I said so" parent, but explanations to our son and Amy typically generated debate. Did "social" Amy need a different style of parenting than we "brains" knew how to provide? Would it have made a difference?

Perhaps intense dyads, as Amy formed in succession since fourth grade, should be a red flag for schools and parents. But young girls often form very close friendships, and Amy did make other social connections. Maybe the behavior to watch out for is when the dyad manipulates the adults around them. It may be better to overreact than underreact. But reacting assumes the availability of competent resources to assess, recommend, and treat. And too many adults seem unwilling to take a stand. We've evolved into a society where speaking up could subject someone to recrimination. It is not an easy space to navigate.

September 2003, Ninth Grade:
Reflection Paper
difficult choices _A-_

Although sometimes it seems difficult, when you are in a tough situation you must always

keep up your hopes and pray that everything will turn out well in the end, because

The decision about where to send Amy for high school was fraught with tension. I was concerned about how she would fare at the Regional Public High School (RPHS). While excellent academically, the school had its liberal traditions, features my husband knew firsthand from his four years there. I feared for Amy's ability to use her freedom wisely—for example, the open campus policy for seniors. I worried about the trouble she might find after dismissal and on days off when I was at work. As a ninth-grader, she would overlap with our first daughter's senior year, and I was concerned that having both girls in the same school might be difficult for her sister given how Amy might act out.

The alternative to RPHS was Blessed Virgin Mary Preparatory (BVMP), the all-girls high school where I'd started teaching math after leaving the high-tech industry when Amy was in seventh grade. I had great respect for my colleagues and wanted Amy to have the benefit of their subject matter expertise and values. I liked that our Catholic tradition would be reinforced by Masses or prayer services held for religious feasts and school traditions. I longed for a few short years of commuting with Amy, concluding our conversations as we drove up to the wooded campus. I imagined the satisfaction of walking into the imposing classroom building with her, and how she would enjoy seeing the younger students on the campus. My husband and I hoped that by being a small high school of 200 students she would be less likely to fall through the cracks and act out.

Amy wrote us a letter expressing her thoughts on the matter.

Hey Mom and Dad,

_I am writing to talk to you about the BVMP decision. I know you
really want me to go there, but I have soooo many reasons why I know
it would be better for me to go to RPHS. Over the years I have changed_

schools about 6 times. For once in my life I thought that I would actually be able to stay set where I am right now and actually go into high school with my friends…I am completely sick of all the new friends I have had to make, and lose. For once I am becoming very very very close to a lot of kids at my middle school, and now you are trying to take that away from me. You say that you will let me stay very close to my friends, but that's also what you said when I left for fifth grade and I ended up staying close with one friend, and that was because she lived less than half a mile away so I could easily bike to her house. (With people like Lily, I can't do that because they live much farther away.) Still my friend and I only saw each other about 3 times in the full year. I tried an all girls environment in fifth grade and it doesn't work for me. My first choice in school was RPHS, even over boarding school. While I am writing this letter, I'm crying, because I cannot imagine having to change schools again, and again attend an all girls' school. On my visiting day there, the teachers were ok, but I found on my half day at RPHS, the teachers were a lot stronger in what they taught, and they really got the message across to me. At BVMP, I was practically falling asleep during each of the classes, and I didn't learn anything new. Also at BVMP, all I heard was gossip among the students, during classes, recess, and lunch, even church. Now I do know that I gossip a bit, I'll admit to that, but in one 45 minutes lunch period, I probably heard more gossip than I heard in 1 month at my school. With all girls, that is basically all there is to do, and I can't stand it. Fifth grade was like that and the only thing that kept me sane was my friend. Also I do not want to go to a school that my own mother teaches at. When Mom taught religious education for my grade, I completely misbehaved because it felt like I was at home, so I felt like I could do whatever I wanted. I don't want to have to go through four years of high school like this. BVMP doesn't have Latin or Orchestra, and RPHS has both of those plus about 832,647,153 different groups and clubs that BVMP doesn't have. Also, I was kind of looking forward to going to BVMP with someone from my school, and if [she] hadn't had health issues, I would be MUCH more open to it, but now that she's probably not going to BVMP, my opinion has been greatly affected, and even if she were going, it would still be very very difficult. I am just sooooo upset that you already made my high school decision already…and I'm not saying I never want to go to BVMP, it's just that I'm not ready to go this year and I'm begging you to PLEASE reconsider and respect my input, because I know that

I would try really hard at RPHS and I honestly think it is the best decision. If I thought BVMP was the right decision, the thing about my friends wouldn't bother me that much, but I know it is not the right decision. Please reconsider because I am miserable):):):

~ Love, Amy

P.S. I have many more reasons but I think the letter is long enough as it is.

My husband and I considered this input, and decided we would allow her to attend RPHS if she agreed to see a counselor. Yet in August Amy chose to matriculate at BVMP, accompanied by her middle school alter ego Lily. While both of them wanted to attend RPHS, they agreed to attend BVMP if the other one went. Lily's mom had hoped that a Catholic school might provide the structure and discipline to help her daughter stay on a better path than public school. Meanwhile, I was preparing for my first marathon, having stepped up my running as a way of taking care of myself amid the stresses of three teenagers.

The School Year Begins

The transition to BVMP did not bode well. When I was proctoring Amy and Lily as they took their placement tests, Amy refused to move seats when I asked. The school librarian, who was not aware that Amy was my daughter, said to me after observing the defiance, "Can you *believe* how rude that kid was? What kind of girls are we admitting now?" In fact, about one in four of the girls entering the class of 2007 left BVMP, and even with incoming transfer students the graduating class was a mere thirty-six.

Amy's first progress report was mostly Bs and Cs, with comments including, "More seriousness needed," "Needs to come for help regularly for awhile," "Needs to change quicker for gym class," and "Needs more consistency in effort." Her report card comments were all from the negative palette: "Incomplete assignments one to three times," "Attitude needs to improve," "Does minimum requirements," "Inconsistent effort," "Needs to stay for help," "Noticeable lack of effort," and "Inadequate preparation for class." One teacher had pulled her aside to tell her that she had the best research paper in the class, so she now expected to see more work of that caliber. Amy's retort to me was, "I don't like that teacher anymore, because now she thinks I'm capable."

So in yet another environment, Amy was underperforming academically. She opted to not participate in fall sports, citing the high school transition, yet she had not joined any extracurricular activities. The girl who loved hoops declined to even try out for winter basketball, despite being heavily recruited by the athletic director, Ms. Dirath, and the coach. We couldn't figure out why: lack of self-esteem? In all her experiences with musical instruments, she had not practiced in a committed way, frustrating teachers and parents who could see her getting by on her natural ability, and raising the question: Could she work through a challenge?

Amy soon held the school record for most detentions that year. In October, the principal said, "It is not beyond the realm of possibility that she will be asked to leave." She cited numerous incidents of Amy being late for class or wandering, almost always with Lily, repeating the dyad pattern from grade school. The principal mentioned how Amy always argued, never said "I'm sorry," and was beginning to really aggravate the students and teachers with her behavior.

Amy's facial expressions often communicated disdain or contempt, which she denied if confronted. Her body language was often "droopy," even in meetings with the principal. Teachers across every class had observed similar affect, which was especially a problem in the honors sections. In January, the principal told us, "Amy must be tested as a prerequisite to staying here." She questioned whether some of Amy's behavior was voluntary, especially her inability to keep quiet when the principal was talking to someone else in her presence.

One teacher reported in January, "Often I have had to get after Amy to pass in material that was due on a certain day. Several times she said she passed in material that I never received. Amy's attitude is quite disturbing to me. She often shows little interest in class. When she is called, you can hardly hear her reply. Dealings with Amy frustrate and weary me. Outside of class I have found her to be defiant. If you ask her to move, she won't. The students in class are quite aware of her attitude. Can this continue?" Amy told this same teacher, when asked whether she had taken photographs of people at school, "You know how sneaky I can be." Another irritation occurred in a class where Amy dropped a pen. Her solution was to slowly inch her desk forward so she could retrieve it with her foot, which proved much more disruptive than other alternatives.

As a teacher, I observed several incidents as well. One was when the principal was talking with Lily, and Amy came up and interrupted. Another was when Amy was attempting to argue with the principal in full view of several classmates about a locker matter, and when the principal had to confiscate food that Amy was bringing into a classroom. Finally, the principal told me that after Amy promised her she would not bring her cell phone to school, she did. Amy's trustworthiness was severely in question. While she had an explanation for every incident, which sometimes sounded viable, the sheer number of them was of great concern. The comments from fifth grade about manipulating what teachers said were ringing true in yet another environment.

I knew that I could not teach Amy, and fortunately she always had one of the other math teachers. But even without being her teacher, I was a teacher and her mother, which often put me in an awkward position. I was not one of those mothers who defended her child against any and all charges, so having to accept so many unfavorable comments was disheartening. But my years in the corporate world trained me to remain professional and to compartmentalize, so I coped.

The concern extended outside of school. When Amy went with her dad and siblings to see a movie, she went out to buy food and did not return to sit with them, claiming she did not want to disturb other patrons. In fact, for an hour and a half, the family was worried about where she was, causing her father to miss half an hour of the film looking for her. We later learned she had snuck out of the theater. It seemed she had crossed the line from creative alibis to outright lies.

Amy continued to vehemently resist counseling. Paradoxically, her career goal was to become a psychologist, with a home office compatible with a private practice and raising three children. Someone observed how Amy had no qualms about imposing on others. We had always been torn whether what she was going through was simply developmental, or symptomatic of deeper issues. We agreed with the principal's insistence on testing to determine whether the latter was true.

Neuropsychological Testing

The testing was conducted at RPHS over several sessions, and it would take several more weeks to learn the results. I prepared a "briefing package" for the testers. I stated how Amy was a high-maintenance child who would rather argue for five minutes about not doing something than just doing it in thirty seconds. It required constant emotional presence to not be manipulated, which was exhausting and not always successful. She would often try to argue herself out of a task by citing a higher-level priority. For example, after having asked her several times to empty the dishwasher, the chore through which she earned her allowance, another reminder would be met with, "But I'm doing my homework, and you always say school comes first."

Amy often insisted she had Obsessive Compulsive Disorder, but what we observed was fastidiousness. She wouldn't eat food that approached its sell-by date or had been opened for more than a few days, much less left-overs! She complained when I microwaved tomato soup, instead of heating it on the stovetop. These quirks made it very difficult to manage meals at home. While the description of Oppositional Defiance Disorder seemed to match Amy to a T, no practitioner ever agreed. She had also requested medical appointments for various ailments, but usually would not follow the prescribed advice.

Amy also resisted limits, some of which was expected at that age, but which made parenting exhausting. We made the mistake of letting her buy her own desktop computer on a payment plan to us and setting it up in her room. My husband installed watchdog software to limit her usage to nine hours a week, but she learned how to change the times. We were unsuccessful at setting a time limit on phone calls, although we prohibited calls after 10:00 p.m. The September 11, 2001 attacks happened when she was in seventh grade, and like many parents we wanted our child to have a cell phone in the event of emergency. But cell phone battles were constant, and my body tensed every time the bill came in. I joked that as soon as surgical phone implants were offered, Amy would be first in line.

In dealing with these challenges, we didn't want to lose sight of Amy's gifts of effervescence, determination, and enthusiasm. She often baked and brought together groups of people with her homemade goodies. She knew how to get things done and done well. She planned parties and trips months in advance. She had no reticence about calling for information to organize events, and she was a very competitive shopper. Perhaps our proudest example was at a town library fundraiser when she noticed that lemonade had been delivered but no one was running the stand. She proceeded to organize the effort and the sales approached $400.

Amy often said how she wished she had a younger sibling and probably would have been a great big sister. When frustrated with a situation, she often reverted to the tirade, "Dad favors my brother, and Mom favors my sister, so I'm the odd one out." Her emotional reality prevailed despite the actual day-to-day connect time she had with us, as well as special events including ball games with dad and travel with mom.

We further questioned the continuing pattern of Amy becoming intensely attached to one friend during any given school year. Amy became the dominant party while the other girl lost her voice with Amy as her spokesperson, and a seemingly puppeteer/puppet relationship evolved. It happened in fourth grade, to the extent where she and the other girl were ostracized, and the teacher said, "It's a mystery to solve." It happened in fifth grade, where the teachers said they'd never seen a situation like that.

This pattern was amplified at BVMP. She and Lily were inseparable during the school day, and, unfortunately, they had all the same classes. They spent hours on the telephone outside of school. The principal cited an example where Amy accompanied Lily to hand in Lily's late document to the principal, upon which *Amy* commented, "Good, now that's taken care of." Similarly, when Lily lost a bag of clothes at school, it was Amy who took her back inside after school, went to the principal, and led the search. The boundary between healthy friendship and one who has "taken over" seemed to have been crossed.

Ironically, I noted in the input to the testing, "We are fortunate that we are not dealing with really awful issues like smoking, drugs, alcohol, promiscuity, illness, eating disorders, trouble with the law, body mutilation, and bad friends." Little did I imagine how many of those pathologies would, in fact, come true. I wrote, "She has carved a niche from which she irritates those around her, and in turn diminishes herself. She is still acting in high school as if she were in junior high, and it's hard to tell what she takes seriously. It appears there are very few adults in her life whom she respects, something we believe must be changed to successfully navigate adolescence. After years of hearing the same comments from teachers, it's time to intervene. We are most curious to learn from the testing!"

The New Calendar Year; Amy Turns Fifteen

Amy had a brush with the law in January of 2004, when a family accused Amy and Lily of Section 43A criminal harassment of their daughter at BVMP. They filed an eleven-page report with the police and went to the BVMP board and diocese, who found no fault with how the principal dealt with matters. My husband and I met with Amy, the principal, the president, and the local police at the end of the month, and the case was ultimately dropped. Both the girl alleging harassment and Lily subsequently left BVMP. We too questioned whether to move Amy, but decided against it, as we were concerned about yet another uprooting. The principal set as a requirement that Amy obtain counseling if she stayed at BVMP.

Those weeks were very difficult for all involved. I remember phoning an attorney from my bedroom closet, where Amy could not overhear me, to ask what kind of legal counsel we might need to line up. Lily's mother and I talked a lot about the best course of action for our daughters. The aftermath was complicated and painful, including the accusing mother verbally assaulting me in line at a coffee shop the following summer, necessitating a call to the police. It also left Amy in a vulnerable identity crisis because she had to reestablish herself without her alter ego Lily.

On January 26th, Amy wrote to my husband, the principal, and me apologizing for her behavior. The letters were insightful, admitting to the adjustment difficulties of high school: ". . . I can't get away with the things I used to be able to get away with," and "sometimes I feel like I am always right, even over people of authority . . . I try to stand up for my opinions but don't always realize that I am being disrespectful to the person I'm talking to, until after I've done it." She resolved to improve during the second semester. I overheard her tell a friend, "Do you realize that if we were in public school, we'd be on Instant Messenger with boys three hours a night?"

The month ended with rumors that Amy was going to be expelled from BVMP, an extremely awkward message for me to hear from my students. Incidents at school continued almost daily involving Amy's work, defiance, and cell phone use. I was starting to see the thinness in some of her stories but would give in to what was plausible. I didn't expect adolescence to be so difficult, and I sometimes made the mistake of taking it personally when she called me "the worst mom in the world." The attempts my husband and I made at imposing consequences proved unenforceable, but he and I were hopeful about the start of counseling, although Amy weighed in that she wanted to see a psychiatrist, not a psychologist. I don't know how clear she was of the distinction between the two and whether she could have been trying to give us a message, or was merely being difficult.

February break provided a much needed respite. Amy and I enjoyed a few days in Florida with my relative. But her overindulgence of fast food resulted in her vomiting on the beige rug outside the bathroom between our bedroom and his. I remember my combined compassion and frustration trying to comfort her and quietly clean up the mess in the middle of the night without waking my relative. This incident seemed symbolic of my role cleaning up Amy's messes while trying to be a supporting mother to her *and* do damage control with those to whom she was an inconvenience.

The First Counselor and Psychiatrist

On February 25th, I took Amy to her first session with Ms. Firther, a middle-aged licensed clinical social worker who also worked in a local urban school district. I received her name from our first daughter's counselor, Dr. Hischolor. Being in crisis and emotionally exhausted with Amy's situation, I felt ecstatic having been thrown the lifeline of a recommendation so I didn't have to "shop" for a therapist. The fact that her office was midway between school and home appealed to my logic of convenience, and being able to schedule the first sessions without waiting for weeks quenched my desperation. In retrospect, perhaps we should have endured our pain a little longer and performed our due diligence, even if it would have meant more driving and waiting to start.

Amy said that Ms. Firther was "great," but she wanted to look around, which Ms. Firther encouraged. But Amy's guidance counselor, Mrs. Guicona, cautioned that we couldn't let Amy control the process, especially as a delay tactic. Amy next met Ms. Firther on March 10th, the day before I had noted figuratively in my diary, "Amy is kicking me when I'm down." Teen girls seem to know when mom is vulnerable and go for the jugular. I felt defenseless.

On February 25th, I started seeing therapist Dr. Sporsy, who was also recommended by Dr. Hischolor. I wrote, "I am a functioning wreck. Wonder how precariously close that is to being a non-functioning wreck."

On March 12th, Amy and I met with the dean of students, who was also one of her teachers. From the start of the year, the dean saw Amy as immature, but that did not scare her, and she had seen some growth in Amy. Inappropriate laughter during class was an issue. But Amy's dishonesty was troubling—for example, saying she came for help and really hadn't. The year had been a runaround, and the dean couldn't keep chasing her. Mrs. Guicona had also advised that Amy's therapy needed to discern what was immaturity/anxiety (cover-up, defense) versus core dishonesty. Ironically, I had met with the dean over the summer about Amy's high school decision. She had played up the advantage of Amy being in a school where she could meet students from other towns. Curiously, on March 2nd, Amy stated she wanted to move to my hometown where her maternal grandparents and other relatives lived, perhaps for a "fresh start."

Testing Results

We reviewed Amy's testing results at RPHS on March 25th. The testing revealed no underlying learning disabilities, but poorly developed inner controls, impulsivity, fragility, low self-esteem, and a very negative global self-concept which the defiance masked. Her inability to concentrate was due to the emotional distractions of depression and anxiety. She was deemed a relationship-dependent learner: If she felt no connection, she was lost. While Amy was less mature, her cognitive abilities were average to very superior. In retrospect, this reassurance of intelligence to intelligent parents is a Trojan horse; Amy later ended up using all her intelligence in support of her drug habits. And we clearly lost focus on the underlying depression, anxiety, and self-esteem issues, which we now know often lead to self-medication with substances. As parents, we trusted that Amy's mental health professionals were working these issues, and that results would take time.

Ms. Firther canceled our March 24th session, and on March 31st we had our first family meeting with her. While she was not technically our family therapist, it is not uncommon for a child's therapist to meet with the family. By mid-April, I was already questioning Ms. Firther's effectiveness with Amy, as well as my value as a parent. I was not enjoying family life. I was feeling a raft of abuse from Amy to the point of tears. I had a respite when she and my husband left for three days of Red Sox spring training. During April vacation they visited his family in the south.

Later in the month, I noted, "I think Amy is cutting," though I can't remember the clues. According to a teen health website, cutting behavior "may also be associated with substance abuse and with other impulse control and risk taking behaviors" as well as a sign of low self-esteem. Amy also asked one of my students if she hated me. I was beginning to think that perhaps it wasn't such a good idea for Amy to attend the same school where I taught.

In early May, I met with Amy's teachers and Ms. Firther at BVMP to discuss the testing results. Mrs. Guicona set the context, saying that Amy could be disruptive, disrespectful, and defiant. Testing was to figure out why, and how much was volitional. The focus was on the anxiety piece. It was hard for teachers to know where to draw the line, not wanting to enable her yet not wanting to add to her distress. What consequences were appropriate, and when? Could she succeed at BVMP if I taught there? Was the harassment allegation still casting a shadow? Were we dealing with adjustment or fit issues, and were they unique to BVMP? Who could help her develop to her potential and, if so, how?

Individual teachers gave feedback. Only one never had discipline issues with her because Amy knew she couldn't get away with anything in this teacher's class. (Ironically, while I never seemed to connect with this teacher personally or professionally, I have the utmost respect for her as the only one whom Amy could not manipulate.) Another added that Amy asked questions, was fidgety, but was starting to grow and, like a seedling, she didn't want to rip her out of the BVMP pot. The teacher mentioned how Amy and Lily "did not bring out the best in each other," and, since Lily left, Amy had settled down and been more consistent. Another teacher was baffled because Amy always had her backpack with her even when other students did not. She saw a slight improvement in Amy's attitude and interest in what was being taught. Another claimed Amy was never a problem in class, and she saw great improvement since Lily had left. But a recent issue was her being in the corridor during lunch. In another class, Amy was still drooped over her desk, mumbled, seemed insecure, and the teacher couldn't hear her. Students were watching the teacher to see her reaction, for example, when Amy would not move when asked. The teacher questioned whether Amy's friendliness outside of class was sincere.

The feedback continued. In the dean's class, Amy acted as a seventh- or eighth-grader rather than a ninth-grader from the start. She always seemed to have a cold or allergies, needing tissues, and was a bit of a "Nervous Nellie." She was showing signs of maturity by asking more questions, but she was not answering. Other students weren't looking at her anymore. The dean believed she second-guessed and doubted herself a lot, and needed tips on how to make friends. This change was perhaps a huge red flag we missed at the time, given how easily Amy socialized in elementary school. Why was making friends now such an issue? Ms. Dirath said Amy was always trying to get out of class. She felt she was afraid of failing, and her bravada was a front. She reiterated how Amy would not try out for basketball, despite deadline extensions and being heavily recruited by both her and the coach. She predicted that Amy would be eaten up alive in a larger school, and the most accepting faction would be the pot smokers.

Mrs. Guicona noted Amy's immaturity, misreading of social cues having to do with friends, her inability to be where she was supposed to be at the right time, and her avoidance of lunchtime in the cafeteria.

The principal summarized how Amy bent the truth enough to pit adults against each other. She had heard about Amy not wanting to be at BVMP. While she improved academically, she looked to get out of cafeteria and homeroom, and wandering was a problem. Looking ahead to sophomore year, the principal noted that adults could be forgiving, but questioned whether the other students could be.

Finally Ms. Firther acknowledged that Amy was very bright, could be very personable, and was very guarded. She was very pleased with how she had improved her relationship with the dean. She added that Amy was more immature than a lot of ninth-graders, and she perceived BVMP as "her mom's school." Ms. Firther believed that Amy was angry at the start of the year and now she felt she didn't fit anywhere.

These conclusions, yet again, should have been a clue that something was seriously wrong. Most teachers had several decades of experience, yet a few cited Amy as one of their most challenging students ever. I was frustrated that despite this experience, nobody seemed to have any answers or ideas for a breakthrough approach. And I didn't feel like we had a whole lot of time to act as Amy's adolescence accelerated.

May 6th was a typical day of harangues with Amy. At 6:50 a.m. I gave her the one-minute warning to leave for school. At 7:00 a.m. she was still blow drying her hair. I gave her a cereal bar for breakfast, and she threw it; I can't remember my reaction but I think stayed calm. We had yet another argument after school over her going to her violin lesson. I questioned if I had to be superhuman to survive her behavior.

I had a fourth session with Dr. Sporsy. We talked mostly about Amy and the legal option Child In Need of Services (CHINS). A CHINS matter is where the Juvenile Court tries to help parents and school officials deal with troubled youth. The person filing the CHINS petition must show the judge that the child regularly runs away from home, constantly disobeys the commands of a parent or legal guardian, misses school on a regular basis, or constantly fails to follow school rules. My reaction was to think that my family wasn't one that would voluntarily put our child into the public "system." We'd deal with Amy's situation all privately. While Amy wasn't a runaway or truant, some of the CHINS criteria rang more than true.

Given Amy's depression and anxiety concerns from the testing, we needed to find a psychiatrist to evaluate her for medications (meds). In late May, Amy had her first meeting with psychiatrist Dr. Loftad, who was a mother of two teens. While the doctor asked me to be present, Amy was reluctant to roll up her sweater sleeve to reveal my suspicion of cutting unless I left the room. But Dr. Loftad took a tough stand with Amy, saying she would not deal with an uncooperative patient. Amy relented, but I can't recall if we saw cuts in her inner elbow. Dr. Loftad prescribed Zoloft for Amy's anxiety.

After my ninth session with Dr. Sporsy on June 10th, I was questioning his effectiveness because I just didn't feel I was making progress in dealing with Amy's behavior. She and I had a blowup but, in a new pattern, she came later to the garden to apologize to me. A few days after the blowup, she actually offered to help me garden. But in my continuing exasperation I asked myself, "What reduces a capable, competent person like me to mush?"

We faced a major crossroads about which school Amy should attend for sophomore year. She and I met in mid-June with a guidance counselor at RPHS and were told that it was "clearly a family decision." Amy was encouraged to listen to parent and school judgments as far as maintaining academic momentum. Amy mentioned that she had "no use for Ms. Firther now."

At a June 21st meeting with the principal, we learned that Amy's effort during the second half of the year had earned her a Grade Point Average (GPA) of 2.3/4.0 and a place at BVMP for sophomore year. The question was whether she wanted to do the work. Amy's comportment was droopy throughout the meeting. Two days later, Amy and I met with Ms. Firther about the school decision but did not reach a conclusion. We scheduled Amy's next session for August 4th.

Summer Stresses

The summer was full of tension involving Amy meeting up with friends. Twice she visited a new friend, Roy, in the next town. Even though I insisted on taking her and meeting his parents, who said they would be at home the whole time, my head and my gut were unsure. Amy visited family friends in Hawaii from June 23rd until July 8th. Three days into her visit, I started shaking and hyperventilating upon discovering a note in her recycle bin about a pregnancy scare, confirming my suspicions about this new "friend." I was extremely concerned about how scared Amy was six thousand miles away. I was actually relieved to have an appointment with Dr. Sporsy that morning. It took me a few minutes to calm down, and he commented how Amy always left a trail as if she wanted to be caught. After men-

tioning the prospect of a rape charge, Dr. Sporsy coached me on having a conversation with Amy. My focus needed to be protecting her, and how I wanted to come across. Amy needed to feel comforted from the phone call, without me conveying anger or defensiveness.

While gardening later that day, I was imagining the horrors of a teen pregnancy, and which relative might adopt a baby if she carried to term. My stomach turned as I remembered her creepy friend and the uneasiness with which I left her at his house. I did *not* want to become a grandmother, or mother to a fourth child, this way. I talked with a school nurse friend, Trina, sharing how Amy had been asking what a "normal" stomach looked like.

After exchanging text messages and voicemails, I told Amy about finding the note. She said she had "pushed him off" and didn't want to discuss dates. We agreed to talk the next day, when I reminded her that she could call me any time of the day or night. My husband and I had dinner that night with our friends, Meyer and Giuliana. But I continued thinking that while Amy probably wasn't pregnant, HIV and sexually transmitted infections were still risks. She and I had spoken frequently about the emotional and physical downsides of teen sex, and she always said what she probably thought I wanted to hear: that she would wait until marriage. Later, we successfully talked things through. She was incredibly relieved when she had her period. In debriefing with Dr. Sporsy, he wanted me to make sure I reiterated to Amy how she needed to remember to make far, far better choices, that she wouldn't want to be in this position again, and to reflect on the lessons learned. Nice words, no change.

In mid-July, Amy resumed oboe lessons, one of her many middle school instruments. She and I went to our family's condo, and her friend from summer camp after sixth grade visited for four days, which was not pleasant for Amy or me. I was feeling "like an emotional wreck" at all her push-back: swimming outside of the posted hours, rollerblading after dark, her Abercrombie & Fitch® "microskirt" and skimpy underwear, her threatening to dye her hair (how benign in retrospect, and something she never did), and threatening to go goth. Amy also started befriending boys who worked at the condo complex. Subsequently, I discovered photos of Amy during that time with boys we did not know in places we did not recognize. We later learned that she started smoking marijuana around that time. She had come back to the condo all upset over losing $20 in the food court, which we later learned from her journal was some drug purchase gone awry. Amid all this agita she was talking about podiatry as a career, and I wondered if adopting a dog would be crazy.

In early August, I was assaulted at a coffee shop by the mother from the January harassment accusation, right before leaving for a week's family vacation at the condo. I felt shaken and scared, as my daughter's actions—real or perceived—had resulted in my being threatened. Incidents like this "weren't supposed to happen" in my family, or to me as a responsible adult.

Lily visited us at the condo, not without dozens of cell phone calls to arrange her drop-off, including calls while on a family hike. But we had some good moments. I always loved reading to my children, and I savored the bonding time with Amy as I read aloud *The Secret Life of Bees*, the BVMP all-school summer reading book, even though she was more than capable of reading it herself.

Amy's BVMP friend, Audrey, joined us for two days. Audrey had filled much of the friendship gap when Lily left BVMP, and seemed a little ahead of Amy in the world of boys and pushing the proverbial envelope, though nothing that seemed dangerous. I had taught Audrey as a ninth-grader and felt comfortable with her parents. I had even worked with her mom before the girls were born. In eleventh grade, Amy and Audrey came up with the same androgynous nickname for each other, as had Amy and Lily.

During the vacation I wrote, "Realizing the large part of my life is spent in emotional pain/anxiety." I became aware of looking at the world through the lens of anxiety, and the girls were commenting on my sighing. I stayed at the condo for a few days on my own, joined by a longtime nursing professor friend, Gail, whose two children were best friends with our son and first daughter in preschool. Even this brief respite was rejuvenating.

In late August, Amy's oboe teacher declared her as the second most talented student he'd taught. His most talented was currently studying with the nation's No. 1 oboist. I wished that Amy would use her talents wisely instead of putting so much energy into being difficult. Soon after, Amy's teacher said that she was ready for a professional quality instrument because she had pretty much outgrown her rental. Amy also started running with me, which provided healthy and enjoyable bonding time. She also prepared an amazing PowerPoint presentation to justify a TV in her room. Our first daughter left to start college on August 24th. And after all our deliberations on which school Amy should attend, she agreed to return to BVMP. Sophomore year *had* to be easier.

Three
September 2004, Tenth Grade: from busted to blossoming

The school year started in late August, with the hurt of Amy snapping, "Go away!" to me. She was complaining about my "strictness" and "needing" four hours at the mall. *No* parent should fall for that line!

In early September, Amy, Audrey, and I went to our condo. They visited a girl who Amy claimed to have met nearby while rollerblading. My husband believed this story was thin. On the 9th, Amy staffed the reception desk for our start-up company's annual reunion. To my relief, the cover charge money reconciled exactly. The next day during a school field trip, Amy made several unexplained calls to Connecticut, Maryland, and Canalboro, the city closest to us. She met with her therapist, Ms. Firther, on September 15th, and they decided they could wait until November 17th to meet again, which seemed like a long gap to me. Amy had made a call at 7:18 that morning to the condo region, and received a call at noon, violating the school policy of no cell phone use during the school day.

The next day, I talked with Audrey's grandmother in the school parking lot about what a good influence the girls had been on each other, saying words that I was starting to wonder if I really believed. Amy made two calls to Connecticut around noon, during the school day, then at 3:04. On the 17th, she called the condo area at 8:02 a.m., then more calls to the southwest part of the state, Connecticut, and the condo area after school. If these details seem excessive, they nonetheless show how I was processing the evolving events. And since the itemized phone bills arrived a month or more after the offending calls, we were always behind the proverbial eight ball, and sometimes fell for Amy's insistence that she had ceased contact with a certain party.

My husband accompanied our son in mid-September to start his sophomore year of college. Amy requested a mother/daughter weekend at the condo, a welcome but atypical request. On Saturday, she went to the mall and said she spent some time with her rollerblading friend. Amy and I had a nice dinner out. On Sunday, I went for my last pre-marathon twenty-mile run, and Amy spent more time at the mall.

On the drive home, I harbored the feeling "our relationship feels too good to be true." We missed being in a serious highway accident by a fraction of a second. I thought about how different our lives would have been had that split second gone against us. Little could I guess that the equivalent of a serious car wreck was less than twenty-four hours away. That evening Amy refused to attend a parent-child Confirmation class, citing too much school work, so I attended alone. (Confirmation is a Catholic sacrament typically prepared for and administered during the early high school years.)

Found with Marijuana

The next afternoon, Amy tossed her purse into my classroom around 2:45 before cross country practice. At about 3:00, the principal came into my classroom to report that Amy was meeting with the athletic director, Ms. Dirath, in the gym. Two teammates had heard that Amy and Audrey were "doing something" after school. They informed the captains, who told the coach, who took Amy and Audrey to Ms. Dirath. I mentioned to the principal that the purse was in my room. I opened Amy's gym bag and found about $80 in cash, then opened the purse and sniffed. It smelled like what I had learned to recognize as marijuana in college dorm corridors. I tucked the purse under my jacket and walked across the parking lot to the gym.

As I approached Ms. Dirath's office, Amy and Audrey were coming out. Amy glared at me and snapped, "I didn't do anything wrong!" (Throughout the ninth grade, one of Amy's trademarks was to look at me and ask if she was in trouble.) Ms. Dirath looked in the purse with me. She identified two pipes, roaches, and a solid dark substance. Definitely weed, she concluded. My heart sank as my mind wondered what we were going to do.

As I walked back to the main building, one of Amy's classmates approached me, saying, "Amy wants to know if you know where her purse is." I basically told the student this matter was not up for discussion. Meanwhile, Amy and Audrey were put at separate ends of a classroom to wait for both sets of parents to arrive. Two months later, we would discover what this experience was like for Amy:

I'm such a fucking piece of shit. I'm in
homeroom rite now. it's
4 PM. I just got caught smoking
pot. Me, Audrey and — went driving after
school. we smoked a couple bowls and
then we came back for cross country
practice. Everyone was like "you guys
are so stoned" and we were like
"um no." n then ~~we~~ the people from my
track team ~~were~~ told the coach
and Dirath ~~we went to~~ on
our way out (the captain) was
like "could you 2 stay back a sec?
Dirath wants to see you" we went
in and coach and her were
sitting on chairs and they were
like "there've been some rumors going
around about you two" I was like "I
know, everyone's talking about us.
I'm feeling rejected" n ~~the~~ Dirath
was like "well do you know what this
chit-chat's about?" and we were
like "no, and it's outrageous that you'd
ever ask somthing like that" and
they were like "okay, well I want you
to know that I've called your mother
down and she's coming down rite
now just so we can let her know
about our situation." we went ~~back~~
out and started strefching
w/the team and everyone was
talking about ~~us~~ us. we were

just sitting there and everyone was like staring and this girl was talking about how me'n Audrey always talk about drugs and stuff. Then Dirath came out and she goes "Amy, your mother found your pocketbook so... we know you lied" and then she started talking about how we shouldn't do drugs and blah blah blah. Rite now I'm sitting in an empty classroom waiting for my dad to get here so the principal, me, and my parents can all have a meeting. Audrey and her dad just got out of their meeting. She came back and mouthed "we're suspended for the rest of the week" and then took her stuff and told me to call her cell phone when I can I just cannot fucking believe this happened. I'm such a fucking douche. My life was not far from perfect. Now I'm suspended, my good stars is going down the shitter, and just omg. this means no Florida, no more internet in my room, no more hanging out w/ Audrey.

My husband drove the nearly forty miles from his office to BVMP and we met with the principal. Amy insisted that there was a "big whisper" about drugs being stashed behind the gym, she and Audrey found them, and then walked off school property to smoke. She heard marijuana was good for stress, and she was upset about her results on a recent math quiz. They had planned to throw the paraphernalia in the woods but decided against it.

The principal and Ms. Dirath had searched behind the gym and saw nothing to corroborate Amy's story. I turned the illegal contents over to the principal to provide to the town police, which felt like the right thing to do. I could not deny what had happened.

Amy and Audrey would be suspended for the rest of the week, and they would not receive any credit for work done during those four days. Per state Athletic Association rules, they would be off the cross country team for two weeks and required to be in counseling. My husband took Amy home, while I prepared to meet parents, some of whom had daughters on the cross country team, at "Back To School Night." The principal had to address parents, and had spent the afternoon dealing with the marijuana incident. I could not believe I was in the middle of such a situation. I fulfilled my professional duties that night, weary as I drove home to our new situation.

My husband and I agreed that Amy should not be left alone, and he stayed home with her on Tuesday. We had a slight concern about her harming herself. She met with her psychiatrist, Dr. Loftad, which seemed to go well. She was home with my husband on Wednesday, and met with Ms. Firther in the afternoon. In retrospect, I have to wonder how well coordinated the "meds provider" was with the "talk therapist." While this "split" model has become the norm, it did not appear to serve Amy well. She and I attended the evening meeting for fall athletes and their parents. While most families were probably thinking of varsity letters, I self-consciously felt as if I were wearing some scarlet letter because of my daughter, all the more complicated because I taught so many of the athletes in that room.

On Wednesday, I met both with the principal and Mrs. Guicona, Amy's guidance counselor. Mrs. Guicona raised concerns about Amy's lack of judgment and the pot smoking as a symptom of lack of coping mechanisms. When my husband and I talked with Amy that evening, we told her our paramount concern was truth telling, and that her story about the source of the drugs would not be so thin if she were willing to provide names. Audrey asserted that Amy brought the drugs to school but had not sourced them during our weekend trip. For years after, I had imagined that on *my* deathbed, Amy would ultimately reveal the true source of the drugs.

On Thursday, Amy went into work with my husband, and we let her stay home on Friday, then she and I ran at 5:00 p.m. On Saturday, she came to my weekly running group with me. Despite the incident, Amy kept up well with her academics. She just as easily could have said, "Forget it." She let me help her with her homework on Sunday, and she had an oboe lesson, so we were gravitating back to some semblance of normal.

On Monday, we met with the principal, and Amy signed her contract to return to school, including consequences in the event of future violations. Ms. Dirath herself, and not the coach, told the cross country team that Amy and Audrey were to be welcomed back. "Everyone makes mistakes," she said, "and they should be treated as you would want to be treated." Amy saw Dr. Loftad on the 28th, and she made a cell phone call during lunch.

Amy was wearing me down concerning plans she wanted to make with an older student, Sabine, in her math class. Amy made a call to Connecticut at 11:11, Maryland at 12:10, and Canalboro at 12:15. She saw Ms. Firther at 3:30, which included an outburst at the end of the session about being at BVMP. Apparently, Amy convinced Ms. Firther that their next meeting could still wait until November 17th! I was *not* comfortable with this gap of nearly two months given the recent marijuana incident and all the issues at play.

On the last Thursday of the month, Amy was going to have a sleepover with Sabine, since there were no classes on Friday due to a faculty professional day. I'm not sure why my husband and I hadn't grounded Amy; looking back, it seems like such an obvious action to take. I talked with Sabine's dad around 5:00 p.m. to verify that the sleepover plans were okay. He said, not very convincingly, the adults would be home watching  the presidential debates. My mind flashed back to what had happened when Roy's parents said that they would be home, and I felt uneasy.

Mid-evening, the landline rang. It was one of my colleagues who felt awkward calling, but said that a student who cared about me and knew Amy overheard her saying that she was going to break out of the house that night, presumably Sabine's. This tip-off was one of the rare examples when someone came forward with information about Amy's safety. I thank my colleague to this day.

I called Amy, but I did not share that I'd received the call. Instead, I told her that her father was feeling ill and asked her to come home. She groaned but offered no real resistance. When Sabine dropped her off, Amy went right to the phone, looked at the caller ID, and asked accusingly why my colleague had called. I was truthfully able to say it was because of the faculty retreat the next day. Amy, my husband, and I watched the debates. When reviewing this manuscript, my friend Corinne observed that maybe we had rescued Amy from a situation she didn't want to be in, and having her come home was actually a relief. On Friday, I returned home by early afternoon, hoping that nothing would have gone seriously wrong in those few hours since Amy woke up.

On the first Sunday in October, I took Amy and her friend, Lily, to the mall in the afternoon, then brought them to Mass, after which they had Confirmation preparation class. Amy did not sit with me. In scanning the rather small church, I never saw her. Her teacher did not see her on the side of the church where Amy insisted she had been sitting. Amy said she went downstairs early to help set up for Confirmation, which a teacher did verify.

On Monday, Amy was supposed to be in the library with Audrey at 3:00 p.m., and I did not see her. She received a detention for a uniform violation; I did not see the form until her backpack search a month later. On Tuesday, Amy took it upon herself to apologize to the cross country team. The next day, I drove her to Walmart after school, where she bought herself a TV with her own money based on having convinced us with her summer PowerPoint presentation that she had a responsible plan. On Friday, she made two calls during her after-lunch study. That evening, I took her to Audrey's around 9:00 p.m. so they could go to cross country practice together on Saturday morning.

Marathon Weekend

Amy did not want to fly out of town with my husband and me to watch the marathon and visit her brother and sister. My husband and I decided she could stay home. I did not want a balky teenager distracting me from my second 26.2-mile race. I had trained hard all summer and was hoping to run it in four hours and five minutes, which would qualify me for the Boston Marathon, my goal. We agreed that a friend who used to work for me, Kalli, would spend both nights with her. Amy asked me to stop by Audrey's on my way to the airport. I felt flattered, but in retrospect, she may have been trying to make me feel good and assuage her guilt as she was perpetrating another scheme.

After my flight landed, I was underground in the airport terminal when Kalli called. Her friend was in crisis, and she needed to be with her that night. Kalli said she could bring the friend with her to our house, or have Amy sleep at the friend's house. After numerous phone calls, my husband and I decided that Amy would spend the night home alone, since she was going to be babysitting from 6:00 until 10:00 p.m. anyhow.

Kalli arrived Sunday around noon. She took Amy shopping and out for dinner, spent the night, and left for work on Monday morning. I returned home mid-afternoon on Columbus Day. My husband would be away the rest of the week. Months later, we learned from Amy's journal that she had had people over to the house to do drugs on Saturday night after babysitting. The phone bill showed many incoming and outgoing calls that day, and while she told me she went to sleep as soon as she returned home from babysitting, calls continued after midnight. I wish I had called the town police to do a well-being check, or insisted that a neighbor or friend or relative pick her up for the night. "Conned by Amy" became our phrase of exasperation. As my husband notes, perhaps some readers will ask how could we have fallen for this stuff. But, at the time, the choices we made always seemed reasonable, or not sufficiently unreasonable. As Corinne says, we try to do the right thing as parents, but the reality of choices can be so very difficult in the moment.

On Wednesday, October 13th, after PSATs (a preliminary standardized test for college admission), I gave Amy permission to go home with Audrey and her grandmother at noon, and then return for practice. Amy later told me they went to the mall instead. She made calls throughout the afternoon, including several to an unknown number in Canalboro. On Friday, she called the Connecticut number right before school, made a call during her math class, and during lunch to Maryland and to Connecticut.

The unsettling patterns continued. Early the next week, she called Connecticut mid-day, went to Audrey's after school, and when I picked her up in the early evening I learned she hadn't been to cross country practice. The next day, she made a call before school. After school, I had a dentist and doctor appointment that took longer than expected. Amy was supposed to call me; she left no message until 5:10. She made numerous phone calls after school, withdrew $20 at a gas station ATM, and apparently had been with Sabine. Amy reported a rumor about a Friday "sick-out" at school. I said "no way" could she lie and call in sick and miss school.

I had to have a follow-up heart stress test the next morning, which would have been completely unnecessary had the doctors really listened about the behavioral stresses in my life. Amy had her phone on, again violating school policy, but she claimed it was so she could receive any messages from me. She made a call at 7:45, received one at 11:33, made one at 12:06, and received one at 12:31. She received four calls during her biology lab. I was exasperated trying to chase this moving target of calls that seemed to have taken on a life of its own. I hope that anyone in a similar scenario will be more assertive than I was.

At the end of the day I collected Amy and Audrey, who *had* skipped school, in Northwood, the city next to BVMP. We spent an hour at the electronics store where Amy was all excited about buying a new camera phone. I talked with Audrey's dad from Northwood, with both girls in the car, saying my husband or I would bring Audrey home afterward. The girls were going to work on a biology project at our house and were debating whether to go to a dance at the high school in Audrey's town. Around 8:00 p.m., Audrey's dad showed up at our door; the girls had called him to pick them up, contrary to the expectations I'd set in Northwood, which they claimed they did not hear. The dad's jaw dropped when I mentioned that there had in fact been school that day. Audrey had convinced him there was not, and she had spent the day at work with him.

On Saturday, Audrey's mom took the girls to a cross country meet in Broton, where Amy made and received numerous phone calls. Audrey was picked up early. I went to collect Amy, only to find out she was not supposed to leave yet. I spoke with her coach about recent erratic attendance at practice, but neither of us could offer the other a solution.

On Sunday, Amy worked diligently on her biology project. I dropped her at Audrey's, whose parents had bought her concert tickets and arranged limo transportation as a birthday present. Amy was invited, and again made and received numerous phone calls. Apparently the performance ran late, and they were not back at Audrey's until about 1:30 a.m. I arrived on Monday morning to pick up the girls and take them to school. Audrey's parents said "never again" to a concert on a school night. Audrey had no biology project.

That afternoon, Amy withdrew money from a non-bank ATM, which I could see online because her account was linked to mine. On Wednesday, she had one incoming and three outgoing calls before school. This continuing pattern of phone calls and cash withdrawals felt wrong, and in retrospect was a huge red flag. I felt powerless in dealing with it and was increasingly frustrated that the professionals from whom I was seeking help didn't seem to be providing any help that was actually working. I feared the cash withdrawals and phone calls were drug related, but confronting Amy was like trying to hold a wet, flapping fish.

At this time, one of Amy's teachers requested a conference with me about Amy's recent behavior, which sounded a lot like the immature patterns of the previous year. I called Ms. Firther because I felt like we were dealing with increasingly serious issues, and too much could go wrong in the nearly two-month gap between scheduled sessions. My therapist, Dr. Sporsy, had expressed concern at my November 2nd session that Ms. Firther wasn't getting Amy to talk, and he also encouraged me to call her.

Ms. Firther responded that Amy's behavior was within the realm of normal. Often with adolescents, she explained, you see how long you can go between sessions, because you don't want therapy to seem punitive. She encouraged Amy and me to meet with teachers to see if we could resolve matters on our own, and she hoped I could handle it. She said to call back if I didn't get results or something didn't feel right. She could meet on the 10th, and while I felt an urgency to prioritize the session, I was torn. I decided that it was more important for Amy to attend her cross country banquet at that time to keep her school life more normal. Also, the time slot was too early for my husband to attend a parent meeting, and I didn't want to impose yet again on his work time.

The Retreat Debacle

On Thursday, November 4th, Amy called Connecticut at 7:40, 12:05, and 2:11. After school, Amy had a podiatrist appointment, and I made sure to let the coach and Ms. Dirath know why she would not be at practice. The next day Amy had incoming calls at 8:50 and several after school. She did not bring her cross country clothes, citing her overnight Confirmation retreat that weekend. Once home, she called the nursing home where she had volunteered a few times to schedule Saturday volunteer work at 2:00 p.m., although the retreat ran until 6:00 p.m. As we pulled out of the garage, Amy also swore she left her cell phone in her bedroom. I should have demanded the phone before we left, but I suppose I wanted to believe her, and I was feeling increasingly anxious about delivering her late.

When we arrived, I told the leaders about Amy's Saturday plan, perhaps defending her by saying at least she'd be present for most of the retreat. They unambiguously replied, "No way. She's tried to get out of things before. If she doesn't stay for the whole time, she'll need to redo an entire retreat at another time." I left without informing Amy of this news. Once home, I checked her room in obvious places for her cell phone. It was nowhere to be found. I called the nursing home to tell them Amy would not be coming on Saturday. I now see that this sequence of my behaviors might be viewed as enabling by not letting her feel the full brunt of the consequences. But my daughter was only fifteen, and I didn't want to appear as an irresponsible parent or family.

I collected Amy from the retreat on Saturday around 6:00 p.m., expecting a major eruption. There was none. Perhaps I had again relieved her anxiety by enforcing limits. I told her I had decided that the final four hours at the retreat were better than twenty-four more hours later. Amy talked about meeting Audrey for breakfast, wanting to make it a Sunday tradition. But she slept until mid-afternoon, making breakfast a moot point.

On Wednesday, November 10th, I awoke at 5:20 a.m. so I could drop Amy at Audrey's by 6:00 a.m. to finish one of Audrey's projects. I had understood that Audrey's mom was going to wait for them at breakfast. But Audrey's dad dropped them at a restaurant, the girls (it turned out) smoked marijuana, then Audrey's mom collected them and drove them to school. Audrey was not present in my class, and I sent first period attendance up to the office, writing, "Please advise."

Twenty minutes later, halfway through the class, I heard a knock at the door next to my classroom. I opened the door for Sabine, who was walking in from the parking lot. She was constantly tardy, but 8:17 was unusually late even for her. Just then, Audrey's mom's car pulled up, and Amy and Audrey climbed out. I very firmly told the mother this tardiness was unacceptable. I had told Amy that under no circumstances was she to be late for school, and they could have called. I canceled Amy's and Audrey's sleepover scheduled for that night. I had to walk back into my classroom and continue teaching. Amy opted out of cross country that day while I was in a faculty meeting. Amy insisted later that Audrey's mom thought I was "psycho" in how I communicated my frustration.

Amy slept in on Veterans Day while I attended a professional day on preventing child sexual abuse. I had not realized how so many perpetrators are very strategic in their planning and plotting, a behavior pattern that I now see applies to addicts. My husband later found a text message that appeared to come from Roy, "Amy, did you smoke yesterday?" and her reply, "Hell, yes!" Bravada, or breaking the rules at home?

On November 13th, my husband and I decided to visit our condo and, uncharacteristically, Amy came without a fuss. She wanted to have a sleepover with her rollerblading girlfriend. We offered to host the sleepover, but Amy begged to stay at her friend's since they had just acquired two kittens, and she even showed me photos. I called and talked with the woman who said she was the friend's mom, who assured me that she was an experienced mother of teenagers and wouldn't let them get away with anything. She was allegedly out getting pizzas when we dropped off Amy around 4:30. My husband and I stopped by again on our way to dinner and met her to make sure all was okay. I didn't feel particularly comfortable with the setup, but at least we had taken this step of due diligence. We even offered to take the girls out to breakfast.

The next morning we collected Amy at 8:45, and her friend was not available for breakfast due to a doctor's appointment. On a Sunday morning? Why hadn't this fact been mentioned the night before? Further, Amy had always been hypersensitive to cigarette smoke, yet she said it really didn't bother her at their house. The phone bill later showed that Amy had numerous calls all evening. Reading her journals subsequently revealed that it was a night of substance and sexual experimentation, involving more than her girlfriend. Upon returning home, Amy attended Confirmation class that night.

Alcohol Allegations

During lunch on Monday, November 15th, I was providing extra help for students in my classroom. Near the end of the period, one of my students walked in and said she needed to speak with me, and not in front of the others in the room. We stepped into the hallway. She said she didn't want to be seen, so we stepped outdoors.

She told me that, at lunchtime in the cafeteria, Amy was passing around and drinking alcohol. She wanted me to know as Amy's mom, citing the fact that she had siblings of whom she felt very protective. She also said Amy was using cocaine (also known as coke). I thanked her, and the bell rang. How could I tell what was true, especially given the marijuana incident? Once again I questioned what I should do.

As I walked upstairs to my 12:32 meeting, I saw the dean walking into the faculty room. She had had cafeteria duty that day; I shared the allegation. She did not recall seeing anything unusual and would talk to the principal. She was previously assistant principal and in charge of discipline, and as the mother of several grown children, she was well versed in adolescent behaviors.

I stepped across the hall to check my mailbox and found a note from Mrs. Guicona, saying, "Please see me ASAP." Thinking the note might have been about the cafeteria suspicion, I went straight up to the guidance office. In fact, another disturbing matter was at hand. Mrs. Guicona mentioned how, a few weeks earlier, Amy had come to her office during a study period and, instead of talking, proceeded to take out her books and start homework. She found this behavior odd, but allowed Amy to continue working. A few minutes later, Amy prompted Mrs. Guicona to turn around and took her picture using her cell phone. Mrs. Guicona asked Amy to erase it, which Amy claimed she did. Mrs. Guicona asked to talk to me because, in retrospect, she found the incident troubling, a real betrayal of trust. I gave her a heads-up about the cafeteria suspicion, and went late to my meeting.

When I went downstairs for my 1:16 class, the principal was waiting for me. She said that she could not ascertain enough evidence about the cafeteria allegation and thought it would be best if I asked Amy about the accusation that evening, which I did. Of course, Amy denied it. She thought she was being framed. I asked why. She posited that perhaps others were jealous that she'd done well on her report card. We confiscated her cell phone due to the incident with Mrs. Guicona and asked her to apologize, especially given how often she had gone "above and beyond" supporting Amy.

On Tuesday morning, Amy and I had a "fight" regarding Sabine. It might have been over a math project. At 8:10, I went to ask the principal for her counsel since Amy had denied the cafeteria incident. She suggested I talk with the student informant and ask if she actually saw, smelled, or heard anything and if she was willing to confront Amy. She said, "It's *not* a matter of getting Amy in trouble, it's a matter of getting her the help she needs." She also commented that the way that Amy and her friends isolated themselves set them up for being the target of rumor.

The principal also noted that Amy passed by her office twice after lunch, something that had not happened in a while. Amy had study hall at that time, and cell phone records later showed a call made at 12:30 to Audrey's town, then at 2:32 to Maryland, and 2:51 to Connecticut. Later that afternoon, I met with Dr. Sporsy. Amy accompanied me and stayed in the waiting room. He vented that he felt like pulling Amy into our session because it didn't seem that Ms. Firther was getting her to talk, but he didn't. Ironically, exactly five years later, on November 16th, 2009, I would be in the meeting where Amy admitted to being a heroin addict.

At report card conferences that night, I met with the parents of forty-one students. Meanwhile, my husband met with Amy's teachers, and without a doubt received the best reports we'd ever heard. Of particular note was the project she did for health, which was to portray yourself on the cover of *Time* magazine in thirty years. Amy projected herself as just having been named the first female General Manager of the Red Sox, and married with three children. The teacher was astounded how Amy's project was perfect in every detail, including the current twenty-something manager portrayed with gray hair in the 2034 passing-the-baton photograph.

In addition, I conferred with Amy's math teacher, who was also my department head. Amy had mentioned that she was going to do a project with Sabine. A few days prior, I ran it by the teacher, asking if that was legitimate. She said absolutely not. If students wanted to work in groups, they had to let her know in advance, which they did not. Also, Amy needed a good grade, which she doubted would happen working with Sabine, and she believed that Amy would end up doing most of the work. The teacher reported a few days later that she talked to Amy, who was furious with her. Amy was also angry with me, yelling, "You don't want me to have friends!" A few weeks later, I learned that Sabine did not hand in a project.

At 9:20 p.m., Dr. Loftad returned the call I'd put in to her after school. She felt the issues I was describing were more behavioral than medication-related. She asked if Amy was having thoughts regarding cutting or hurting herself. How would I have known? She said Amy wouldn't come close to being eligible for drug treatment or hospitalization. I didn't think to ask why not.

More from the Student Informant

On Wednesday, November 17th, my student informant came to talk with me at 11:30. We prayed to start the meeting, an aspect I liked about teaching in a Catholic school. She provided details about the Monday cafeteria incident, including that Amy and her friends were bragging about it. She questioned why Amy was drawing so much negative attention to herself. She was at the table across from Amy and her two friends. She claimed they'd been bringing in Dasani® water bottles filled with gin for awhile. It was being passed around the table and thrown in the trash at the end of lunch. She said it had been happening so much that people were noticing, and given that it was a small school, word spread. She said that Amy had told everyone that someone had come to tell me about what happened on Monday.

Frighteningly, she provided additional input, which I did not share with Amy. She said Amy hadn't stopped carrying weed to school. She asked, as if answering, why Amy *always* carried her backpack. She said Amy was hanging around with the wrong crowd, and had been going for car rides with older students pretty frequently. I asked how easy it was to obtain drugs at school, and she said you could ask one particular student today and have whatever you wanted tomorrow.

She went on to say that drugs were the main problem for Amy, and all other problems led from that. She asked me about the source of Amy's money. I said she babysat a lot and earned some allowance. She said coldly, "You might want to start checking your wallet." She claimed Amy was using cocaine, even though she had not actually seen her, admitting that it can be difficult to catch someone in the act of snorting. She agreed to think about whether other students would be willing to come forward along with her.

At 11:50 I called my husband and left a message for Ms. Firther. I decided I wanted to sleep on this news. I walked upstairs and found the dean, and we went to the school prayer room. She emphasized that I was dealing with drugs, not my daughter. It was a "survival thing" at this point for Amy and kids would lie, steal, and cheat. In retrospect, she thought maybe we should *not* have told Amy about the alcohol accusation, because it gave Amy a chance to clean up her story and be one step ahead of the adults. Also, we decided that I should not share with Amy the money and cocaine information, because that could impede any investigation. She also advised that talking with Amy would only confuse me.

At 3:00 p.m., I took Amy to her first session with Ms. Firther in six weeks. I believe I had to leave yet another faculty meeting early, adding to the tension I felt between being a responsible mom and a professional. I noticed that Amy's eyes looked funny and one of her pupils appeared larger than the other, but I couldn't be sure. Now I know I should not have second-guessed myself.

Ms. Firther told me, probably when I spoke with her privately either just before or after Amy's session, that what was normal varied per kid. She said we needed to let the school handle the investigation. I do not recall receiving any suggestions from her about the cocaine and cash concerns.

I later told Amy that the truth would prevail, and I reminded her that when she was caught with marijuana on September 20th her first assertion was a defensive, "I didn't do anything wrong." Amy argued that the principal being in my classroom during the last period on Monday meant it had to be about her. I countered that a principal could have many reasons for being in a teacher's classroom. It seemed to me that Amy was connecting bizarre dots.

Meanwhile, BVMP asked the faculty to step up vigilance at lunchtime. I thought back to a day when Amy and Audrey broke the school rules by leaving the main building before lunch to buy a drink from the vending machines in the gym. When Amy told me before heading home from school that day that she had agreed with the music teacher to bring candy for the upcoming sophomore field trip to the symphony, I made a mental note to verify her claim with the teacher.

That evening, I discussed the day with my husband and asserted that Amy should not be allowed to babysit until we had a clearer picture of what was going on. He did not feel this step was necessary yet, and I deferred. He did a preliminary screen of Amy's text and voice messages and, due to the concerning nature of some of them, planned to do a more thorough screening over the weekend. I ended that evening thinking that if a greater good were to come from all this scrutiny, it would be to create a safer environment for all BVMP students.

I also left a message for the principal that I needed to fill her in face-to-face about my conversation with Ms. Firther. It was clear I needed to be out of the middle so that the school could investigate, but I would help however I was needed. Also, per Amy, Audrey knew about the Monday accusation, even though I had specifically asked Amy to not share that information. I should have realized that such a request was not realistic because Amy had no sense of confidentiality.

The principal was going to be meeting with Audrey's parents on Thursday morning regarding some other matters, and I told her I thought it was fair to tell them that the school was beginning to investigate the Monday cafeteria incident and any ties to substance abuse issues, so not to be surprised if the school was in contact in a few days. Meanwhile, I suggested that she ask Audrey's parents to keep a close eye on their daughter. I also shared the Wednesday morning breakfast incident so she would not be caught by surprise. I recommended that if Audrey did not have an after-school commitment, she should be picked up at dismissal, which her parents agreed to do.

On Thursday, November 18th before the sophomores left for their field trip, I checked with the music teacher about Amy's candy purchase. I was relieved to learn it was legitimate.

The Locker Search

At 8:45 a.m. I met with Mrs. Guicona and the principal to discuss the status of the investigation. I started by recapping the week's progress. Most recently, the principal had just met with Audrey's parents at 7:00, and reported that Audrey's dad would call me. We decided it would be appropriate to search Amy's locker and backpack due to the reported suspicions, and it was a good day to do it since the sophomores were out of the building. We agreed we would take the same action if it were any other student, that we were more comfortable searching together, and we would search during lunch when the other students would be in the cafeteria. The principal said if the drug issue were really pervasive, they would involve the police. She emphasized that dealing drugs was very different than using, and the school had zero tolerance for dealing.

We discussed my student informant, and the principal said that the student would run the risk of more exposure if others stepped forward, so to tell her to scratch that idea. She also posited that if rumors were that rampant, others would be hearing it. We ended the meeting by talking about Amy's lack of honesty and poor judgment, including the cell phone photo of Mrs. Guicona. They advised me as a parent that until my husband and I could really trust Amy, we should not entrust other people's children to her and thus not allow her to babysit for the foreseeable future.

I called my husband with these updates at 9:40 a.m., and I called our first daughter's counselor, Dr. Hischolor, to see if she could meet with my husband and me about how to handle the current situation as parents. We felt that her knowledge of our family would provide some helpful perspectives, and we had come to trust her over the years. At 10:00, I talked with Mrs. Guicona, who said that Ms. Firther had used the term "characterological" in reference to Amy. This was the first time I'd heard this ominous-sounding word, and I made note to learn more about it later.

During lunch, the principal, Mrs. Guicona, and I went to the lockers, with Mrs. Guicona guarding the entrance to the area. I did the actual searching. In Amy's backpack, I found pictures of her with guys I did not know, but nothing else. Her locker contained several air fresheners and more photos. I called my husband. While we were both relieved, not having found any alcohol or drugs provided hollow reassurance because we knew that Amy could be steps ahead of us.

Entering my last period class, my student informant slipped me a copy of a handwritten note saying under her breath, "I thought you might want to see this." I recognized both Amy's and another student's handwriting.

let u know if I hear anything.
What did the principal say? Seriously
just go to your mom ; be like
look what it is, someone is
trying to get me in trouble ;
I didn't do anything! but all
upset ; shit. See if you can
get her to tell you who it
was, then we'll jump her. lol!
haha- dude we think it mite b that girl

from my grade). the principal and the dean actually
took my side . The dean was like "i didn't
see anything weird" n the principal told my
mom that it mite just b rumors.. i'll

just cry n b like "ppl just want me
outta the school"...wtf tho-- who does
that? Yah my parents deffinetly don't
believe me at all but i'll hopefully
change that. Whatever

I never told Amy I had that note, and I gave a copy to the principal.

That evening, I spoke with Audrey's dad. He asked about my concerns, and I shared that one was the girls isolating themselves from classmates. We agreed that rumors were generally not without base. He said that Audrey was grounded over the breakfast incident, citing a one-hour timeline discrepancy. Amy's version had been that they went into the convenience store, bought candy, went into the restaurant, and about eight customers were ahead of them. They had coffee first, ordered, and the food took a while.

That evening, I confronted Amy about trustworthiness. She admitted that she did take the cell phone on the Confirmation retreat. I also mentioned her violation of school cell phone policy, and the calls I discovered she had made when I was away at the marathon. Later that night, I went through her bank records, noticing withdrawals in surrounding towns on days I was not with her. The bank was very helpful, providing me with the times so I could confirm they were made after school. But even armed with information, confronting Amy was like walking on eggshells, knowing she'd have some alibi I usually couldn't counter on the spot, or she would erupt in a tirade.

More Cause for Suspicion

On Friday, November 19th, when we parked the car at school, I noticed that Amy left her purse in the trunk. During my late morning free period, I received a message from Ms. Firther about scheduling a family session on Wednesday, and I decided to search Amy's purse. I found $80 in cash, a single-edged razor blade, a small mirror, a small zip-lock plastic bag, and a questionable wrapper. I called my husband. I went over to see Ms. Dirath, who shook her head, saying that these items were telltale signs of coke, including money for her weekend hit. She connected back to the concern the cross country coach had raised to her about Amy always showing up for practice jittery and needing tissues for her nose. The coach had also asked me a few weeks earlier if Amy had a cold because she always needed tissues at the start of practice. Ms. Dirath agreed that I should take the bag to the town police for testing.

Just before 11:00 I called my husband, and we agreed I'd confiscate the four items, and return the purse to the car. Eight minutes later, Mrs. Guicona came downstairs to bring me a booklet about drug use and a website URL. She held the door open for me while I returned the purse to the car, which I always parked across from my classroom. I gave her the confiscated items in a plastic bag for safekeeping. At 11:10 I called and left a message for Audrey's dad. On my way to my class before lunch, I stopped by the principal's office and informed her. We agreed that I should cover lunch duty as scheduled. I noticed Amy with her usual friends in the usual spot, with a few others. She had not come to my classroom to collect her purse at lunchtime as I would have expected, not even to ask for lunch money.

After lunch, I had a brief talk with the dean. She warned me to beware of Amy's sweet talking, including her admitting that she'd lied about using her cell phone at the retreat. I had read a book that asserted how all teenagers lied, the question was how to deal with it. I remember not wanting to accept that lying was a given. I still wanted to believe in the eighth commandment, especially with my daughter.

I called Audrey's dad after lunch, and he was home searching her room. He had a flexible work schedule, unlike his wife who held a corporate job, which was also why I typically spoke with him instead of her. Audrey's counselor had recommended random drug testing. He and I agreed we were fighting a war we had to win. I called my town's police station and arranged to stop by after school.

After my last period class, I was ready to leave, and Amy said she wanted to go home. I said I needed to check my mailbox and headed upstairs. Amy's math teacher stopped me to say that Amy did not have her homework. The principal also stopped me to let me know of two more questionable incidents. The first was from Thursday when the music teacher told her that Amy tried to bring her backpack on the field trip, clearly contrary to expectations. It took Amy seven or eight minutes to return to the bus with her lunch bag, jacket, and pocketbook. Ten minutes before the concert, Amy asked if she and two friends could go for a drink. The music teacher told her no. During the concert, she asked and was told no again. During intermission, the teacher let the girls go one at a time.

The second incident occurred on Friday, when another teacher noticed that Amy brought what appeared to be closed can of seltzer into the classroom, a violation of the school rule on clear water bottles only. The teacher had her leave it at the front of the room. At the end of class she picked it up to give to Amy. It felt light, and Amy was drinking from it. While sometimes people opened soda cans only a little bit, it was concerning that, once again, Amy needed to go against the flow with a minor infraction. As Dr. Sporsy would say, the example was not in itself significant, but adding them all together revealed a major pattern. It brought to mind how my student informant questioned why Amy needed to draw attention to herself in a negative way.

Amy, anxious to leave at 2:10, was nowhere to be found ten minutes later, so I had her paged at 2:27. She claimed she had forgotten her math and English homework and wanted me to fax it when we returned home. Amy also complained that I was being mean.

Meeting the Police

We arrived at the police station around 3:00 p.m. Amy asked why we were there. Without telling her why, I gave her the option of coming in, which she accepted. The officer instantly recognized her from middle school dances, so they had an immediate rapport. I placed the confiscated contents on the table. I recall Amy's body language and speech as neutral, neither defiant nor withdrawn. He asked Amy about the plastic bag. "It's from earrings I bought," she said. "So what's the razor blade for?" he asked. "Cutting myself," she replied. He continued, "Where?" Amy pulled up her left sweater sleeve to reveal a cross-hatched pattern on the inside of her elbow. The discussion immediately shifted to one of personal safety.

"Why?" he asked.

Amy responded, "I was so stressed out about the rumors from Monday about the drinking."

The officer noted that sixty percent of the time rumors ended up being true. He emphasized to Amy how much she had going for her. I asked to talk privately with the officer at the end and relayed the information from my student informant that I had not shared with Amy. He told me about the CHINS program that Dr. Sporsy mentioned and also about hair testing which is considered the authoritative way of establishing type and duration of drug use. But his main concern was for her safety. I was beginning to feel overwhelmed by this plethora of presenting pathologies.

We arrived home at 4:00 p.m. I canceled Amy's 4:00 p.m. Latin tutoring and asked her to keep her bedroom door open. I called my husband to update him, and then the principal to tell her that we had met with the police and discovered cutting. I asked her to confiscate the photos from Amy's locker. Next I left messages for Dr. Loftad and Ms. Firther.

Our friend and neighbor, Trina, her husband, my husband, and I were scheduled for our twice-a-year dinner that night. I asked her if she could instead come and stay with Amy while my husband and I met with Dr. Hischolor because I did not want to leave Amy alone. At 4:20, Audrey's dad called to report he found nothing when searching her room, though later mentioned some letters. I told him of Amy's cutting. He said Audrey had no known history of cutting, but a mutual friend did, and he wondered if Amy's attempts were copycat. I had discouraged Amy's contact with this girl whose father seemed clueless about what the girls were up to when I dropped Amy off one evening. Audrey's dad also said that his daughter admitted to having smoked pot since September 20th, but she said she had not used cocaine.

Ms. Firther called me back at 4:50, and we talked for almost an hour. She said to keep Amy at close range because we were very worried and concerned. She said we did not need to debate with Amy about who was right. She cited the delicate balance parents face between knowing enough versus having proof or evidence. She felt that until the school could tell me that the alcohol accusations were unfounded, we would have to be overly cautious. I said that the cutting scared us, we were concerned about Amy's after-school time, and we needed to batten down the hatches until we were more comfortable. "Concern doesn't always have to be rational," she said, advising that if Amy cut further we should take her to the emergency room (ER). While she claimed Amy was not overtly suicidal, she noted it was a vulnerable time. She recommended that Amy should lose the privilege of Internet in her room but could earn it back. She said to make sure that Amy was with me after school and to tell her it was because I didn't know where she had been. Ms. Firther agreed we'd talk before the Wednesday appointment, and she said we might need to work together on the safety issues. Finally, she said to tell Amy that she was willing to talk with her if it was helpful and also that we would cancel her babysitting.

Dr. Loftad called and said that even if we took Amy to the ER, there was no guarantee of hospitalization. She urged me to count Amy's Zoloft antidepressant pills, and we discovered she had lapsed taking them in recent weeks, something I should have monitored. But Amy had convinced me to trust her, despite Dr. Loftad's warning to the contrary. She reiterated that she did not specialize in kids with drug problems, and while she could order the test for multiple drugs known as a toxicity (tox) screen, the question was whether it was worth doing. The results of a hair test would take at least two weeks. She recommended calling the local probation officer and leaving a message to request some advice. She also urged me to slow down so as not to transmit more anxiety to Amy.

After my phone call with Dr. Loftad, Amy came to tell me she had cut herself with a pen cap and *not* the razor blade, which she had been using to scrape residue off her locker. "So you lied to the police officer?" I asked.

Trina arrived around 7:45, and my husband and I left for the appointment, confident that Amy would be in the best of hands given Trina's calming presence, her experience as a mom, and medical background. My husband revealed that he'd found some disturbing letters in a cursory search of Amy's room that morning. I pulled my thoughts together. We didn't know how sick Amy was. We didn't know the extent of her problems involving illegal drugs, alcohol, sex, stealing, lying, cutting, and deception. I worried whether her involvement could extend into weapons or gangs. How would we navigate trust? How long had I been fooled? How would Amy's issues impact our first daughter who felt so protective of her little sister?

Dr. Hischolor asked about the six-week gap in Amy's therapy from September 29th to November 17th. If "what's normal for Amy" was being cited by Ms. Firther, she said that sounded defensive on Ms. Firther's part. She didn't think Amy's therapy was working. She reiterated that experimenting with cigarettes, alcohol, and pot could be seen as acting out, though *not* normal within our family system. However, she said that coke could wreck Amy's life really fast. She was alarmed about cutting, saying it wasn't normal, and urged us to make sure Amy was current with her tetanus immunization. If Amy were institutionalized, she added, all her rights would be taken away and she'd have to earn them back. We didn't want to over-pathologize, but we had to somehow break her down so she could start rebuilding. And supporting Amy's highest level of functioning was key. She was *not* at rock bottom, Dr. Hischolor claimed, which was the first time we heard that term.

We returned to a calm house. Amy and Trina were watching a movie. At bedtime as I was rubbing Amy's back, I gently mentioned the adage that "you are only as sick as your secrets" and told her that either she needed to tell Ms. Firther about her summer sexual experience, or I would have to. She mumbled in a childlike voice, "You read my diary," to which I reminded her, "No, I found the page you crumpled into the recycle bin."

That evening, I reflected on the phrase "she who doth protest too much." As a ninth-grader, Amy had talked about "all the druggies" at BVMP and those with *real* lying problems. She had been verbally adamant about waiting until marriage for sex although she was experimenting. I also noticed a pattern to her asking me, "Do you think so-and-so is nice?" In fact, most of the girls she named were ones whom I would not put beyond suspicion of drug use. I felt like I was in an action movie: *Guidance*.

The ER Decision

On Saturday, November 20th at 7:00 a.m., I called the cell phone company to reset Amy's voicemail password so my husband could go through those messages. I went to my running group in no state to run, but forced myself to do about a mile. By then I was near the home of my nursing professor friend, Gail, so I stopped in. Her sister was a nurse in the adolescent psychiatric ward at City Pediatrics Teaching Hospital. After relaying the week's events, Gail and her sister convinced me to take Amy to the ER at City Pediatrics, saying people would do so for a lot less than what we'd been through. The goal would be to have her admitted to a clinically based facility for safety and detox. They were telling me in no uncertain terms that right now we were *not* talking about trust.

Around 10:15 I called my husband to update him; he had gone through seventeen of Amy's voicemails, finding some disturbing ones. One cryptic message on March 20th was about a boy named Justin, "Leave him alone or I'll go to your mom, I know where she works." In ninth grade, one of Amy's teachers had raised a concern when seeing "I love Justin" scrawled on Amy's notebooks. When I asked Amy about Justin, she claimed it was the name of her cell phone.

Another message she received during our family vacation was about drug dealing from a former classmate. "You really ought to be more careful about leaving messages when you're high." A message during Audrey's birthday concert from another former classmate referenced specific quantities, types (including mushrooms), and costs of drug purchases.

At 10:45 I called Amy's pediatrician, Dr. Pedreia, and told the office I was taking Amy to the City Pediatrics ER, and asked if they would call ahead for us because Gail had told us that would help. They did so without question. Gail, her sister, and I discussed contingency plans if Amy resisted. I arrived home about 11:20, and she was still asleep. Dr. Erchild from City Pediatrics called to obtain some pre-admission information. I woke Amy, telling her we had a noon doctor's appointment for a tetanus shot, and we needed to get going before they closed. She did not resist or push back with "I need to shower" or her often-used expression, "I look like poo."

My husband, Amy, and I stopped at a Dunkin' Donuts® to buy her breakfast. I silently feared that she would use that stop as an opportunity to run away and was relieved when she did not. At 12:30 p.m. the three of us arrived at City Pediatrics, and my heart went out to the parents filling the waiting room with their physically ill little ones. I felt a little guilty because these other kids were here for real medical problems, while Amy's behavioral health seemed like an avoidable choice that was burdening the system. We were ushered to the "safe" treatment room by 1:00, and the nurse came in at 1:10 to explain the standard procedures of the searches and the room sitter (someone who is paid to sit outside a hospital room and call security if the patient tries to escape). Dr. Erchild asked Amy about her cutting. She replied that she had started with the razor blade but it hurt too much so she changed to a pen cap, which was the third version of the story. We met privately with Dr. Erchild, and then he met with her.

Shortly before 3:00, Dr. Loftad called to caution us about "sequelae" (aftereffects or secondary consequences) with friends if Amy were to be admitted, and she warned us she might not be. She said to ask for a tox screen, despite questioning its value the day before, and thought we did the right thing by bringing her to the ER.

Just past 3:00, Dr. Erchild told us he was going to consult with his supervisor, and at 4:00 p.m. my husband and I were allowed to rejoin Amy, who was watching a movie and about to order lunch. At 5:45 Dr. Erchild returned to say that an inpatient admission was indicated, our health insurance provider agreed, and she would go by ambulance to a nearby inpatient psychiatric hospital. We were a bit surprised to hear that all her lab results were negative. He said the other hospital would help us put together a plan. Amy seemed to take the news in stride. As Dr. Erchild left, I started sobbing. I was finally having a still moment to let all the pain, confusion, and tension of recent weeks come to the surface.

A few minutes later, I asked to speak briefly with Dr. Erchild. I questioned whether any one piece of information was the "tipping point" in deciding to hospitalize Amy. He said, no, the decision was based on a constellation of risk factors, even though she had a clean tox screen. I then asked if we did the right thing bringing her in. He looked at me almost in disbelief, and replied with a firm "Absolutely." I called Gail's sister, who said the available facility was not her favorite, and we wouldn't be thrilled when we saw it, but that it would hold Amy safely.

Hospitalization

My husband and I drove behind the ambulance with heavy hearts (and at what dollar cost, I worried) through unfamiliar city streets as the wet autumn evening darkened into night. True to Gail's sister's prediction, we were *not* thrilled when we saw the facility. Six years later, the online reviews of it are horrifying. I remember the system of door interlocks, the dim dinginess, and the sense of despondence. The population appeared much sicker than our daughter, and we were concerned that being among them might only make her worse. We addressed some of our concerns with the nurse, who greatly reassured us. My husband and I left shortly thereafter. He said it was the most difficult day of his life. I left wondering, "Is this for real?"

However, once home around 9:30 p.m., an almost giddy relief came over me. I realized how, for the first time in years, I could go to bed without worrying whether Amy was safe. I left voicemail updates for the principal, Mrs. Guicona, Dr. Hischolor, and Dr. Sporsy.

On Sunday morning, I faxed Amy's physical and vaccination records to the facility. I left messages for Ms. Firther and Dr. Loftad. Mrs. Guicona called, and our talk was punctuated by a call from Dr. Pedreia, who commended me for the action we took. I shared with Mrs. Guicona that Audrey had admitted to her dad that she and Amy had been smoking marijuana since September 20th. Mrs. Guicona was thrilled to hear that news, because she saw it as step out of denial. She reiterated her concern about all the manipulation and deceit, despite what she believed was an underlying desire in both girls for things to *not* be that way. Mrs. Guicona had told them, "I want to believe you, but I'm not sure I can."

Amy and Audrey had not been seeing her regularly, and Audrey had expressed in anger to Mrs. Guicona, "We have to get out of this school." As their guidance counselor she replied, "When you're not supervised, you're getting into trouble."

Amy called around 10:00 a.m. with a list of items to bring when we visited. I talked with Audrey's dad, suggesting he check Audrey's voicemails and text messages, and that we should possibly meet. I was concerned about how the girls manipulated both sets of parents at the condo, the Wednesday morning breakfast, and over Audrey's birthday concert. I told him about the unsettling photos, dated around the time Audrey visited us over the summer.

We told Amy we would search her room and asked if she wanted to direct us to anything in particular so we wouldn't have to search so minutely. She said no. We found about a half dozen lighters, lighter fluid, and more photos from questionable circumstances. We stood by our promise that we would never read her diary, but we considered loose papers fair game, and we discovered several of concern. One was the very sad piece she wrote at BVMP on September 20th while awaiting my husband's arrival, describing her devastation upon being caught.

We also found an instant-message transcript from December, about sneaking out of the movie theater to be with others during the time she was missing for an hour and a half. There were also instant-message transcripts from middle school, and we pined for those days of innocence. Most disturbing were additional photos of her with young men whom we didn't know at places we didn't recognize.

With these discoveries, I was starting to worry whether she was scoring drugs at our condo. The photos and dates were suggestive, in more ways than one. That could explain why she was so anxious to have the mother/daughter bonding weekend the day before she was caught with drugs at school. While Amy stuck to her "behind the gym" story, Audrey still told her dad that Amy brought them to school. Even after Amy's death, Audrey thinks the drugs did not come from the condo visit.

My husband returned home from church and noticed that the security lock was back on Amy's phone. She had removed this code on Monday night. Could she have possibly relocked it? My husband may have left her phone in his jacket in the hospital room. Would she have dared relock it even in the presence of a room sitter? Amy denied it, but we didn't know how it could have reset otherwise.

Ms. Firther called early that afternoon. I told her she had been manipulated by Amy, as had Mrs. Guicona and both sets of parents. She agreed. I asked her to explain what she meant by "characterologic." She explained that Amy's behavior over the last year had a mood or affective component. The medications were treating the depression and anxiety, she said, but the behavior we were now seeing was something more deeply seated, more of an orientation to life that was much harder to work with. It was not alien to Amy, so nothing felt wrong to her, thus she had no impetus to change unlike with depression or anxiety, where you could feel you needed help. She didn't know what we'd see when Amy was not taking illegal drugs. She agreed it would be good to obtain another viewpoint and to not let Amy out of the hospital until a barrier was cracked.

That evening, I recapped this conversation with Gail's sister, who asserted that characterologic was a good word to leave out if it were being used casually. On Saturday, she had been incensed that Ms. Firther would have disclosed this use of the word to Mrs. Guicona without telling me first. She cautioned that Amy was still a child with a core of innocence, a little girl in a big mess. Manipulation, she said, was another word for survival. What was making Amy need to have a secret life? What did she feel? Gail had mentioned on Sunday that it probably was not helpful when our first daughter would give Amy grief for never crying, accusing her younger sister with words like "you're dead inside." How empty was Amy feeling inside? Gail urged us to keep taking small steps and to maintain regular routines as best we could. She said she wouldn't be surprised if Amy were discharged without a plan.

Visiting Hours

My husband and I visited Amy on Sunday afternoon for a half hour. She seemed to be much more easygoing about her hospitalization than we were. The facility, and some of the residents, gave me the creeps.

We stopped at Gail's on the way home for some grounding. She said that the treatment plan must include some really good family and individual therapy. It was okay to tell Amy to keep her distance from some of the other kids at the hospital so she didn't learn bad stuff. It was *not* okay to say that we weren't sure why she was there. Gail was concerned about Amy's over-compensating, as if she were saying she didn't want people to see who she really was. Gail mentioned the self-fulfilling prophecy of Amy as the "bad girl" in the family in the eyes of her brother and sister, who were away at college and with whom we didn't share all the details of Amy's condition.

On Monday, I shared limited information with people at school. I mentioned to Ms. Dirath that the police declined to test the plastic bag because it wasn't suspicious enough. I mentioned the irony that, at the meeting the previous spring to discuss Amy's neuropsychological testing, she had said that if Amy went to RPHS as a sophomore her self-esteem issues would make her vulnerable to falling in with the crowd that would most accept her (translation: druggies). Yet that acceptance seemed to have happened at BVMP. We discussed how the more structured practice of basketball would be good for Amy, as opposed to cross country where, other than stretching together, supervision wasn't intensive. The basketball coach would be in a better position to watch Amy, and Ms. Dirath would be able to give her "jobs" if needed to keep her under watch between the end of the school day and the start of practice, which could sometimes be several hours. I was grateful again for her support.

At 1:20 p.m., I called the facility and was told that Amy had yet to be seen by the evaluating team. She was asking to go home and saying she didn't belong, a theme which would repeat in her 2009 rehab journals. The nurse characterized her as a polite and courteous kid, which was unusual in that facility.

I talked with Audrey's dad at 2:00. He asked if Amy was at the hospital, because she called their house around 7:00 the previous evening. I said she was still being evaluated. He said he had a genuine feeling from Audrey that she and Amy had not gone beyond marijuana, and in his gut he did not believe they'd done harder drugs. I called the facility to notify them that Amy had breached phone security by calling Audrey when she was not supposed to call anyone but immediate family.

At 3:00, I talked with the social worker at the facility, Ms. Sparrow, and we agreed to meet on Tuesday at 2:00. Amy requested some items, including her hairdryer, which she said she'd checked was okay to bring. After school I stopped to have her phone unlocked. We had a short visit with her that evening and learned that the hairdryer was in fact a prohibited item. I went online and transferred the money from her bank accounts into an escrow account so she would not have access. I had my husband put password protection on my laptop. I did not like the feeling of having to take security precautions in my own home.

I awoke early on Tuesday, and went through Amy's bedroom trash basket. I found a plastic bag that looked like it contained marijuana residual, but the pencil shavings in the bin led me to doubt my instinct, though I did take it to the police department. I also went through her recycling. I always did that with the kids, and have found money, items of high sentimental value, and one of their passports. I found a draft of an assignment Amy did for health: If you could have lunch with one person, who would it be? She proceeded to describe her fascination with the protagonist in the movie *Catch Me If You Can*.

Around 8:00 a.m., I wrote a "big picture" summary of the situation with Amy. She was crying for help, and we didn't know how sick she was. She maintained high-level functioning, though oboe and cross country were slipping in recent weeks. I was concerned about her schedule overload. I recapped the battles not worth fighting, such as any having to do with food. I recalled her previous resistance to any kind of family or individual therapy. When did she start using drugs? When was the last time? Who were these boys in her life? Did we finally have the right professionals involved? I called Audrey's dad and told him we were receiving the results of Amy's evaluation at 2:00 p.m.

Meeting with the Clinical Team

My husband and I arrived at the facility, having left our workplaces early, again. Amy expressed disbelief at the academic caliber of her fellow inpatients as the three of us walked into the meeting. "They can't even spell," she exclaimed. The presiding psychiatrist, Dr. Notting, was older, overweight, and did not appear very energetic. Ms. Sparrow was young and had clearly established a solid rapport with Amy; I wondered if their racial differences had actually helped that connection. At the outset of the meeting, we asked if the scope of Amy's assessment incorporated the input from the hours at the City Pediatrics ER. Dr. Notting admitted that the connection between hospitals was not smooth. I chafed at this fragmentation and cost to the healthcare system. He mentioned that Amy was "really oppositional and defiant, with major depression recurrent." Yet as much as I doubted Dr. Notting's demeanor at first, in retrospect his assessment was spot on.

We clarified that the role of the hospital was to stabilize, then refer out. Dr. Notting said that after talking with Amy for an hour, the reason for hospitalization was not just the presenting issue of drugs. And while he said they were ready to discharge her, he was observing "a strange dance" and wondering "what was the music?" Almost an hour into the meeting he told Amy that we had run into a major stumbling block, and he didn't fully understand the mixed picture. The breakthrough into Amy's defenses came when Ms. Sparrow mentioned the possibility of Amy going to a forty-five-day diagnostic program. Amy started crying, hiding her face behind her long brown hair. Yet Ms. Sparrow later told us that she had observed Amy appearing to smile and smirk, as if she enjoyed upsetting her parents. The team agreed to keep her another day, and Ms. Sparrow asked how many of us would join Amy for Thanksgiving dinner.

During the meeting, Dr. Loftad called to say we needed to find a new psychiatrist. She did not deal with patients who cut; she had originally planned to refer Amy out but kept her because she had responded so well. In addition, she would be doing more work with her husband's practice and would have less time for her patients. Therefore, all things considered, it would be better for us to work with someone else. As dejected as I felt at the prospect of trying to find Amy a new psychiatrist, I gave her the benefit of the doubt and thought perhaps she was recusing herself from a case for which she wasn't a great match, which was the most ethical stance if Amy's case was truly out of her realm of expertise. When I later told Dr. Sporsy, he was incensed, citing this action as "dumping" a patient. So here was yet another example where I felt torn between the conflicting opinions of two professionals.

As we walked out of the meeting, we gave Amy $5 for the snack machine. She asked if she could call Audrey, and we told her no. I said that before the girls met again outside of school, I wanted both families to meet. My husband and I left around 4:15, and for the next several hours I made numerous phone calls in pursuit of assembling a new care team. That night we discussed how the hospital had wanted to discharge Amy that day, but we didn't feel she was ready. Now, we had to advocate whether she'd stay for Thanksgiving weekend. We were concerned about the lack of services during the four days and whether staying would do Amy more harm than good. She was clearly in with a very sick population. It was a tough decision, but we agreed we would advocate for discharge.

BVMP was closed the day before Thanksgiving. At 7:35 a.m., Audrey's dad and I talked briefly; he and his wife were open to having a family meeting and would be pursuing drug testing. I then spoke with Dr. Boyd, a psychiatrist neighbor, who observed that Amy had been ripe for intervention, and that it probably came as a relief to her. She needed a genuine, authentic therapy relationship. The best would be a child psychiatrist who could do meds *and* therapy *and* knew substance abuse, but they were a dying breed. He gave me words to describe her situation: fifteen-and-a-half-year-old substance abuser who manipulated adults, including licensed social workers Ms. Firther and Mrs. Guicona. She had a false self, a veneer of success masking real pain, and needed to connect in therapy.

After more phone calls, my husband and I drove into the city for our mid-day meeting. We stopped to buy the chicken Caesar wrap that Amy had requested for lunch. The same group of five who had assembled less than twenty-four hours earlier was back together. Amy asked when she was being discharged. Dr. Notting said it depended, as it was sort of a question of fact. "For us to believe," he explained, "we need the truth." Her first reaction of tears was when confronted again about attending a forty-five-day program, an option that almost seemed to be more of a threat since it was never seriously pursued or subsequently recommended. Dr. Notting told Amy she wasn't helping anybody out by denying her drug use. She then admitted to using several times, and said meekly, "I do lie." Around 12:30 I took out the lighters and photos I had found in her room. As I placed them on the table, Ms. Sparrow observed how Amy's eyes shot anger at me. Amy could not deny this evidence, but the discussion quickly proceeded to the option of Amy having a day pass for Thanksgiving.

Dr. Notting agreed that, since I had lined up appointments with Dr. Loftad and Ms. Firther for December 1st, the facility could proceed with a full discharge. Ms. Sparrow told Amy that, as a prerequisite, she needed to look up *stubborn, anger, rage,* and *rebellious* in the dictionary, then write *Webster's* definition, her definition, and an example. In typical Amy perfectionist form, she did a stellar job on the assignment as the adults continued talking. Ms. Sparrow also suggested that Amy attend some teen twelve-step meetings, an option no other professional would mention to us again until after Amy admitted that she was addicted to heroin.

Release for Thanksgiving

While the facility generated the discharge paperwork, Amy took a lot of time having her "Goodbye Book" signed by the other patients. We left to fight the pre-Thanksgiving traffic and to await our son's and daughter's flights home. I'm not sure how we came up with the idea of a ten-minute nightly meeting, but my husband and I talked with Amy to clarify academic expectations. We underscored that we *didn't* expect her to be perfect, and that using drugs to enhance performance would *never* be acceptable. We praised the progress she had made during her sophomore year, and we reiterated that we were very pleased with her results considering the suspension.

Thanksgiving weekend was amazingly unawkward. Sibling interaction was relatively normal despite all that had just transpired. Our family joined my husband's relatives for dinner, and I thought how glad I was *not* to be eating at the psychiatric facility. We even took our annual family Christmas card photo, although Amy displayed her hospital bracelet.

On Black Friday, she and I went shopping at 6:00 a.m. She caught up on a lot of Latin with her brother. Our ten-minute Friday meeting was about friends. By Saturday evening, though, she was fighting us about going to church on Sunday. Our ten-minute meeting went "badly." We saw the reappearance of our sarcastic, oppositional child. She accused me of making "mean" facial expressions. We unsuccessfully broached how to monitor her after-school whereabouts going forward. She reminded us that she could be like a girl in the ghetto living with her boyfriend, a standard Amy tactic of comparing herself to those doing a lot worse. She expressed her skepticism for family therapy. Our Sunday meeting, all of five minutes long, was calmer.

Return to School

The Monday after Thanksgiving, our son and first daughter returned to college. Amy kept her hospital bracelet on for her return to school, which I suspected was a way for her to broach the topic of her hospitalization. My student informant seemed angry, and I felt like she was avoiding me. Amy had a run-in involving iced coffee; the principal saw Amy carrying it out of a class, tucked under her clothes, a clear violation of school rules. As the principal was addressing her, Amy pulled out the drink and sipped through the straw. The principal left the confiscated container in her office to remind herself to inform me after school.

Amy had a 4:00 p.m. appointment with a new psychiatrist, Dr. Adderoth, who was referred by Amy's pediatrician. A balding blonde with no trace of an East coast accent, I did not think to question his expertise in dealing with a patient like Amy, nor did I comparison shop since I felt we were in crisis and needed a new psychiatrist immediately. Amy also had basketball tryouts, so I decided to attend the meeting alone, which was probably good so I could provide him Amy's detailed history. Dr. Adderoth said Amy's diagnosis was not clear. He wondered if she could internalize what was going on. He characterized her approach as, "If I can get away with it, it's not a problem."

On Tuesday, my student informant still seemed angry and evasive. At 4:45 p.m. my husband and I met a prospective family therapist referred by Gail's sister who advised that our first priority had to be basic safety. The therapist said we might need to think of an even tighter environment for Amy, and how she might need a fresh start. Talking after the meeting, my husband and I decided not to work with her, feeling perhaps that she was too much of a generalist for our specific crisis. I then returned to BVMP to collect Amy from basketball tryouts at 6:40. I wrote that night how she still asked me to rub her back at bedtime, and we were no longer doing our ten-minute nightly meetings.

On Wednesday, Amy met Dr. Adderoth at noon and at 6:30 had what would be her last session with Ms. Firther. During a gentle car conversation on the drive home, Amy insisted that September 20th was her first time with drugs. We discussed ADD (Attention Deficit Disorder, which she claimed she had) and impulse control, but I do not recall the tone or outcome of the conversation. My husband and I sparred at dinnertime about enforcing Amy's whereabouts after school. He believed it was a "no brainer" since I was right there at BVMP, and I felt it was emotionally and logistically arduous.

Thursday, December 2nd, was a blessedly calm day, and my husband and I cleared Amy to resume babysitting. Everyday life felt more settled, and returning to a more normal routine would probably be better for her. On Friday, my student informant and I met the principal, and she removed us from the middle of the investigation. The student was scrupulously consistent with what she had told me in November. She added that students have been known to go into teachers' pocketbooks when they're not in their classrooms and take small amounts of money. Usually the amount was not enough to arouse suspicion, though maybe a little doubt, but the amounts added up. The investigation subsequently concluded that there was not enough evidence.

Late in the evening, waiting for Amy to return from babysitting, I started looking for patterns in her cell phone calls. I was deeply disturbed to still find several days when calls were made right after we arrived at school, at the start of lunch, and right after dismissal. These calls were primarily to Canalboro, Maryland, or Connecticut. I feared she could be involved in distributing drugs. In talking with a running buddy on Saturday, it occurred to me that Amy's "normal" to which Ms. Firther constantly referred might be pathological.

On Monday, December 6th, the principal, Mrs. Guicona, and I met to discuss ground rules moving forward. We agreed that I would primarily be in touch with Mrs. Guicona about any issues involving Amy, as would any other parent. We agreed that we still didn't know how sick Amy was, but she *had* gotten in trouble and *was* at risk. I met later with Mrs. Guicona, who affirmed our decision to find a new therapist for Amy. She stressed the distinction between behavioral and emotional issues. She was concerned about how Amy had missed guidance appointments with her.

Amy did *not* find me at dismissal as she was supposed to. Her friend said she was not at the 2:15 meeting where basketball uniforms were distributed. I found her at 2:40 making up an English test with her teacher. My student informant stopped by around 5:30 while Amy was at practice. I was very concerned because it seemed like being "in the middle" had taken an emotional toll on her.

I met again with Mrs. Guicona on Tuesday, who said she would send a memo to teachers asking them to note until vacation if Amy were ever tardy or asked to be excused. We agreed that it was up to my husband and me as parents to monitor her after-school whereabouts. Later, I called the police lieutenant, who did not believe that the bag I found in Amy's trash had contained marijuana. He still was checking on Amy's cell phone call numbers to see if they corroborated with any possible "persons of interest" in the drug enforcement community. We never heard a conclusion.

After school, I drove to Northwood to buy Amy a mouth guard so she could play in the basketball scrimmage. We attended the 6:00 p.m. meeting with Ms. Dirath, winter athletes, and their families. I knew that if Amy had another confirmed incident she would be ineligible to play more basketball.

On Wednesday morning, I very calmly held firm about Amy not taking her coffee into school. "But we'll waste it," she protested, using a line she knew would appeal to my frugality. "I guess that's what'll happen," I let myself say. Yet again she was the only student not wearing a uniform sweater at the Mass for the feast of the Immaculate Conception.

Amy and I had a nice dinner out before my husband and I had our 7:30 "closing" parents meeting with Ms. Firther. Amy did homework in the waiting room, and then joined us at the end of the session. Ms. Firther said she supported us looking for a new therapist.  As parents, we needed to be comfortable "letting go" before Amy left for college. She talked to Amy's immaturity, and while Amy was mature beyond her years in some ways, she clearly was struggling with the different growth paths of being in different places, much like her brother had. She urged us to reinforce Amy's positives and clarify expectations for choice of school next year. My husband articulated the mistake of dealing with a sick person as if they were healthy. In hindsight, perhaps we should have pursued family therapy when Amy started with Ms. Firther to increase Amy's sense of confidentiality with her. But I was already seeing Dr. Sporsy, and it was not clear how much more therapy our family system could have handled, in time or in cost.

On Thursday, December 9th, Amy met for the first time with her new therapist, psychologist Dr. DeSantos, an avuncular figure referred by Dr. Sporsy as the best in the area. Prior to the meeting, I let Amy use my cell phone to order pizza. She threatened to obtain a Virgin Mobile® cell phone because she wouldn't need parental approval. She then went down the path, not unlike what we heard in Ms. Firther's office in September, about how she hated BVMP and had no friends, and used a lot of surly "*whatever*" and "*okay, mom*" phrases. Hearing those sentiments was difficult, but I stayed composed. I reminded her she'd had huge violations of cell phone trust. She claimed she didn't know she was signing to obey school rules when she returned on September 27th after her suspension. We ate our pizza and ice cream, and she had a great first meeting with Dr. DeSantos, with plans to meet every other week for individual therapy. He and I subsequently spoke often, and we had a few family meetings.

The following morning, I told Mrs. Guicona that I was concerned to hear that Audrey was now manager of the basketball team. It seemed like the prospect of the girls being together after school could lead to trouble. She said she'd talk with Ms. Dirath. She mentioned that one of Amy's teachers saw Amy and Audrey in the hallway after the bell had rung, so they should have been in class. I then received a note at 1:08 to see her ASAP, and subsequently learned of another incident involving Amy, Audrey, and another teacher. Mrs. Guicona believed this teacher might have overreacted. I decided to wait for this teacher to contact me, since when we met in early November we agreed that in the event of future incidents we would have a three-way meeting. I never heard back.

While driving Amy home after her scrimmage, I mentioned how we were planning a family meeting with Audrey's family. Amy became defiant, insisting that she wouldn't go and she wouldn't talk. She felt everything had been taken away from her, protesting, "Even Mrs. Guicona thinks you're being too harsh." She complained that she didn't receive enough praise. I remained grounded and consistent. I told her I wanted to have a normal life, including resuming my running and adopting a dog. I didn't want to regard everything with suspicion. I reiterated my concerns about the September 20th drugs, and my pain at wondering whether our mother/daughter trip to the condo was genuine or a con. I then shared a story from when I was sixteen and how another parent had cared enough about me to intervene when I was making a poor decision. The conversation ended calmly. Audrey's dad called to say that the weekend would not work for a family meeting.

On Saturday, December 11th, Amy spearheaded the purchase of the perfect Christmas tree, and she decorated it splendidly. She loved to celebrate holidays, and we could always depend on her for the special touches. On Sunday, she had practice at 7:30 a.m. for two hours. She, my husband, and I went to lunch, although the decision about where to go seemed unusually tension-filled.

On Monday, we talked on the way to school about her last drug use. She said it was a few months ago. She shared that her drug use was a maturity issue. That afternoon I attended a teachers' meeting, at which increased vigilance was urged, and the names of students of concern were correlated.

On Wednesday, Amy had a noon appointment with Dr. Adderoth. When he finally greeted us at 12:20, she told him that she needed to leave because she was going to be Chlorophyll in the biology lab play at 12:30. He agreed he would prescribe her meds, but not be her therapist. I gave him a copy of the ADD survey I'd filled in for Dr. Loftad. He believed Amy's claims of ADD and prescribed her Adderall to take as needed. (Adderall, like Ritalin, is a stimulant used in treating ADD/Attention Deficit Hyperactivity Disorder [ADHD] and is highly abused.) I was not convinced about the diagnosis, but he was the doctor and I was only the mother.

Since Amy died, almost every mother I've met whose son is marijuana dependent and/or a heroin addict has said how their child had learning differences and ADD/ADHD when they were young. The National Institute for Drug Abuse (NIDA) has recently published the statistic that one in six teens who tries marijuana will become dependent. Today's marijuana has been bred to contain about ten times as much of the active ingredient THC as it did a generation ago. The detectives in Broton say that while not all marijuana users become heroin addicts, they have yet to meet a heroin addict who hadn't smoked weed. Recent NIDA statistics agree: only one in 1,000 heroin addicts never smoked weed.

Ms. Firther then called to cancel what was supposed to be Amy's last session with her at 6:30 because she was sick. I was a little disappointed, but the cancellation did make life easier. In the car, I asked Amy how it was different after her hospitalization for her to interact with the people who had influenced her about drugs. She said she hadn't been influenced.

On Thursday the 16th, I learned that, yet again, Amy had not given me a detention slip to sign, this one for a recent incident with the music teacher. I wrote the teacher a note, requesting a three-way meeting. The next morning, Amy was being difficult about which car we drove. I asked her who specifically was the "everyone" who thought our 1991 car was a piece of sh--. She offered no names. She also said that Audrey was not her friend, which I noticed she'd been saying recently.

The Christmas Pageant Incident

That morning, the last day of school before vacation, I was unusually, and unfortunately, sitting two rows behind Amy in chapel for the Christmas prayer service, a lovely event including song and dance and a little pageant. She spontaneously turned around and snapped, "Why are you giving me dirty looks?" I said it was because instead of her school sweater she was wearing an oversized hooded sweatshirt. She took it off and sneered, "Now are you happy?" I gave a weak smile, still dismayed because she was once again the only student in chapel out of uniform.

Into the service, I noticed that Amy was slumped over, with her head between her knees. I was going to ask another faculty member to intervene, but I was too late. Mrs. Guicona had noticed from the choir loft, and summoned the nurse, who took Amy to her office where she concluded that Amy's pupils were dilated. Mrs. Guicona had also seen Amy close up and corroborated what the nurse observed. Mrs. Guicona then signaled me out of chapel. Due to correlation with other information the school had received about Amy and cocaine, they requested that Amy go for a drug test. We abruptly left BVMP so Amy could see Dr. Adderoth at noon. She was adamant that a tox screen would be negative. Dr. Adderoth offered that Amy's pupils could have been dilated due to the dark chapel and having had her eyes closed.

We returned to BVMP to pack the car, with Amy dawdling at her locker. I took the opportunity to check her purse when I put my course materials and presents from my students in the car. I found roughly $80 in cash. Amy was angry that the principal said she could not stay at school to watch the afternoon movie, say goodbye to her friends, and finish delivering Christmas presents. (In addition to her friends, teachers, and staff, Amy always made sure to give a present to every cafeteria and custodial worker.) The principal also did not want Amy to attend the basketball game on Friday, or the Sunday or Monday practices, until the tox screen results were known.

Once home, we spent several pleasant hours organizing some kitchen shelves. To this day, I smile wistfully when I look at the spice racks we installed on that ambiguous afternoon. I confronted Amy about the cash, having told her on September 20th and November 19th that I didn't want her carrying that much money to school. She claimed it was there from mid-week, when she thought she'd need money for her friends' Christmas presents at Walmart. Yet when we shopped, she usually asked me to pay for presents. I was suspicious once again.

I spoke with Dr. DeSantos. The tox screen results came back negative on Monday, which was a relief. But my concern returned on Tuesday when Amy gave me $200 in cash to deposit, and even if I asked her where it was from, she probably had an answer which would seem plausible enough to me. I happened to see Ms. Firther at a Northwood store and told her that Dr. DeSantos agreed that it was not necessary for Amy to have a closing meeting with her.

Amy had her second meeting with Dr. DeSantos on Wednesday, December 22nd. The next day I reflected in my diary, "You know it's been a tough year when your kid (in this case our son) has a car accident and it doesn't even register on the emotional Richter scale." Fortunately, our son was okay, but that reflection tells how overwhelmed I was with distress over Amy.

The five of us traditionally drove to my hometown the day after Christmas to spend a few days with my side of the family. The time away went smoothly, but I always wondered in the back of my mind how much of Amy's compliance and good mood we could believe, and how much was more sophisticated deception, consciously or unconsciously, manipulating us so that we would ease up on her. We did not return in time for Amy's basketball meets.

Ringing in the New Year; Amy Turns Sixteen

I could not begin to imagine what the new year would bring. The year 2004 had brought truth that was stranger than fiction, events beyond imagination. We still didn't know how sick Amy was. My husband and I questioned how to understand the events leading up to her hospitalization (knowing we might never have all the answers), how to "process" the hospitalization, and how to move forward as parents. At BVMP, students apparently knew the faculty was being more vigilant, so they were being more careful. I was concerned about Amy being over-committed, yet her most important work was getting healthy. We also would have to make decisions about her summer plans, and what school she'd attend for junior year.

Lily stayed the night on New Year's Day, but when it looked like the girls weren't doing their homework, which was part of the plan, we sent her home. Amy responded without drama to the limit setting. The next day she worked on her *Thirteen* movie project all evening. At 10:30 p.m. she asked me to make her ravioli. At 1:00 a.m. she asked me to read the project. I was blown away at how thorough and insightful it was. I wondered what she was saying in her project about some of the life experience she had just been through. She couldn't exactly remember with whom she recently saw the movie. We had talked about watching it together, something I wish we had eventually done.

My husband and I looked forward to beginning family therapy on January 6th with Mrs. Ladaco, a licensed alcohol and drug abuse counselor. Amy would be having her third session with Dr. DeSantos in parallel, and the two therapists conveniently had offices in the same suite. She came highly recommended by Dr. Sporsy and Dr. DeSantos. Our hopes, however, became a letdown. We met twenty-two times over the next fifty-three weeks, seemingly to no avail, and I rarely noted anything in my journals. Or was it working, because the time between Amy's incidents seemed to become longer?

The following day, I met with Dr. Sporsy, who observed the pattern that part of Amy went out of her way to arouse suspicion, but then she'd be outraged when she was a suspect. She wanted it both ways, creating drama in the process. On January 9th, Amy made note in a diary or journal entry that she hadn't used since November 14th, a week before she was hospitalized.

She obtained her driving learner's permit the day after she turned sixteen, having brought inadequate identification on her actual birthday. (Later I found a journal entry about the prospect of her driving: "I'll be able to go out and lie about where I'm going." I worried about how we were going to manage that new stage.) I started seriously looking for a dog to adopt. That included some reading, including *Mother Knows Best*, by Carol Benjamin, about dog training. She wrote, "Perhaps the most difficult part of discipline is understanding when the dog is genuine and when the dog is trying to pull your leg." Substitute "student" or "child" for "dog" and the caveat seemed spot-on!

For my forty-ninth birthday in February, Amy baked me a chocolate cherry truffle cake from scratch. She recommended *Queen Bees and Wannabees* by Rosalind Wiseman, the book on which the film *Mean Girls* was based, a movie we'd intended to watch together and regrettably never did.

Queen Bees and Wannabees provides an insight into the incredible power of cliques among adolescent girls. It nicely complemented a book recommended to me by Mrs. Guicona and written by Chap Clark called *Hurt: Inside the World of Today's Teenagers*. His thesis is that today's adolescents are experiencing "systemic abandonment" by adults. As a result, they form "clusters" with other youths who really become their family, but without the guidance that adults traditionally provide. While at one level they appear more indulged than ever, in fact so much of what they receive is what is convenient for the adults, rather than what they need developmentally. These ideas definitely provoked some soul-searching as a mother and a teacher. I realized that in both roles my instincts about developmental needs may lag what the research, especially in neuroscience, currently tells us.

During February vacation, Amy and I again visited my relative in Florida while my husband took care of the home front. I then went on to visit friends in Houston, and felt so rejuvenated from these nourishing, long-term relationships. Amy stayed in Florida when I traveled to Texas, and I know she enjoyed shooting hoops and tanning, but I'll never know the whole story of what else she did.

In early March, Amy attended the sophomore semi-formal dance, taking it upon herself to find dates for herself and two friends. Unfortunately, plans did not solidify until 4:30 on the afternoon of the event, which meant I spoke multiple times with the parents of the five other friends that day given all the last-minute drama. I later reflected in my monthly letter, "We do need to do a better job of sticking to deadlines with Amy," which was a polite way of saying I was totally stressed out. To capture the drama from the week leading up to the semi, the day of the event, and the aftermath would take at least another ten pages.

I flew to my hometown for Easter, and I was "just short of livid" that my husband did not confirm Amy's plans with the parents of the friends with whom she would be staying. I was worried that she would be perpetrating another scheme, especially since her plans would involve some of the boys from the semi.

Battles over cell phone usage continued. Amy signed up for spring track, admitting that the three weeks between basketball and cross country were a bit long, and in the gap she was becoming better at wasting time. She flew on April 8th to visit her sophomore brother and freshman sister for the weekend. Her plans to go away during April vacation went through numerous gyrations, ending up with my taking her and her classmate, Nancy, to New York City for an overnight. I let them sleep in the beds, but that was really so I could sleep on the floor across the door of the hotel room to make sure they didn't sneak out during the night.

Escape with Lily

On April 15th, Amy joined my husband and me for dinner with his former colleagues, including the father of the family she visited in Hawaii. I thought how good it was of Amy to join this group of adults when she really didn't have to, although she never refused a good meal, especially at a nice restaurant. She then asked if she could have a sleepover at Lily's. "You can pick me up at 7:55 and we can go to the 8:00 a.m. Mass together." It sure sounded wholesome, and I fell for it.

At 7:50 Sunday morning I arrived at Lily's house. Her mother reported that she had gone to check on the girls at 2:00 a.m. and noticed pillows had been placed in the beds to look like occupants. The girls used the fire escape ladder to leave the house and meet up with some guys Amy knew from the condo. Lily's mother and I lectured the girls in no uncertain terms about the dangers of their choices. I had my husband call the house of the protagonist and tell his mother that her son must cease contact with Amy. His house was about two hours from ours, and I started to worry whether Amy was at risk for running away. My diary entry said, "Shattered, angry, resentful … her chronic lying?"

The next day my family watched the movie *A River Runs Through It*. I couldn't help but see Amy as Brad Pitt's "Paulie" character, a close-to-the-edge thrill seeker, and wondered if she was on the same track to an early demise. Meanwhile, I felt like the withering mother becoming ever more unable to deal with her errant child.

On April 23rd, we adopted River, a seven-year-old black Labrador Retriever from the south. Amy came with me to collect him from the transport and was the first to spot and interact with him. She comforted him in the car on the way home. I was hoping this bonding would bode well. Amy always had a soft spot for the underdog whether canine, feline, or human.

I was feeling suspicious on April 26th about an event involving Amy and $40 and her needing to mail some letters. In my journal I asked myself, "How many years the manipulation, deceit? Feel like last November freefall, no handholds. Can we trust ANYTHING?" The family therapy did not seem to be helping. Mrs. Ladaco also raised the CHINS prospect before Amy became too old.

On May 1st, Amy was at the mall from 11:15 to 4:15. Or was she? She received the sacrament of Confirmation on May 6th, taking the name Augustine, after the saint who engaged in profligate behavior for many years before his conversion. I wanted to take hope from her choice of saint that perhaps she was contemplating changing her ways.

The next morning during my running group, I took a call from Dr. DeSantos. I welcomed his calls at any time with any updates he could provide. He raised concerns about Amy's sneakiness and not coming clean, the *Catch Me If You Can* mentality. She clearly had self-esteem issues, he said, and would use "downward comparisons" as a way to rationalize why she wasn't doing as badly as she could, but she never compared "up." He noted her poor decision making and anxiety.

On May 19th, Dr. Sporsy reflected at our twenty-eighth session how Amy constantly hid or changed her stories. Why did she feel the need to overexplain? Why was she so burdened by guilt? We discussed random drug testing, where he said the issue wasn't whether *she* was using, but why *I* was thinking about it. While I can appreciate his psychoanalytic tack, in retrospect, there clearly *was* a serious issue about her using. It seems that you shouldn't question whether you smell smoke when you're being burned by flames.

Around 11:30 that night, I came across a note in the "homework folder" from one of my classes. "Mrs. W., I would keep a closer eye on Amy if I were you. Just a tip." I left messages for Dr. Sporsy, Mrs. Ladaco, and Dr. DeSantos. I have no record or memory of what ensued.

We started blocking out summer plans; we had a fair amount of structure in place already for Amy. I hoped to train for a fall marathon, but later wrote in my monthly letter, "We'll see how much energy I have left given how Amy's summer goes." On May 24th, I searched her purse and found a small vial of urine and body jewelry, corroborating rumors of a piercing on May 9th. I was concerned about the urine being a substitute for hers if she were drug tested since sometimes users obtain "clean" urine from someone who has not used. Belly piercing would be in defiance of our discussions. We did learn subsequently that Amy's navel was pierced by someone who illegally provided the service to minors. Of the four pieces of jewelry removed during her autopsy, one was a belly ring.

On June 2nd, her first period class was in the room across from mine. While I was outside my classroom door greeting my students, she placed a sticky note with the humiliating words "F--- everything" on my back. Another student removed it and gave it to me, and Amy swiftly apologized. I was more saddened than angry, and stayed composed. She met Dr. DeSantos at 5:00 p.m. that day.

On the 8th, another incident left me feeling tired, stressed, and upset. It involved Lily coming to our house without permission while I was at the dentist, replete with all sorts of stories that didn't add up as we talked via cell phone. When I arrived home and refused to drive Amy somewhere, she countered, "I'll walk there with the dog." Instead of relenting, I let her take River on his leash down the driveway. When she reached the road she bawled, "Mom, where are you?"

She ended her sophomore year with a 2.8 GPA, but the question of which school she would attend for junior year still loomed. Her academic standing was acceptable, and she seemed to be more stable behaviorally. I knew the principal would not agree to let Amy remain at BVMP just because I taught there. I also believe that even though the school was struggling financially, the principal would not let the school's income from our tuition dollars influence such a decision.

A Smoother Summer

As of June 6th, Amy's major summer plans were in place for vacation, which included a structured pre-career program, a running camp, and driver's ed. On the 9th, we learned that Amy had been the passenger of a junior automobile operator a few times, a flagrant violation of state law. We probably reminded her of this fact, but her choice was out of our control if we chose to give her any freedom. This incident was one of many underscoring the difficulty of balancing the ever-increasing need for independence in high school children with very real concerns about what they are doing. I had to hope the values with which we raised her entered into at least some of her decision making.

At the closing faculty meeting, I spent much of the lunch period in my classroom crying. I had flashbacks to two summers ago, when the stress of all three children resulted in my turning to marathon training as an outlet. I thought back to the previous year, when I still trained for a marathon despite Amy's summer antics, including a pregnancy scare, starting to use marijuana, and her new "friends." In 2004–2005, we endured Amy's traumatic autumn, and I was battered from the last month of her behaviors. Did I have another marathon in me, literally or figuratively? At least our son was doing well, but I was concerned about whether our first daughter had chosen the right college. My daughters were living in different worlds, and I was not in a position to bridge that gap.

On June 11th, I searched Amy's old purse for some reason, finding matches, a lighter, and more drug paraphernalia. In mid-June, Amy spent a few days with my husband's friend Dan and his family in California, then flew home with them to Hawaii on the 17th, returning home July 4th. I trusted that she would be on her best behavior, and her time away was indeed low drama, except for losing her passport. We appreciated our friends' generosity in taking Amy under their wing, and being around their two young children seemed to bring out the best parts of her, what I still believed was the real Amy.

In my diary on June 24th, I questioned the effectiveness of Dr. Sporsy. My husband and I met Dr. DeSantos on June 30th, where I asked what progress we had made on what really mattered since her hospitalization, given *eleven* subsequent major incidents which I detailed. Dr. DeSantos believed Amy was still immature and impulsive, but she had no psychiatric illness.

Looking back, we had clearly lost focus on the anxiety and depression noted in the testing and at the psychiatric facility.

Dr. DeSantos felt it was easier for her to hang with "bad boys" because she was smarter and could "do circles around them." But he had a lot of hope and had seen some improvement, though the question for the upcoming summer was whether we'd see a "rise versus slide." She and Dr. DeSantos had been debating whether she should take the honors classes for which she was eligible, and my husband contended how he'd love Amy to have choices when she went to college. Sadly, we all lost focus on how her choices around substances would ultimately render academics and graduating from college moot.

On July 5th, having been home for a day, Amy departed for a ten-day program with the National Youth Leadership Forum on Medicine. She shadowed medical professionals and attended a variety of seminars and social events. Several BVMP students who had attended said it was a win either way as you'd realize you definitely *did* want to pursue a medical career, or you *didn't.* The pre-drama was over clothes. We needed to buy Amy some professional attire, and in her "the-rules-don't-apply-to-me" way she kept arguing the criteria.

On July 11th, I wrote in my diary, "Realize that anticipation of her return is all stress and limit testing and arguing." But upon her return she said her ten days at "Med Camp" were one of the best experiences of her life, and my husband and I were encouraged. Largely due to Amy's work, her team won the prize for the best project, a public health awareness campaign for breast cancer.

She was home for a few days, and then we drove her to cross country camp at a college in a nearby state. I was shocked upon arrival to learn that Audrey was attending the same camp. I felt shattered and calmly mentioned to the director that the two had a history. But they made it through the week without any reported incidents. One of the camp workshops was on sports psychology and given by none other than Dr. Sporsy, who was able to see Amy in action. He saw the enthusiastic and engaged "best of Amy" bringing out the best in others.

Soon after, one of Amy's "Med Camp" friends visited for a long weekend. The two of them made an elaborate chocolate cake for my husband's birthday in early August; Amy always put her whole heart into remembering others' birthdays. We also let Amy visit a "Med Camp" friend for a long weekend, where she was in awe of being in a university town where her friend lived close to everything. She also had a new friend, Liam, who lived in an adjoining town, whom we all liked for a change. We were very cautiously optimistic that she was having a relationship with a guy who would be a positive influence, although we could never obtain a straight answer about how she met him.

Amy had also wanted to attend a week of skateboard camp. I was leery, but Dr. Sporsy told me to suspend my stereotypes, because such camps actually attracted some good athletes. However, Amy realized her summer was already packed and never pursued it. Driver's education started for three weeks on August 1st. At the end of the class, Amy was offered a job at the auto school as a part-time receptionist. At the time we were pleased, thinking that her winning personality was finding an acceptable outlet. In retrospect, I wondered whether she could have been part of a drug "front," especially when she worked alone. After all, who would suspect intelligent, beautiful, athletic, and engaging Amy?

Cross country practice began August 24th, and Amy, the only junior on the team, was elected co-captain. The decision to stay at BVMP came fairly smoothly because she was on an academic "roll" and looked forward to some of her junior year teachers and courses. I actually felt recharged at the end of the summer. We'd had no major crises as in the previous few summers, and having Amy away for five and a half weeks really helped. I trained well for my third marathon. Distance running was how I was taking care of myself.

My dearest mother,

I'm so sorry. I'm sorry for the pain **Four** le you deal with throughout my life, especially during the past year or so. Sitting at the restaurant this evening I looked over ... smile I've ever seen. It reminded me of all the amazing times we've had tog... (and of course hitting up Tulips) listening to classic oldies and, of course, laughing about your ever-famous attempts at hitting that mailbox in the town

September 2005, Eleventh Grade: running with the bad boys (& girls)

Classes resumed on August 31st, and within weeks Amy was already at odds with one teacher. Amy passed her road test on September 12th. She had been driving responsibly, and it felt like a net energy gain to let her drive. For example, I could count on her to reliably run a grocery store errand on the way home. But we had an increasing concern about guys she met but who never met us, which her new mobility could exacerbate. On September 17th, she drove to Saturday cross country practice for the first time. On the 19th, she drove to the mall after school, "forgetting" to attend math club. On the 22nd, she drove herself to school for the first time. It wasn't long before most days we drove part or all of the way to school separately, usually due to her job or appointments. I felt a little sad not having that time together. Part of my vision in her attending BVMP was our shared commute time, and the inevitable tapering felt like it came too soon.

Amy was finishing second or third for her cross country team, and ran a 6:10 mile. She saw an orthopedist who diagnosed her stress fracture, by then healed, but referred her for physical therapy. Amy accompanied my husband and me to the 2005 marathon. It was an unforgettably special experience having one daughter under each arm supporting me when I finished ninety-eight seconds shy of qualifying for the Boston marathon. I was sorely disappointed after all my training, though I found some consolation having finished in the top quartile for women and top quintile for my age group.

Overall, the autumn was going calmly, though I did find a lighter in the car on November 2nd. This discovery may have been when I asked Amy about it and she replied that it was for lighting birthday candles, a plausible answer I wanted to believe despite not believing it. Amy was spending more time with a younger student, Liza, who was also on the cross country team. Amy convinced her to attend the reception after the BVMP "Ring Day" ceremony, when juniors received their class rings. Since underclasswomen were not invited and Liza had missed class, yet another meeting with the principal ensued.

Amy had her first car accident on November 6th, when an older man clipped her as she was turning out of the BVMP driveway on an unauthorized trip to the mall. While our car sustained less than $100 of damage, the other driver claimed $3,000, which thus classified Amy as having had a major at-fault accident, resulting in a surcharge and a more expensive class of insurance. The next day, I noted in my diary the "stress of Amy's decision making." But the report card conferences mid-month were overall positive, and my husband and I were cautiously encouraged by her academic traction.

Right before Thanksgiving, the principal met with Amy, who was accumulating detentions and not always serving them, needing to be paged, or showing up late due to sitting in the hall or wandering. The principal did not believe Amy's stories. I checked in with Amy's psychologist, Dr. DeSantos, who truly believed she was clean. He felt the two major issues for her were first, liking herself and making good decisions since her judgment could still be shaky, and second, starting to prepare herself for going away to college. He asked her to start comparing herself to valedictorians and looking up, rather than at those in trouble and saying that she wasn't as badly off as they were. He was trying to convince her to play basketball for the teamwork, the structure, and because free time was still dangerous for her.

Amy slept at Liza's the night before Thanksgiving, and her dad took them to run a local road race in the morning. Amy had Thanksgiving dinner with us, and then spent the evening with Liza at her dad's house until 10:00 p.m., a time limit Liza's parents had set.

On Friday night, Amy had an older BVMP friend, who was also one of my students, stay the night. I felt better having them under our roof than her friend's. On Saturday, we attended the funeral of the mother of my dear colleague, Sr. Juliann, who was also Amy's Confirmation sponsor and ninth-grade English teacher. Amy and her friend were the only students from BVMP at the services. (Since Amy died, we learned the two had been drinking illicitly during the sleepover, and the friend had become sick. She did *not* go home with the flu as initially reported.)

The Sunday after Thanksgiving, the mother of Amy's friend Liam showed up at our front door in no mood for nonsense. Something was awry involving the return of one of his $60 sweatshirts. She didn't say exactly what, but apparently Liza was involved. This episode was yet another emotional drain since I knew I would never know the whole story. I wrote the mom a check, then obtained reimbursement from Amy, despite her protestations of innocence.

I was having little faith in the family therapy since nobody could convince Amy to attend. My diary entry on November 30th was, "Getting really down on mental health professionals," and on December 19th, "Where are the people who know what they're doing?" I was so frustrated because I knew we needed help and we were enlisting trained clinicians, but it still didn't seem to be making the difference I somehow believed it could.

In mid-December, I analyzed Amy's cell phone numbers and wrote, "Still scared re: dealing or secret life." On December 20th, I wrote in my diary that I was trying to stay more even-keeled, but the constant pushback was a drain. Amy had started volunteering at the local hospital and was there from 9:00 a.m. until 1:00 p.m. She spent almost all of December 23rd wrapping presents. Our family made a very quick visit to my folks because we left River at home in the care of a neighbor. We made it through our holiday rituals without any major behavioral incidents.

Ringing in the New Year; Amy Turns Seventeen

The evening of the 30th, we received some phone calls about Amy's whereabouts that we could not verify. I noted the theme that every time we received an explanation from Amy, it was slightly different. On New Year's Eve, she slept at Liza's mom's house. I delivered her and spoke at length with the mom who said she would be monitoring the girls closely. Amy even called me at midnight to wish me a happy new year. Still, I had a very uneasy feeling about what the girls would perpetrate, especially since Amy's classmate Nancy was also there. While no crisis ensued, I seem to recall learning later that alcohol had been snuck in.

I spoke with Dr. DeSantos a few days later. He said he and Amy talked a lot about the company she kept. He told her, "Don't pretend in your heart that the guys you've been hanging around won't like you." He wasn't convinced that a year ago she owned being attractive. "You can't pretend they won't ask you to sneak out," he added. "They don't have as much at stake as you do. What do *they* have to lose if you go downhill? Do you think any of these characters will foster trust? It would be so much easier if Mom and Dad knew who you were with. What quality of life do these guys live if they can't even afford a phone?" The ongoing concern was the caliber of these characters. "Nothing good can come of it," Dr. DeSantos emphasized. Yet Amy seemed to have an innate drive to save kids, or found them interesting and intriguing, which Dr. DeSantos didn't like. He was waiting for her to say some day that she had met a valedictorian. That day never came, despite the repetition of the concept.

The next day, Amy and I had our first discussion about artificial sun tanning. She tried to convince me that the dermatologist of her fair-skinned friend actually recommended it so that she wouldn't burn when she went to Florida. I was always fearful of melanoma since I knew several people who died from it, so I discouraged Amy although I no longer seemed to have the power to forbid her. I learned in July of 2010 that tanning is one way that some addicts compensate for their wan complexions, especially those who are trying to keep up appearances to evade suspicion.

On a January 7th walk around the block, Amy and I started talking about colleges. Everyday life was going more smoothly and I savored any hour of respite. Amy opted to not play basketball. She was still working at the auto school, though it did seem strange one day that their number was forwarded to her cell phone. She claimed she went to the car to retrieve her cell phone and didn't want to miss any office calls.

The BVMP college planning kick-off meeting was on January 18th. I wrote in my monthly letter, "Amy appears to continue progressing. In the absence of living from crisis to crisis, I feel like my emotional energy is the highest it has been for a LONG time." While I knew better than to declare premature victory, I treasured such times. For example, one day when I was going to be late coming home, she walked the dog on her own initiative. Another day I returned to see she had done a load of laundry for me. We missed the days we didn't commute with each other, and tried to drive to school together at least once a week.

Amy spent the night of her seventeenth birthday at Nancy's. She made the honor roll. For my fiftieth birthday, she made me a mix CD of songs that were special to us, and I was really touched by all the effort she put into such a customized present. The last song was by Kanye West, with the chorus:

Hey Mama, I want to scream so loud for you
'Cause I'm so proud of you, let me tell you what I'm about to do (Hey Mama)
I know I act a fool, but I promise you I'm going back to school
I appreciate that you alive for me, I just want you to be proud of me (Hey Mama)

I spent the weekend in my hometown because the mother of Tara, my best friend from childhood, had died. When I returned home, Amy seemed touchy when I tried to talk with her.

On Valentine's Day, I spoke with Dr. DeSantos, and Amy had not told him about another incident involving detentions. He noted how she was always willing to make up a story rather than admit she had messed up. When he'd challenge her about identifying with people who were not going to be successful, she'd admit he was raising a good point. She also agreed he was right when he told her, "For someone who doesn't like to get in trouble, you like to get in trouble."

On February 25th, I was suspicious again of her latest cell phone bill. Two days later we had a blow-up about her not keeping up with her online pre-calculus course and I wrote in my diary, "I'm tired of motherhood."

Amy's best friend, Audrey, spent the night the first Friday in March. On Saturday evening, I went to a friend's fortieth birthday party, leaving my husband in charge of Amy. I was annoyed that I had to field cell phone calls when I arrived at the party about some irregularity in Amy's behavior, and she had a friend spending the night. Yet the next afternoon Amy asked me to join her at a meeting about a post-Hurricane Katrina service trip to the Gulf Coast, over April vacation, and she decided she wanted to go. I was taken a bit aback but encouraged, even surprisingly pleased.

Vicodin Discovered

When our first daughter was home for spring break, she and Amy said they went to the movies. I learned later they'd gone to the house of a drug-using friend. I had no reason to suspect my first daughter was having any issues with drugs, but I hadn't been thrilled by her description of the friend. I searched Amy's room and found Vicodin in her purse, a marijuana baggie under her bed, and liquor. Given what I now know about prescription drug abuse, this discovery should have raised immediate alarm among all the professionals.

On Monday, I needed another action plan. I talked with my husband's relative and with our first daughter's counselor, Dr. Hischolor, who felt the Vicodin was a big tip-off that Amy was experimenting more than we thought. We knew that Dr. Hischolor could only share limited information while still maintaining confidence with our first daughter, but it seemed so unfair that I as the mother couldn't know more of what was really going on because of "confidentiality."

Dr. DeSantos noted that Amy hated structure but was asking for it. He assumed she was generally clean in contrast to "very clean" on January 2nd. But he worried about the people she was in contact with and thought she might therefore rationalize that she could dabble again because she was doing less than before and less than the people she knew. He said a standard line for kids was that they were holding the substance for someone else, which is what Amy must have told him about the Vicodin. While Amy would complain that she needed Mom and Dad off her back, and he told her that was a good goal to shoot for, he said she needed to be smarter, not sneakier.

On Monday, I also took Amy for a tox screen; I can't recall whether I told her in advance. Her psychiatrist, Dr. Adderoth, said he did not need to see her and that, while she had never been in any sort of program, she had to admit she had a problem. In retrospect, it seems like the job of an MD treating a teen with a history like Amy's should be to help them see that they have a problem, not just keep prescribing Adderall. I still feel angry when I think about his laissez-faire approach. Even Audrey now feels that he was essentially a drug dealer. I talked with Amy that night and I noted that it went well, although that conversation was unfortunately followed by another confrontation about her cell phone.

On March 7th, I suspected Amy was using and the next day I had no feeling of trust toward her. The tox screen came back confirming that she was using over-the-counter drugs and alcohol. On the 9th, I had a strategizing phone call with Dr. DeSantos, who would see her later that day. We agreed I wouldn't "ambush" her with the tox screen results, but I would come in and share them with Dr. DeSantos present. He was hearing Amy starting to complain about him "taking sides." I was glad to have his support. I don't remember what happened after discussing the test results.

Two days later, I was conned by some scheme involving Amy and Audrey and basketball, and I was too weary to record the details. The next day, Dr. Hischolor recommended that Amy not make any unsupervised visits to her siblings. She could not say specifically why due to confidentiality.

At 6:00 a.m. on Monday, March 15th, Amy claimed that she had a headache. We agreed she could sleep until 6:45. Then we agreed she'd come in for third period. Later we agreed she would try for after lunch. We talked around 12:20, and she said she still had to get ready and pack up her schoolwork and would try for 1:15. She arrived at 1:20, went to the nurse, and left for work without checking out in the school office. I told her that in the future, if she didn't go to school, she couldn't go to work. She claimed that since I called her out of work the previous Monday for the tox screen, she didn't want to miss two Mondays in a row. On the 15th, I wrote in my diary "Amy and feeling suffocated." I'm not sure if I was referring to her, me, or both, but the next day I entered, "Feel like I need an emotional IV" and I lamented, "You don't become a parent to be appreciated!" I now wonder if a hangover or dope sickness (opiate withdrawal) caused her headache.

Spring track started on March 20th, but the next morning Amy didn't arrive at school until 10:25. She left for work at 2:10 thereby missing practice, having told a classmate to tell her coach she was sick. Given that she took literally the "no *school*, no work" warning from the previous week, I spelled out specifically that if she missed *practice* she could not go to work. In hindsight, all of the sick days raised a big red flag pattern that no one saw at the time. I spoke with my therapist, Dr. Sporsy, about her diagnosis/prognosis, and we discussed a drug treatment house in Canalboro as another local resource. He wondered if Dr. DeSantos was being direct enough with Amy. We discussed that Dr. Hischolor would not be contacting Dr. DeSantos despite our suggestion because she felt she didn't have a whole lot to add. Dr. Sporsy thought that perhaps our first daughter should talk with Dr. DeSantos to provide some firsthand information about what she saw Amy doing.

Dr. Sporsy also gave me a script to use in calling some of the suspicious numbers on Amy's phone bill. "My name is Melissa Weiksnar. Your number is showing up multiple times on my phone bill, and I would like to know who you are." I could never bring myself to do that and we never explored why. He proposed that if Amy couldn't identify the callers, she had to pay the full bill, but I didn't feel I could implement that consequence without more pain from Amy. He said she had to take responsibility for creating the context for the lack of trust and pay for her stories. Why was she presenting herself as the perfect girl instead of "fessing up?" he wondered. But talking with Amy about the phone bills was like walking through a minefield. She'd always claim whatever "problem" I accused her of was already in the past. We also discussed a MySpace page issue that was probably the least of my worries at the time because I don't even remember what the problem was.

Later in the month, I noted for the first time that she was going out with a new friend, Chauncey. On March 28th, she and Audrey were late for school. I was in the middle of a failed attempt to track her car mileage. At the month's end I learned that she missed practice, claiming she needed to study for five tests. In early April, she said she had Indian food with Chauncey and his grandmother and brought me my favorite Peshawari naan as a treat. She also grocery shopped for me. On April 3rd, I wrote in my diary, "Very concerned re: Amy falling asleep while studying," which I now know could have been a symptom of opiate use.

Gulf Coast Mission Trip

On April 4th, Amy and I attended a meeting about her upcoming Gulf Coast mission trip. Her junior year job shadowing at a hospital fell through because she needed a chicken pox vaccine. She was still behind on pre-calculus, she weaseled out of an appointment with Dr. DeSantos the next day, and she had an eyebrow waxing that lasted a *long* time. We later learned that she chose to see Chauncey instead of Dr. DeSantos. We started exploring her taking a summer biology research program at an out-of-state university, which we thought would provide the advantage of academic focus while being away from troublesome local people and places.

Amy and I flew to my hometown for my dad's eighty-fourth birthday, and when we returned, she took a cab from the airport to see a basketball game with Chauncey. I wished she had come home with me, but I knew she loved the home team, yet I felt so torn about wanting her to choose good activities but never knowing the whole story. She left for the Gulf Coast on the 15th, and we heard good reports from her about tutoring and volunteering in a library. At the trip debriefing, I learned that she had been a challenge to the chaperones, pushing one to the brink of deciding that this trip would be her last. Yet Amy's eloquent essay on her experience would never suggest anything but altruism.

After three and a half years at a high school with a total enrollment of less than two hundred, I've become very familiar with (and expectant of) strong and effective leadership. This may have been the reason for my response to the virtual absence of leadership during a volunteer program I participated in last April. I arrived...with a group of 20 adults and teenagers who hoped to help rebuild the Gulf Coast after Hurricane Katrina. While none of us knew exactly what to expect, we could not have predicted that the volunteer center at which we lodged would be almost as disorganized and devastated as the town. With two adult leaders in charge of a camp of about 150 people, simply retrieving job assignments was chaotic enough; actually making it to work sites and carrying out tasks in an orderly manner was nearly impossible. While many were discouraged, given the circumstance, others used this as an opportunity to take the initiative and become leaders. I worked with other members from my group to organize various methods of transportation to work sites and sanitize molding garments. At the school where we were cataloging donated library books, the librarian was clearly new to her job, but based on our experience of having grown up around well organized libraries we were able to make effective suggestions to help the process move forward. Eventually a group of about forty people had merged to create an effective working environment. The experience was so unique because there were no power struggles between adults and teenagers; everyone was a leader and everyone was doing the best he or she could to rebuild the town. From this experience I not only tested my ability as a leader but also gained the confidence in my leadership that I'll need for college and beyond.

Classes resumed on April 24th, and I couldn't help but feel a bit proud of Amy. So many of her classmates had been on fancy vacations and she had chosen to do service. A few evenings later, I attended a talk by Dr. Henry David Abraham, who wrote the book, *What's a Parent to Do? Straight Talk on Drugs and Alcohol.* One of his tenets is that every day we lose more control of our kids, and like holding sand, the harder you hold, the more you lose. Every day you have fewer and fewer cards to play, so you have to play them well. I wondered how much sand and what cards remained in my hand. He also provided a useful five-point spectrum for substance consumption: abstainers, experimenters, users, abusers, and addicts. He even asserted that some experimentation is likely to result in a more psychologically resilient child than one who abstains.

Amy's BVMP prom was at the end of April. I wasn't exactly thrilled that by searching on Google we found an arrest record, albeit relatively minor, for her date, Chauncey. I stopped in at the prom to "ooh and aah" at my juniors and seniors, and sighed wearily when I saw Amy and her date and another couple out at his car, breaking prom rules. I was not pleased to be in the position of informing the chaperones, who had not noticed them slipping out. I was going to leave it to the adults in charge to assign consequences. I stayed up until 1:45 a.m. awaiting Amy's return home.

Amy was really pushing for a strong year-end GPA given upcoming college applications, and she took the SAT on May 5th. She was busy with track, and I still felt her auto school job was too much, even at six hours per week. She continued to walk the line with her behavior that so often made me want to quit motherhood—and I *never* was a quitter.

On April 30th, I made my first diary reference to Lonny, a boy with whom Amy had become close on the mission trip. I wrote in my monthly letter, "Parenting 17- to 21-year-olds continues to be more than I'd expected. But no matter what you're going through, someone else is going through worse, and you usually don't have to look very far into your circle of family/friends/acquaintances to find them, so I do remain thankful for all the blessings we do enjoy!" I was trying to stay positive despite my deepening suspicions to the contrary.

On May 1st, 3rd, and 4th, I wrote diary entries expressing my concern with Amy's sleep and studying patterns. I spoke with Dr. DeSantos about how often she appeared wiped out and tired. He claimed that we never would be far away from worry with Amy. He claimed she needed "crap" to happen before she "gets it," and her fears of success and failure were constantly pulling at her.

On May 7th, I noted in my diary a call about Amy and Lonny and possibly liquor, and a question about their whereabouts. On May 10th, she was home sick, but the car odometer showed that she had driven twenty-six miles. I knew confronting her would result in denial, so I spoke again with Dr. DeSantos on the 18th. He reiterated that Amy was walking that fine line of being potentially a great student and athlete versus getting into fairly major trouble. She still hadn't shown the ability to manage her free time. He thought her pattern of three to four bad decisions per year was more worrisome than isolated incidents. I felt the ongoing stress of Amy's behavior on our family, yet wasn't feeling that the professionals we were entrusting for effective advice were providing much.

The next evening I drove Amy to the condo so she could attend a prom with one of the boys who worked at the complex. I spoke with his parents ahead of time and we agreed to meet, much to Amy's annoyance. The stress of the Friday rush hour drive across the state dominated my emotions. I can't even recall how Amy looked or whether she enjoyed her time. The only pleasure I derived as mother of the prom girl was that she was back on time and seemed okay.

In early June we finally agreed that Amy would attend the four-week biology research summer program. My husband and I were again hoping that this setting would help her rise to her academic potential by being among a better cast of characters. Only after her death did we learn that her *research* went pretty far into the realm of substances, not just biology.

I noticed she was very irritable on the 12th, and at her meeting with Dr. Adderoth later that day he ordered a random tox screen. The reaction I noted was, "She went berserk." My husband and I questioned whether she was using the landline in lieu of her cell phone to evade detection, since the landline bills were not itemized. She finished school on June 14th, but she required numerous extensions to complete her anatomy and physiology class. She managed to earn a 3.55 GPA and was thrilled to have a cumulative GPA above 3.0 as she approached her college search.

Positive Tox Screen for Cocaine

On June 16th, the morning before Amy was due to fly to the research program, I flew to New Orleans as one of seven chaperones with eighteen students for the BVMP mission trip to the Gulf Coast. As we were waiting by the curb for the rental car shuttle, and I was dreading having to drive a fifteen-passenger van across Louisiana, I retrieved a voicemail from Dr. Adderoth at 12:50 central time. I quickly stepped away from the group as I listened to the alarming message. While Amy had told him on the 12th that she was clean, the tox screen came back positive for cocaine. He was in the office until 2:00 eastern time, ten more minutes.

Could my life become more surreal? Did I need to return home? Should we even send Amy to the research program? How was I going to be able to talk with people to figure out what to do in just a few hours while renting the van and driving to Mississippi and performing my responsibilities as a chaperone? When our group stopped to visit a recent BVMP alumna at her college, I excused myself to talk with Dr. DeSantos, who agreed that a change of scenery, routine, and people would be better for Amy than her familiar environment. My husband and I agreed he would put her on her flight the next morning. When I spoke with Amy she denied cocaine use and wanted me to research the chances of a false positive, which I did later.

While on the mission trip, I didn't feel like I could talk with Mrs. Guicona, Amy's guidance counselor, even though she was a fellow chaperone. I remember calling Audrey's dad from outside the church hall where we were staying, not far from the row of portable toilets which everyone was using because the indoor plumbing at our "camp" was broken. I could see from the layout of the grounds and the sleeping arrangements how Amy could have gotten away with a lot when she stayed here during her mission trip in April.

I returned home on June 21st, and learned that my husband found a bag of Amy's pot. While disheartening, this discovery felt relatively minor given that cocaine now seemed to be the issue. I realized that my trip had a symbolic end. I had brought along a package of baby wipes, which proved invaluable for cleaning our sweaty hands and faces and respirators. On the flight back my few remaining wipes leaked onto the two precious documents I brought for comfort: my fiftieth birthday card from Amy, and a card she made me the summer before about all the things she wanted us to do together. Printed in permanent metallic ink, with her inimitable childlike watercolor illustrations, she listed reading, running, gardening, laughing, and taking hip-hop classes. Most of the words and pictures were no longer legible and some were faint. I felt sad that these endearing documents from Amy were permanently damaged. But I now had the firsthand perspective of how my loss was miniscule compared to what people lost in Hurricane Katrina. And I realized that in the grand scheme of the Gulf Coast cleanup effort, the accomplishments of our mission trip were merely "baby wipes."

My husband and I had a few weeks to regroup before Amy came home from the biology program. Business school had taught me to make action plans, but I never imagined I'd be making one about my daughter's positive tox screen for cocaine. I decided I needed to keep my various notes better organized and selected a blue Five Star® spiral notebook that our son had partially used. On the first page I made a list of people to contact. I had a long talk with Tara on the 23rd, knowing she could offer some no-nonsense guidance. My husband talked with a relative at length to obtain insights.

A few days later, I talked with one of Amy's beloved teachers about her college search. She claimed that Amy was not happy at BVMP, and her behavior was a response. She observed how Amy ate constantly and how drugs made you have the munchies. She believed that Amy would love college but counseled, "To have the headroom she needs, she needs to follow enough of the rules," something that had been a problem from toddlerhood. Meanwhile, my routine switched to summer mode: Instead of preparing for classes and correcting student work, I was gardening, overseeing house repairs, catching up on financial matters, and training for another marathon.

The itemized cell phone bill came in on the 27th, with more suspicious calls, which again made me wonder if Amy could be dealing drugs. I had expressed this deepest fear to both Dr. Sporsy and Dr. DeSantos, but no action plan ensued. Maybe I should have gone to the police. The possibility of hiring a private investigator was raised at one point, I believe by Dr. Sporsy. At our appointment the next day, he suggested a meeting with him, Dr. DeSantos, Amy, and me, saying it was time for Amy to acknowledge the truth. He captured my feelings as "betrayed, taken advantage of, heartbroken, beyond devastated, astonished Amy would do this to me." He suggested I use words with Amy like: "I need a guarantee when you return to engage dad and me in honest, mature, and detailed conversation around your coke and marijuana use and your contacts with friends. And if you cannot give me that guarantee, then you are done. It's time to grow up: no more stupid, immature denying." He suggested telling her that my husband and I needed a "reevaluation of what we mean to you and what you mean to us," and said that we couldn't do with "eroding trust." None of these recommendations actually felt helpful.

My big question (noted in all caps) was WHAT WILL BE EFFECTIVE? Somehow I didn't see the proposed script working with Amy. But I typed a letter which I never gave her, so that exercise wasn't exactly effective, either:

Dear Amy,

I would like to begin this letter with "Dearest Amy," but right now I am feeling so hurt, so betrayed, so deceived, it is almost difficult to write "dear."

I really thought I could trust all the good things that happened this year. I wasn't expecting perfection, and I know there might be steps forward with occasional steps back.

The most recent step back, the positive tox screen, is devastating. I can't tell if you're crying for help, or mocking me. You were positively thrashing the last two weeks of school. Maybe I should have intervened given how you resisted all of my overtures to help.

While so much looks positive that I can see, it's what I can't see that has me really scared. Who <u>are</u> these people you call? How much trouble are you in, substance-wise, money-wise, socially? How lonely are you? Why are you choosing to keep your social life a secret?

There have been too many things this spring that have added up to a disturbing picture…the incident with your purse and your sister in March and what we found in your room … that tox screen … the incident with Lonny … the most recent tox screen. TOO MUCH! Yet here's a girl who

- *Gives her mom a framed three-generation photo for Mother's Day*

- *Volunteers at the local hospital*

- *Does some outstanding academic work*

- *Is a much beloved babysitter*

- *Gave her mom an incredible birthday card and mix CD*

We have to figure out a way to make the rest of the summer and senior year work. We need to have honest, detailed conversations around your substance use and "friends," and friends. These need to be mature conversations, commensurate with the privileges we have given you; which you probably want to retain, but I'm feeling VERY reluctant about. Amy, this is SERIOUS. You have crossed a severe line. I don't know how many times, but even once is too many. It cannot get worse.

I love you too much to want anything but the best for you. But if my love is going to be manipulated and exploited, that is going to put me in the position of taking steps I would have thought unthinkable. But I am not a martyr, and you are almost an adult, and I want us to have a relationship that lasts both our adulthoods. As far as we've come, we have much more to do. Will you?

Much love,

Mom

I also spoke with a woman at the Canalboro drug treatment house. We talked about how marijuana can be traced or laced with cocaine or heroin, so that's how Amy could have had a positive tox screen. But marijuana had *not* shown up. She said we needed to believe what Amy was saying momentarily, but that a hair follicle test would be conclusive. She cautioned, "It's not so easy to be honest, especially about an illegal substance."

On the 29th, I was wiped out emotionally. I started going through Amy's room for any more evidence of use and had to stop to attend my appointment with the new police chief, who was a lieutenant when Amy and I saw him in November of 2004. I shared my fear of Amy getting into cheaper heroin and asked whether to pursue a CHINS. He empathized with my concern but offered no action plan. I also spoke with Dr. DeSantos, who was definitely going to try to reach Amy at her program. I then left him messages as my discoveries in her room continued to scare me: references to 420 (the National Marijuana Day is April 20th), a baseball cap with a cannabis leaf emblem, a lighter, and rolling papers.

The next day I wrote, "Not seeing a way through. Read Amy's diaries (she has lost right to privacy) and she is SCREAMING for help. Talked with my husband's relative and my brother. Need to change her environment. Tomorrow will be my last race for awhile. All the lying…" My husband's relative reassured us that Amy would be fine, that we were experiencing a huge bump in the road. She also mentioned how she heard Amy was hanging out at a Broton trailer park. She thought it preferable for Amy to be fighting with me rather than the cops.

The next day, my husband's relative tried to help us see things from Amy's probable point of view. "Amy thinks what she's doing is 'cool'," she said, "and she doesn't see it as a risk." She felt my husband's and my influence was limited, and believed the only weapons we had were the car and college. She suggested saying, "You're not going to convince us the tox screen is wrong. Employers do tox screens. Do you think you wouldn't be fired?" She suggested accentuating Amy's positives. My first of two younger brothers, a Franciscan priest, offered, "Give thanks that she's alive, and do not downplay that your love is not unrecognized."

I now, with Amy gone, give thanks that she lived as long as she did, and I know my love was recognized.

On July 1st, I tried calling Isabel, my friend struggling with raising her teen daughters in Britain, for advice. Her husband answered and assured me that he had faith that all would be fine. He underscored that Amy had to *want* to change. When Isabel rang me back, she reiterated that it's all about trust and that Amy was at a risk-taking age. She counseled that it was important to not destroy the relationship and to seek out all the extra support I needed. She suggested that if Amy gave me grief about searching her room, I tell her that nobody has the right to absolute privacy.

My husband's relative referenced Dr. Phil's "Commando Parenting" and mentioned how programs for at-risk kids micromanage them. She followed up the next day with an email. She believed that Amy needed social contact like most people needed air so we had to accept that aspect of who she was. The question was whether we could help her channel that need into pursuits that could also build her self-esteem, such as tutoring. She thanked us for bringing her into our circle of support. She reminded my husband and me to reach out because we did *not* have to handle Amy's situation by ourselves. She was even willing to take Amy if we wanted.

When I was on the phone with Tara, Amy called to request that I let her spend an overnight in the Midwest with one of her friends from "Med Camp" and I told her no. For the first time she argued, "I'm almost eighteen." My body tensed. My diary entry was "It's going to be SO hard."

On July 3rd, I became shaky when I heard the "Amie" song that inspired her name, realizing that my happy anticipation of a third child had become a living nightmare. I journaled, "Nobody deserves to go through what I've been through the last four years." My husband and I had spoken with Amy that day and she attacked my occasional attempts to reach her as "obsessively" calling her. On the 4th, I visited my nursing professor friend, Gail, after my running group. She asked if there was any adult to whom Amy wouldn't lie, and whether we should be open to a CHINS. But my pride kept telling me that responsible parents take care of their own children and do not hand them over to the state. To me, a CHINS would be admitting I had failed as a parent and as a citizen. Gail emphasized that I had to be steady and take it slowly. Our parenting was *not* at fault, she reassured me, but some tough interventions might be needed, though she did not mention a formal intervention. Could Amy get better while living at home? Meanwhile, if she babysat, she said I would need to check in on her.

Babysitting seemed to be one of the ways of accentuating the positive in Amy and helping her confidence and self-esteem. She really enjoyed being with the kids, they specifically asked for her, and she always went above and beyond, bringing little gifts and genuinely engaging and interacting with them. Families would mention how responsible she was with their children, pets, and house, and none of the professionals we dealt with ever suggested that babysitting was a bad idea. So except for right after her sophomore year hospitalization and her return from her summer biology program, we did not stop her.

....

After Amy died, several families commented on how she was their favorite sitter. Sherryl, a close friend of Amy's who babysits frequently, adamantly agreed with me that Amy would rise to her most responsible self when caring for others.

Gail also loaned me *What It Takes To Pull Me Through,* a book by David L. Marcus about youth who go off to wilderness treatment programs for their severe behavior. It didn't seem like Amy was quite that badly off, but in many ways she was close. It was tough imagining a scenario where she'd be whisked away in the middle of the night, or we'd be deprived of contact with her for weeks or months at a time. Little did I imagine that two very close and accomplished corporate colleagues would have to do exactly that with their children. I wrote "scared of 7-15," Amy's due date home.

On July 5th, I drove across the state with our first daughter to meet up with a high school friend and her family, a pleasant outing. I also talked with two of my husband's relatives, who estimated that on a spectrum of "trivial fun and games," "moderately serious," and "dangerous," Amy's condition was in the middle. One reiterated how Amy's sense of self was not as strong as it should be, and observed, "She's very slippery, guarded, knows the game, and is tricky." She mentioned how a certain class of antidepressants can counteract the effects of cocaine, a lead we never pursued.

My husband's other relative relayed a conversation with a contact who works with kids in trouble. He suggested that we have Amy assessed. "If she's a chronic user," he said, "then there's no talking to her, she won't 'get it.'" He added, "Be very, very confident that the counselor has the level of competence with adolescent and family drug issues and how the crisis infiltrates the entire family. Share with her that this is no time to let up, or you could have a dead kid. We have no idea where the stuff is from, and what's in it." He further stressed, "The biggest issue is that she's seventeen and a half. If she's uncooperative and belligerent, take her to the police and charge her. Most people in the system are very empathic and helpful. She has lost sight of the fact that she has parents. You need new discussion, dialogue, goal setting, and limits." Despite this strong advice on *what* to do, I still couldn't figure out *how* to do it, so I simply remained stunned. And the fact that I "could have a dead kid" was something I didn't really hear. I hope, dear readers, that you do.

Several points in *What it Takes to Pull Me Through* spoke to me. One was that "Principals spend lavishly on wireless classrooms but won't hire enough competent guidance counselors to ensure that students have the human contact they need" (p. 319). I've seen schools whose boards seemed to believe that technology was a panacea for the school's future. At one, the guidance secretary position was cut, leaving two guidance counselors for two hundred girls and all their issues. This ratio was rationalized by the argument that in most public schools the ratio is one per two hundred, which is also inadequate but they have other support staff. I knew that when I was teaching math, there probably wasn't a single girl in front of me who wasn't dealing with at least one item from the list of smoking, drugs, alcohol, promiscuity, physical or mental illness, eating disorders, trouble with the law, body mutilation, "bad friends," or difficult/abusive relationships. And now I know to add sexual identity. Yet guidance counselors were expected to deal with all these conditions, plus any academic challenges, student/teacher issues, college counseling, and parental concerns. They are among the unsung heroes in our schools. And to be fair, it's not necessarily principals pushing technology; it's often those higher in the administration who are not with students day in and day out.

One girl in the book was quoted saying, "Every night I go to bed praying that this isn't happening, but every morning I cry because it is" (p. 278). I felt the same way many days. It was said of the same girl, "Some kids like [her] are so smart and charming that you don't know when they're being sneaky and dishonest. Those kids are more self-destructive than the kids who go around punching walls" (p. 290). Amy sure fit the former description. It was helpful to have the distinction between being a mother and being a friend reinforced (p. 132). And I loved the line, "Your reaction tells me more than my suspicion was telling me" (p. 109).

A quote from the VIRTUS "Protecting God's Children" training program that as teachers at a Catholic school we were required to follow also spoke to me: "We must never forget that perpetrators are cunning and manipulative. Appearing trustworthy and reliable is their mode of operation." The connections between those perpetrating sexual abuse and drugs are stunningly similar.

My husband's relative then emailed me:

This could have all started when she had the first problem within her social group. She went from being the center of everyone's universe to not being the center of anyone's universe. She had carefully carved out a niche for herself there and she felt more connected to those children than to any adult in her life. Although you guys tried to help her navigate that time, she did not end up happy with the results, and probably told you what you wanted to hear regarding how she was doing in an effort to stop the dialog about the problem (as it was too painful for her). What had to follow was a series of bad behaviors which probably was met with discipline but might have warranted family therapy. Floundering for a connection like the ones that were lost and so desired, where she felt like the most important opinion in the room, and therefore validated as a personality, she decided that if she got in trouble for everything she did anyhow, then she might as well be bad. And unfortunately, as is so often the case, she found acceptance. The counterculture world is full of people who do not have a lot of positive relationships with role models and place a lot of importance on their peers.

The rub here is that the cure is something that she will struggle against accepting due to resentment and anger. The cure is cultivating that strong healthy relationship with adult role models: mom, dad, and anyone else you can. But since she is now meeting her own needs with the relationships she has formed with her counterculture group, she will not want to do this. Why give up being important and having your opinion valued? So what if you are engaging in risky behavior?

I appreciated her insight but still didn't know what to do.

The next morning, I had coffee with Gail, who didn't like the idea of the four-way meeting between Dr. Sporsy, Dr. DeSantos, Amy, and me. I deferred to her professional judgment and don't remember asking why or why not. She lamented, "Coke is so addictive." I reread an account of the year to date and journaled ". . . am sick to my stomach. To where was she driving?" I wondered about secretly installing a GPS in the car to track its location.

I met with Dr. DeSantos, who verified he and Amy had spoken prior to his vacation. I asked about an assessment of her chemical use and character, whether she could get better at home, and if BVMP would be okay for her senior year. I was also concerned with balancing sanctions and the risk that she might run away. He thought she was doing "okay." In the eighteen months they'd been working, he said, she had grown up and matured, but she was still making bad decisions, and was very naïve about the risks of hanging out with losers. He said no treatment program would take her because, while she admitted use, she denied she had a problem. He performed drug and alcohol evaluations for the courts, so I trusted his opinion. I told my husband that while Dr. DeSantos was getting more information than we were from Amy, she probably would not give the full story even to him.

That evening, my husband's relative and I bounced around the mantras, "Act your age—if you act thirteen (or eighteen) I'll treat you like you're thirteen (or eighteen)," and "Raise your level of deserve." I confessed that sometimes I felt so angry at Amy that I wanted to threaten, "In some countries, your behavior could warrant conviction and sentencing to death by stoning, even at your age." This relative suggested I share that thought with Amy, but I never did. Yet after talking with her, I was feeling optimistic.

On July 7th, I was feeling more confident about the "act your age" approach, and spoke with my daughters' pediatrician, Dr. Pedreia. She said we needed confidence about Amy's safety and suggested her therapist conduct random drug tests. I spoke with Dr. Adderoth who gave me the details of the $345 hair test that would "only" show PCP, stimulants, cocaine, opiates, and cannabis and would estimate how far back the use went. Despite being armed with this information, we ultimately did not pursue the testing, probably because we anticipated Amy's protests and were concerned about how we would deal with the actual results. I reported to Amy over the phone that the Ph.D. whom I tracked down said the chances of a false positive on a cocaine screen were virtually nil. Amy retorted that she would do more research. I also started another letter to her, which I never finished or shared:

Dear Amy,

It's now three weeks since your positive tox screen, and a week until you arrive home. I hope your time in [ ] has been good for you—intellectually, socially, and keeping clean.

When you return home, there need to be some changes. But the most basic one, that permeates all, is that I want to treat you like a 17-year-old, not like a 13-year-old. We need to be able to talk about what's really going on. No more lies. No more b.s. No more denials, evasions, tantrums. I've had enough. And I'll bet you have, too.

We have to make the rest of the summer and senior year work. We need to have honest, detailed conversations about your future, and how

we move you from your substance abuse and "friends," to being in a
healthy place with real friends. These need to be mature conversations
commensurate with the privileges you've been given.

On July 8th, one of my running buddies offered that you can't control kids, you can only put in place the structures. I felt up and down that day, but more down. I questioned how my husband and I were using the two weeks prior to her return. He and I went on an overnight to our condo to try to recharge. My feelings about Amy's homecoming ranged from "confident to terrified," and I wrote:

The rest of the summer promises to be full of challenges upon Amy's
return. She has to complete the assessments for her online pre-calculus
1a course, and will be taking the 1b at Canalboro University. The
online course became more of a power struggle over assignments than
about math, much like piano lessons at age five became more of a power
struggle over practicing than about music. Amy misplaced her driver's
license going to her program, but found it amid her many belongings
upon arrival. The night I returned from the Gulf Coast she thought
she'd lost her cell phone, so I went through the hassle of suspending ser-
vice, only to have someone find the phone a few hours later, and going
through the process in reverse. She still hasn't found her Palm Pilot.

Nothing with Amy was ever easy.

I attended her first summer pre-calculus class at Canalboro University since she was still away. I spoke again with the woman at Canalboro house because of a tip I'd received about Amy "ccc"-ing. A Google search identifies this behavior as using Dextromethorphan, a cough suppressant, one of whose street names is ccc and is also used recreationally as in "robotripping." This substance had come through on one of Amy's tox screens. The woman's response was, "It's not the end of the world." She was more concerned with Amy's overall well-being.

I checked in with Dr. DeSantos, who was back from the long weekend. He said to not force Amy to see Dr. Sporsy, but if she wanted to it was a good idea. But he wasn't sure what she would get out of it other than worries and concerns. He said to drug test her when she returned, and if she was clean to do a random test in two weeks, then weekly random tests. He suggested my husband and I get her settled upon her return on Saturday, discuss rule changes, and have her see him on Tuesday.

I also spoke with a drug counselor named Mr. Coolwater, who was referred by Gail. He taught sections of her nursing curriculum on substance abuse, and she had the utmost respect for him. I liked him right away when he prefaced his remarks about Amy's demographic with, "This age group is about the smartest dumb age group on this planet." He said that generally the kid is in big trouble by the time she realizes Mom is right. He reminded me that a parent's job is to protect, and the question was whether the latest behavior required intervention. He was interested in her drug of choice, which I said was stimulants. Amy liked them for a reason, he said. "Maybe she's self-medicating. The drugs can help her to organize/energize what she sees as a vulnerability." We agreed to meet the next day.

I made a list of concerns to address with him, including how to be her mother and not a friend, the extent of her secret life, what was going to be effective given how far back the problem went and how much change would be required, and the ethical issues in communicating with the school and other parents. He began by saying that the fact that Amy was very bright didn't help. "Her intellect gives her a false sense of control," he warned, "and you can't use intellect to 'get over' substances." He told me my job now was to protect her as best I could, and to protect her from herself. He noted that a lot of cocaine is cut with stimulants, and there's no quality control on street drugs. Adderall could be crushed and snorted, or exchanged for other drugs. College kids often won't be prescribed such stimulants, he said, because they are so commonly abused. While her character was malleable, a lot of the basis was formed. So far I really liked what I was hearing from him.

He asked questions that other practitioners had not, such as had she suffered head injuries, and was she taking multivitamins, drinking at least four to five bottles of water a day (because college kids were perennially dehydrated), and did she consume at least fifty grams of protein per day? He advised that B complex could help with stress. He also raised a reality I hadn't realized with respect to her driving. If she were to have an accident and someone else were hurt, and she had a positive tox screen, all her records could be subpoenaed and probable cause would be found. How would we cover that scenario financially?

His approach was holistic. He tried to understand why a particular drug worked for a patient. If the patient couldn't tell him "what's up," he'd draw blood to determine any underlying organic reasons. He could not help, he admitted, unless he knew what the patient was doing. His goal was to have an educated consumer as if they were buying electronics (another one of Amy's fortes) including knowing physical, social, legal, and academic consequences. He was familiar with some colleges that were "draconian" about drugs. For example, with a marijuana violation, the first time you're out of university housing for a year, the second time for the rest of your college years, and third time you are asked to leave the school. Drug use could also cost a student their financial aid.

He added that he no longer attended psychotherapy conferences, but rather sought out brain science meetings. He explained that women's brains aren't developed until ages twenty-one or twenty-two, and adolescent brains are so vulnerable to chemicals. Seventeen-year-olds can't bear conflict. A perfectionist is in denial because they have no fallback position, they are face-to-face with their own incompetence. The fallback is to pursue an education.

He noted that Amy had survived so far, and that she was experimenting, probably not dependent, and probably not abusing. He would be educating her about how to handle stress. Also, he believed a baseline and random drug screening was the best defense: the drama ends, parents are off your back. I was wowed by his knowledge and insight, and expected that Amy would like him, especially his referring to the Dalai Lama and the movie *Kundun*.

July 14th was a flurry of activity preparing for Amy's reentry, and I attended her second pre-calculus class that evening. Amy was feisty on the phone about her homecoming the next day: She wanted an eyebrow waxing appointment and did not want to go out to dinner, I suspect because she did not want to face my husband and me about the cocaine.

Return from Research

On July 15th, my husband and I agreed that when we collected Amy at the airport we would go straight to a restaurant to eat and talk in a neutral location. Our time was fairly calm, and Amy shared her epiphany about wanting to be good at a lot of things, drugs not being one of them. She slept past noon on Sunday, and I forsook a party with some friends to stay around her. I took her for a random test on Monday, and Dr. Pedreia said her office could set up standing orders, meaning we could take her in at any time.

Every month, I gave each of our three children a nominal monthly allowance for clothes. I had tired of being constantly asked to pay for individual clothing purchases, so came up with the idea that if I gave each child a set monthly "budget" they could buy their own clothing, including saving up for more expensive items. It was their choice if they spent the money on something other than clothing. I thought at the time it was a way to encourage responsible spending habits. On July 18th, Amy blew up about her clothing budget, arguing that it wasn't enough, and she wasn't spending money on anything bad. I did not increase her budget, though I wish I'd stayed with having the children produce clothing receipts to be reimbursed up to the budgeted amount. The extra transaction time would have prevented providing cash in advance that could be diverted. But now I know that if someone wants money for drugs, they find a way. But at least I wouldn't have been making it easier for Amy.

While driving Amy to her 1:00 p.m. session with Dr. DeSantos, she told me that she thought she was receiving a caffeine pill which ended up being the cocaine in the positive tox screen. We talked about there being no quality control on street drugs, and she said she was scared, too. That evening she started attending her pre-calculus class.

Of far greater import was the first reference to Calvin, a guy she said she met at a cross country meet, so I naively assumed he was one of the runners. She asked to meet him for ice cream at 2:15, so I dropped her at the restaurant after her appointment. When he dropped her at home around 4:40, she told me they had gone to his house and she talked with his mom. Meanwhile, Beirut was bombed, and one of my overseas friends evacuated to Cyprus. I felt that both of our worlds were under siege.

On July 19th, Amy cleaned the family TV room, and Calvin was at our house for two hours at lunchtime. I had my annual summer lunch and swim with two of my former colleagues who would have been an excellent source of street-smarts about handling Amy, but, unfortunately I didn't come close to disclosing the pain in our family. Calvin came to take Amy to go to a local park, then to his house for dinner. I cried while walking River at 5:00 p.m. thinking, "How am I parenting Amy? Can I trust her?" I felt so nervous about her being with this guy. She called around 8:15 to say she was coming home. I asked that he come in and meet my husband, but have no memory of what that was like.

The next day, I was at school for a scheduling meeting and talked in generalities with two colleagues about the challenges of parenting young adults. I was concerned whether my parental "bark" was bigger than my "bite." Although Amy's most recent tox screen had come back clean, I felt more skepticism than relief. On Friday, Amy and Calvin went to breakfast, and, after my meeting at school, I picked her up. I jotted later in the day, "How to talk to my husband, Amy, ANYONE?" I was not feeling heard even when I tried. At 11:30 p.m., when my husband was almost asleep and heard Amy's cell phone, he went to confiscate it despite her protestation, "Dad, you're hearing things."

On Saturday morning, my husband and I listened to Amy's eighteen saved voicemails, which included drug references. Yet we accommodated her by spending $50 on a used ping-pong table. She had played quite a bit at the biology program, and we figured it was better that she be in the basement playing than out somewhere unknown. We needed to rent a small truck. It took the better part of an afternoon to relocate the unwieldy table, even when folded, across town. The next day, I referred to a "debacle" concerning my husband's annual family picnic: He and our first daughter went. I stayed home because Amy had set up volunteering at the hospital. Calvin then collected her and they came to our house, and I did not trust having them alone in my home.

On Monday, July 24th, Amy came to 9:00 a.m. Mass with me, and she went to Calvin's for dinner. On Tuesday, I spoke with Dr. DeSantos again. He reiterated the usual themes, that Amy liked to walk on the edge and that when he told her that she only had a year for her parents to develop confidence in her ability to make right decisions, she'd say, "Mom and Dad worry too much." He added that she was either lying to herself or incredibly naïve because she had trouble believing most boys hope for "something" but once limits were established they could be friends. He reiterated the constant struggle of trying to have her compare "up" and not "down." He believed it was time for Amy to start pulling away from Audrey. Finally, he cautioned, even if we saw no signs of use, she should be drug tested at least once a month.

Amy went to the beach with Calvin that afternoon. To this day, whenever I see a car like his, my stomach turns.

Two days later, I took Amy to Mr. Coolwater for an assessment. She went in angry, and came out mellow. He told me that she agreed he could share some things about their meeting. During our quick debrief, she looked at a meditation book in the waiting area. Mr. Coolwater reaffirmed my parenting. He said Amy was curious about substances and had a healthy respect for them, but was vulnerable. We stopped for ice cream on the way home, and that night she played ping-pong with my husband and me and cleaned her room. She made a point to us that she did not see Calvin that day.

On Thursday, July 27th, I dropped Amy at a pizza shop so she could accompany Calvin while he drove his mother to the airport. He also drove her to class, which she verified with a text message. I was not liking this relationship. Amy's behavior seemed unnatural around him, and she endeared herself to his mother, despite the reservations Amy herself mentioned.

I articulated to myself how all the various therapy appointments felt like lily pads, with the time between them like the interstitial pond water as I waited to jump from one to another in hopes of progress. At my next meeting with Dr. Sporsy, he provided various statements I could use with Amy, including, "Until you acknowledge you've done this, it won't get better. You've been lying to others, to yourself, and you're being a victim." Her argument for not going to the family picnic was that she didn't want to watch older people smoke and drink. Dr. Sporsy said my comeback should have been that, if none of the incidents had happened, she wouldn't have to. The price of freedom was about being honest, straightforward, and making the right decisions. He said I should have told her, "You've absolutely earned all the restrictions and suspicions." He echoed a pattern that Dr. Hischolor had observed: Amy was not taking ownership that she was dependent on transportation and that other people had lives. Her playing the victim went back to fourth and fifth grade. He suggested setting the expectation, "I can only be lied to and manipulated and hurt so many times; you could lose me." Great rhetoric, but what did it really mean? And I never remember him asking me if I followed his suggestions and, if not, probing why.

On Friday, Amy slept until 10:30 a.m., watched a movie with her sister, and worked on pre-calculus. But she left at 2:40 with Calvin, took her books, and said he might give her a ride to class, which he did. On Saturday she volunteered at the hospital from 1:00 until 5:00 p.m. On Monday, July 31st, we learned that Amy's tox screens on July 17th and 27th were clean; I question if she faked them by providing someone else's urine or using a scheme she could have found on the Internet. On August 1st, she went to breakfast with Calvin and his folks, then he took her to Dr. DeSantos's office, and I retrieved her. That night she and I argued as I drove to her class. I cited a discrepancy between the time she told me she went to the pharmacy and what was printed on the sales slip, and she insisted that the time printed on the receipt was wrong. I tried to frame the discussion by saying that it would be better if I heard the truth directly from her, rather than discovering it on my own. She countered that she felt she couldn't enjoy life because she was under a microscope.

The following Wednesday, we were in the midst of a brutal heat wave, but we had a good day, which included discussing "forgetting" versus lying. On Thursday, she had lunch with Calvin. My first daughter and I were commenting, not favorably, on Amy's choice of shirts; the girl who in seventh grade fretted that she'd never have a chest was now very well endowed and flaunted it. Amy's immodesty, also expressed in very short shorts, contributed to my weariness about underlying sneakiness and dishonesty. I was not going to whip Amy over her clothing; I knew someone whose father did that to her when she was sixteen. But that's not to say my exasperation didn't sometimes make me imagine that option.

The Calvin Calamity

On Friday, August 4th, Liza slept at our house. Amy was okay with me saying it was too late for Calvin to come back. I was pleasantly surprised that she didn't push back; I should have been suspicious. The ensuing hours were "too strange." Amy asked to sleep in the basement, something she'd never done. I talked her out of it, citing something that would surely convince her, namely that the cats had been known to have occasional "accidents" on the carpet. Then she went out for "fresh air" at 12:30 a.m., something else she'd never done. She said she needed to bring in the lawn chairs and basketball from the rain, but they'd been outdoors for weeks. At 5:30 a.m., I noticed the house alarm was not on. Since I'm a very sound sleeper, I wondered what else I missed in the wee hours.

Dog walkers notice very small changes, and while taking River on his morning walk I saw some water bottles by the side of the road. When I checked, their code matched the remaining bottles in the case in our basement. I saw two empty vodka nips near our house. I left a message for Dr. DeSantos saying, "I want to be able to trust my daughter." But he was away. Did his absence provide the backdrop for Amy choosing to act out then? I also left a message for Dr. Sporsy. I began to think it was better that the sleepover had been at our house because too many things seemed unusual. I hated the "guilty until proven innocent" approach with Amy, but she had earned it. Liza's dad collected her mid-morning, and I think Amy volunteered at the hospital, because I noted a call having to do with long pants, which were part of the candy-striper uniform.

On August 6th, Amy went to a mid-afternoon cook-out with Calvin. Later in the afternoon my husband's relative was hosting a birthday celebration for him at her house. I decided I would do that day's seventeen-mile training run by running to the party. Calvin, with Amy in the passenger seat, drove past me around mile sixteen as he took Amy to the party. That moment defined the shattering of my plans for a fall marathon. I just could not keep training under the anxiety of their relationship. I felt like I was melting from sadness and despair.

Amy made her father a strawberry cream pie for his birthday on August 7th. The next day, she committed to babysit for one of her favorite clients; I'm not sure if we had explicitly lifted the ban. I let her drive to Liza's the next day while I was in the car and noted her hot foot. She was going out to dinner and then to a movie with Liza, her dad, and the brother of some BVMP girls. I felt uncomfortable leaving her. Although I knew the boy was from a good family,

I was starting to learn that upstanding parents are no guarantee about the trustworthiness of their child. Two days later, I attempted an eight-mile run, and I stopped several times to cry as all the emotional pain surfaced.

I flew to my hometown to visit my folks on August 11th, and I was anxious about how Amy would fare with my husband in charge. The following afternoon, I drove six hours with Tara to her city. I had a dream that Amy and I were in an earthquake, not an inaccurate metaphor for our summer, which had been filled with tremors and aftershocks. On the 14th, Amy flew to join me at what would be my last visit with my friend since age fifteen, "Aunt Hattie," now ninety-five. I savor the memories of how patient and delightful Amy was with my stroke-ravaged friend. We also visited two colleges, opted out of a third, and flew home that night.

The next day, another student informant came forward. My diary entry was simply, "A wreck." She told me that Amy was not referring to Calvin by his real surname. He had license restrictions and a young child. He had allegedly hooked two girls on heroin. My informant questioned whether he was buying drugs for Amy. I checked the old phone bills, and his number first appeared on March 4th. I left a message for Mr. Coolwater and Dr. Sporsy, and went to see the town police.

The sergeant said that Calvin was almost twenty-one, and "one of the worst" in his town, "one hundred percent the worst." He could be involved with heroin. He said we didn't want him at our house, "any time, any place." He talked to the chief and said we could have a certified letter that if Calvin trespassed on our property, he would be under arrest. I talked with Tara, who said the situation might not be as bad as it seemed, or it might be. She urged me not to overreact. I finally felt that someone was acknowledging that my fears were legitimate.

Mr. Coolwater called back and said Amy in her naïveté/vulnerability could be seeing Calvin as her "Johnny Depp," the "magic man." She could be under the illusion that she could handle him better than she actually could. If he really were a loser and using her, if she required anything from him, he would walk away. But most difficult was that she saw him as a "wounded pup" to be converted. But he could also be a predator using her as a mule (someone who smuggles or delivers illegal substances).

The best outcome would be if Amy started feeling uncomfortable and decided to change to a safer way of living. If she were to rebel, an aggressive intervention would need to occur. He noted we still had a lot of power since we controlled the car, her phone, and our home, but she could become defiant and run away. I later talked with Dr. Sporsy and my husband's relative. That evening, my husband had dinner with his friend from graduate school,

Anya, and her husband, who were visiting from out of town. I drove Amy to her class, collected her after, and we dropped by the restaurant for dessert where I said nothing about what I'd just learned. I was straddling dramatically parallel worlds, acting as if everything were fine while I felt like I was in the middle of a collapsing family life.

The next morning, I left a message for Dr. Sporsy suggesting that maybe he, and not I, should be talking directly with Dr. DeSantos so that Amy would keep talking to Dr. DeSantos. I called the police chief, told him I'd received tips, and he agreed to see Amy and me that morning. At the meeting, I told Amy that my concern was for her safety and the family's, and if Calvin came by our house we would execute the no trespass notice. She claimed she hadn't spoken with him in a week. The chief told her she was at a fork in the road and needed to make good choices. I told her we had zero tolerance for larceny. She and I managed to end the conversation with a hug, and although I had to go to school briefly we talked more afterward. Another relative weighed in that moving Amy to another city wasn't the answer. My new student informant called again with more information about Calvin, and I thanked her. Calvin had tried calling the house twice. I carried out the unenviable task of informing two of our neighbors about the risk Calvin could pose.

Mom's Migraine

The next day, August 17th, I had yet another migraine, and I questioned in my journal, "How much can I trust versus what she thinks I want to hear?" Amy wanted permission to drive again. The 18th was also rough. Amy and I sparred about her driving; Audrey picked her up at work. I searched her room in the evening when my husband and our first daughter were at a movie. For the second time, I found a urine sample, which made me worry to what lengths she might be going to "fake" a drug test. The first time was in the spring of 2005, when she claimed that the vial in her purse was from her friend Lily, a variation on "blood sisters." Yeah, right.

August 19th was "the worst Saturday since November 2004," the day we took Amy to the ER at City Pediatrics Hospital. I even missed my running group. I took Amy to work at 9:00 a.m., and it wasn't pretty. She asked about my searching due to her noticing something different about her drawers. I told her the search was part of our due diligence before letting her use the car again. She said two people, whom she wouldn't identify, were accusing me of being mentally ill. I felt this accusation was "below the belt" and almost words of desperation on her part. While I was stressed, I did not feel irrational.

I napped from 9:30 until noon. My husband and our first daughter brought Amy pizza for lunch at work as Audrey was too busy to take any over. I spoke with Mr. Coolwater mid-afternoon, who raised the distinction of abuse versus dependency. If she could go three to four days without using, then she was not considered dependent. He said there were "some remarkable options" for treatment, including outpatient programs, but supervised urine tests were key. Six-month programs were often not doable or useful. Violence couldn't be tolerated. We were facing our last real socialization opportunities for her before college. Generally, no one wants to be supervised, but she needed to be supervised.

I wrote in my journal, "Not seeing a way through." I collected Amy from work and drove her to the hospital to volunteer. Soon after that, I received a message from my new student informant. She said Amy kept meeting new people and finding new sources of drugs and would no longer be completely honest with her. One source was someone from work and another was in his late twenties. I left voicemails for my husband's relative, Dr. Sporsy, and Dr. DeSantos. I was scared. I collected her at the hospital and used the words the BVMP principal had in November 2004, "We're here not to get you in trouble, but to get you the help you need." She pushed back. She said she needed money and that I was blowing things out of proportion.

My husband and I tried to check her purse around 6:00 p.m. before she went out, and she used force to prevent us from taking her cell phone. I made a reference to suspicious text messages and tips I'd received about sources of her drugs. She left around 7:00 p.m. with Audrey, Lonny, and her cell phone. I spoke with my husband's relative, who said Amy needed a lifestyle change *now*. Was she enjoying being part of the counterculture, or the drugs? I collected Amy from a local coffee shop at 10:20 that night.

Dad's Migraine

On Sunday morning, August 20th, my husband had a severe headache, and I drove him to the ER to be checked. I had awoken Amy, who was sleeping with her cell phone, and asked her to come for moral support. I abandoned the request when she said she wanted to go to Audrey's instead so they could go to the outlet mall. I was beside myself because I wanted her to be with me, also because of my fears about her safety, but I was not going to pick this battle. A few hours later, I left my husband at the hospital and collected Amy at home to drive her to Audrey's. She had declined their offer to pick her up at our house and would not consent to meeting them halfway, which was on their way to the outlets anyhow. I should have called Audrey's mom but feared Amy's anger more than my own.

The car ride became ugly. I lost my temper, and took a swipe at her, which was not my style, and indicative of my exasperation. Our first daughter was also quite angry about all the stress that Amy was inflicting on the family. Here my husband was in the ER and yet I was indulging her like a spoiled brat. She responded with the "once I'm eighteen" and "things are going to change" threats. She was arguing that "if you're going to treat me like a ____, then it will become a self-fulfilling prophecy." I tried to state my expectations about her job and cross country co-captainship. What I saw as making myself clear to prevent future misunderstandings she saw as me trying to control her life. She accused me of thanking Audrey's mom for driving the girls as overprotective; I saw it as a courtesy compared to parents who failed to even introduce themselves. These encounters were depleting me, but Amy's history and the current uncertainty made it hard for me to imagine letting go.

That night Amy stayed at Audrey's. I became concerned after reading about people nodding off after using heroin. Given what we had learned about Calvin, my radar was more attuned to making such a connection. Yet I could not bring myself to believe that Amy would cross the line to shooting heroin, in part because she was so particular about her physical appearance. I did not know then that heroin could be snorted, and you did not need to inject to become addicted.

On Monday, August 21st, I spoke with the town police at 8:00 a.m. and learned about a local Youth Substance Abuse Program. I started calling Amy at 9:30 a.m., but she did not answer. When she finally picked up at 10:05, she told me she just walked out of the restaurant and Audrey's car wouldn't start. When she said she "got up late," I replied that it would be a courtesy to let me know that. When I arrived at the restaurant, Audrey's dad was working on the car. She asked to go tanning before her senior portrait photo shoot, and I agreed, but said first we would go for a random tox screen. She said okay with no pushback and left everything in the car except her water bottle, which she took into the bathroom. When she emerged she said that she didn't void very much. We then drove almost an hour to have her portrait taken and were late due to poor directions. I reminded her to cover more of her chest. I was feeling concerned about whether she was high on something.

We had a peaceful trip home, but the calm was shattered when I found two unopened cans of beer in my husband's mini-van. I can't even remember if I confronted her. She left for a movie around 7:50 with Hal, a fellow hospital volunteer, and at 8:00 I discovered that the sports drink bottle in her backpack contained what smelled like gin. I left a message for Dr. DeSantos in exasperation saying, "I don't know when it's going to end." My husband and I talked about what to do. I was feeling anger and pain and was afraid of the ticking time bomb as Amy approached age eighteen. I left a message for Dr. Sporsy saying it was time to re-strategize.

Call to 9-1-1

Amy returned home around 10:30 and refused to let us check her purse. I struggled with her over it, and a drug baggie fell out, which she snatched and ran upstairs. So I called 9-1-1 and the police arrived. While difficult to recall the precise details or their sequence, the emotional pain and desperation are indelibly etched in my memory. I couldn't believe this scene was happening in my house. The officer calmed everyone down, but I don't think we resolved anything about the baggie. As far as the rest of the evening, I just have a note that she and I talked before bed about counterdependence, and in my diary I questioned the way forward. I had to make an action plan of who to call in the morning.

On Tuesday, August 22nd, Dr. Sporsy called around 7:30 a.m. and said he'd call if he had a cancellation. I gave Amy the option of joining me at 9:00 Mass, but she wanted to sleep. I left a message for Dr. Adderoth saying we needed the tox screen results as soon as possible, as well as standing orders set up at another facility, and the option of supervised screens, where the person produces the sample in the presence of a medical professional. I left a message for Dr. DeSantos that life with Amy continued to be out of control, and we later spoke for almost an hour. We discussed the dilemma that if a seventeen-year-old commits a crime, it's not on their record. But at eighteen, only five months away, the parents don't have to do anything because the kid is treated as an adult by "the system." In fact, when the kid is legally an adult, parents really can't do much.

Dr. DeSantos shared that Amy continued to believe that her behavior was because "Mom and Dad are too strict." She continued to argue down, "I'm not as bad as ____." For the first time, Dr. DeSantos also told Amy that if things continued to be this shaky, we could fire him. My husband and I questioned whether it was time to start with someone new, but Dr. DeSantos said he wasn't giving up, and he thought he could be effective. We had been told he was the best in the area, and the idea of changing Amy's therapist seemed overwhelming. She seemed to have a good rapport with him and went to her appointments willingly, which was critical.

He said that he very rarely met a kid who wanted to get caught as much as Amy. He had told her that I was going to find out about Calvin, and that she couldn't continue to lie because she'd be caught. Dr. DeSantos said we could entertain various treatment programs, but if a kid says there's no problem, the program won't take him/her. I mentioned how my husband questioned whether we should enlist a new family therapist. Dr. DeSantos remained hopeful that the start of school would help because Amy would once again have more structure.

Then I called Dr. Adderoth's office to ask about the results of the tox screen. His secretary said, "Oh, we had a problem with one of the samples." Sure enough, it was Amy's: all water. I awoke her and by 10:55 we were back at the lab. I was feeling held hostage again, first as she took her time eating her oatmeal at home, and secondly when at the clinic she said she wasn't able to urinate. We waited until she could provide a sample. I also called the clinic and spoke with two people about supervised samples. They said they didn't do them, but I could go in after her to check that she provided urine. (I subsequently wrote to the medical director and received no reply.) I called Mr. Coolwater and mentioned the incidents of recent days and asked if perhaps he could take on the role of family therapist. When walking the dog, I had the chilling thought that maybe we were dealing with a problem we *couldn't* solve.

Amy and I proceeded to the optical office, and I told the eye doctor that Amy used over-the-counter eye drops extensively. He was appalled, so I asked him to educate her. We ended up with $100 prescription drops. Meanwhile, Dr. Hischolor called me back, observing that Amy was not responding to limits at all, and was clearly acting out. She said we needed someone who played hardball on family therapy. She felt it was frightening that Amy really let herself experiment at a level that could put her in danger, had been at it awhile, and had had some luck surviving it. She added that Amy believed she was invincible which was age appropriate, but she had very little internal superego/conscience.

Sleepover Sequelae

Amid the numerous other calls that afternoon was a message from Liza's mom saying she had some disturbing details about the August 4th sleepover, and she would fill me in when we talked. My husband's relative also called to remind us that we had to send a healthy mind to college. She asserted that Amy wasn't physically addicted, but she was emotionally addicted to the lifestyle, much like people who are addicted to a cigarette lifestyle.

At 8:50 the next morning, I learned the devastating sleepover details from Liza's mom. The phone call started with her assumption that I hadn't been home the night of the sleepover. I told her that of course I was, and she said she thought I would have been. Liza told her that Calvin was in fact the boyfriend of Amy's classmate, Nancy. He snuck into our house at 3:00 a.m., and they were snorting heroin and cocaine. Liza vomited after and was completely wiped out when her dad collected her, and she slept the rest of the day. The mom reported that one of the times the girls got together, someone dropped off the drug ecstasy. I started hyperventilating and became sick to my stomach.

I went into my appointment with Dr. Sporsy at 9:00, and he mentioned a formal intervention as a choice, not a threat. He said we couldn't keep being triggered by hearsay, so to step up the drug tests to every four days with no negotiation, and he mentioned blood tests. He believed that in Amy's eyes, "Everything was a big f---ing joke." I questioned how we lost focus on both the family therapy after Amy's November 2004 hospitalization and the social worker's recommendation that Amy attend a teen twelve-step group. I suspected that, in the former, we were feeling "therapy fatigue," and we *had* tried working with Mrs. Ladaco, a licensed alcohol and drug abuse counselor, to little or no avail. And my misconceptions of twelve-step groups probably kept me from pursuing one for Amy, coupled with the fact that she had individual therapy. After the session, I learned from Liza's mom that at 9:30 she intercepted a text message from Amy to Liza: "I'm so f---ed. In so much trouble. So much to tell you."

Mr. Coolwater called back with the names of one or two places where Amy could be admitted immediately. He also recommended more frequent blood or supervised urine tests. He urged us to stay as empirical as possible. I was kicking myself for not following my intuition to test Amy for drugs after the sleepover.

I returned home to find Amy sitting on our futon reading *Northern Lights*, the BVMP all-school summer reading book. The drive to Dr. DeSantos's for her noon appointment was tense. Amy complained that she had "no summer" and wouldn't be able to do her best senior year. She asked for her friend, Hal, to come over. She said she had no place to express her feelings, except her diary. (How did I miss this red flag?) I did notice she was constantly sniffling. I reflected that while earlier in the summer the various therapy sessions were the lily pads of hope, now we were in a scary poker game with higher and higher stakes. Mr.

Coolwater called again to say he could do the family therapy piece, but the question was how soon.

Amy was in a much better mood after seeing Dr. DeSantos. She and I went to eat at our favorite Italian café and she said she decided to stop f---ing up. We talked of the cigarette culture model her relative had outlined. We went to the mall, picked up Amy's new eyeglasses, and bought more back-to-school items, including what would be her last pair of Birkenstocks. I wondered if the police should still write the no trespass letter to Calvin. Was my family really safe? Amy completed her last pre-calculus 1a assignment that evening. I also learned that the volunteer coordinator at the hospital was the one who suggested that Amy and Hal go out. He was not a stereotypically popular kid, but she knew Amy had a kind heart and would see the good in him.

That night, I was awakened by Amy's cell phone ringing but did not intercept the calls. I woke up feeling sick in my stomach about all the loopholes in dealing with Amy. I was particularly troubled by her comment that sometimes she forgot to sign in when she volunteered at the hospital. I talked with Isabel for support. I found the name of one of the area's most prominent substance abuse psychiatrists, Dr. Herowitz, and called him from my classroom. It was time to bring in the big guns.

In an eleven-minute conversation, he agreed that Amy's story was "complicated" and the number one concern was for her safety. He wanted to meet with my husband and me, then with Amy, and put together a plan, the shape of it being a function of Amy's willingness to engage. He raised the question, "Is she falling or stumbling?" He would not be inexpensive: $200 for forty-five minutes. I then talked with Dr. Adderoth's office, who reported the tox screen was totally negative. My husband didn't believe it. Where was the Celexa, the antidepressant prescribed by Dr. Adderoth? The ibuprofen?

I spoke again with Liza's mom, who also talked with a police sergeant who said they were "very aware" of Calvin, a hard-core heroin addict, in and out of jail, charged with breaking and entering, trouble from day one, a dealer. I went to see the BVMP president and recommended that Calvin should not be allowed on school property, and he should be arrested for trespassing if he showed up. She said she would talk with the town police. When I talked with Amy after cross country practice, she insisted that Liza was exaggerating.

Alcohol on the Carpet

That afternoon, Amy and I met our son's college counselor to consult on her search. Later I spoke with Dr. DeSantos, who said to pull in the reins a little. That evening, our family experienced high drama yet again when Amy's friend, Lonny, came over, and she poured the alcohol from her sports drink bottle onto the basement carpet. I called my school nurse friend and neighbor, Trina, to come over to help. She also smelled the alcohol. Amy's alibi was that she was cleaning out the last of the stuff in her room. Trina pushed back on Amy to take responsibility. I left a message for Dr. DeSantos and phoned the on-call clinician, who suggested we take Amy to the local hospital for an evaluation based on ongoing concerns. My husband and I agreed we would *not* do that, but rather wait on the work we had just begun with Dr. Herowitz, concerned that a short-term action could wipe out the long-term gain we were seeking.

I drove Lonny home and talked with his dad. Amy tried to grill me on the way home about what exactly we discussed. I called Trina to thank her, and she confessed that most medical professionals can't tell accurately whether someone is under the influence. I left Dr. Sporsy an "11:00 p.m. news update" on the day with Amy. My diary entry: "Aargh!"

Amazingly enough, August 25th was a "relatively calm day." But I noted that I'd lost four pounds in the last week, my memory recall was slower, and my attention to detail was faltering. I'd now had fifty-two meetings with Dr. Sporsy, and I questioned their worth. I called the hospital, and the volunteer coordinator verified that Hal was an okay guy, and she corroborated that sometimes Amy forgot to sign in. We had drama surrounding Amy's 6:00 p.m. eyebrow waxing, which she then rescheduled, but my husband said she would be grounded, at least until we talked with Dr. DeSantos. I left him a message that we would not pursue the hospital evaluation since he was away and it could subvert the bigger plan. I said our family was at the breaking point, with high resentment a constant. I questioned whether we were making progress.

That night, my husband, our daughters, and I went out for Italian food with his relatives, and Amy's behavior was reasonable. On Saturday morning, we made Amy come to the airport to take her sister to fly back for her sophomore year of college. I came home to a letter that Amy had written the night before:

My dearest mother,

I'm so sorry. I'm sorry for the pain I've made you deal with throughout my life, especially during the past year or so. Sitting at the restaurant this evening I looked over and noticed you smiling. Mom, you have the most kind, warm hearted smile I've ever seen. It reminded me of all the amazing times we've had together…visiting Aunt Hattie, going on the occasional run, driving to school (and of course hitting up Tulips), listening to classic oldies and, of course, laughing about your ever-famous attempts at hitting that mailbox in the town center with the car for the 2nd time. Seeing you smile made me realize how much I want to have our old, fun times back. I *hate* being the source of your unhappiness and pain. I feel like drugs and alcohol have created a barrier between us that goes beyond what I'd ever imagined they could. I had no idea they could be the cause of such a level of distrust and separation. Honestly, mom, I don't feel I have a problem with any recreational substance. As I've said before, sometimes I'll make the wrong decisions simply to fit into the social scene. It seems ridiculous when I say it like that, but I guess that's what my 'deal' is. You know what I've come to realize though? Not even the best high in the world would be worth risking my relationship with you. I find even the least significant times we have together to be 1000x better than any experience I've ever had under the influence. I just wanted you to know that. No matter how many hurtful things I say when I'm angry, I just need you to understand that I love and care about you so much. And as cheesy as this sounds, I wanna be the one to make you smile some day.

I know this letter is barely articulate and far from "perfect", but I thought it was better to get out my feelings this way than waste time thinking of the ideal words. I hope we can work everything out because I want to have an awesome senior year and I want our relationship to flourish during my last year at home. Feel free to reflect on this letter, but please try to keep it between us as best you can.

Love you so much,

Amy

xoxo

At my running group, I talked with some of my buddies, one of whom raised the question of HIV risk for Amy, and another saying I was doing my best with her, which still didn't feel very effective to me. My husband and I were feeling even more suspicious about what Amy did the day of the family picnic now that we had the detailed phone bill which made her explanation of the day's events look suspect.

I collected Amy from work and bought her pizza while she was at her eyebrow waxing. I commended her bravery in writing the letter, told her she hit the nail on the head about the mistrust, and was glad she felt her summer experimentation would suffice. Always the opportunist, she asked if Lonny could come over the next day, and I told her to feel the pain of being grounded. My husband then took her to the hospital to volunteer. I further analyzed the cell phone bill which looked scary to me, but my husband warned me of the "danger of investigator fever." I collected Amy at the hospital and vetoed her request to travel to another state to visit a college with a "Med Camp" buddy, saying that we'd see how the week played out. My husband and I strategized on Amy's driving privileges. She cleaned the car, made cupcakes, and did some AP calculus summer work. The evening was calm.

On Sunday, August 27th, I talked with Tara, who asserted that Amy was "yanking my chain in the worst possible ways" and was being a real pain in the backside. A carefully crafted driving agreement would be for our family's protection as well as Amy's. I gave Amy my reply to her letter. I'd copied it, written notes next to various items, and added:

Dearest Amy —

I am so glad to receive this letter. It follows your epiphany that you want to be good at a lot of things, and one of them is not doing drugs.

I will help you, we will help you, however you need. You have such a promising future, but we cannot let the last few weeks continue. We will keep talking, finding the help we need, and praying. Thank you so much for writing, and let's keep going from here.

Love always,

Mom

xoxo

In retrospect, the reply made me feel better, but I question what it accomplished. I gave her the driving proposal that my husband and I had crafted:

Dear Amy,

First, remember that driving is a privilege, not a right. As Giuliana once remarked, a driver is behind the wheel of a 3,000 pound assault weapon. Being physically, mentally and emotionally fit to drive is a non-negotiable. However, driving also brings mobility, and the ability to put yourself in risky places and situations. Minimizing these risks requires sound judgment and truthfulness.

When we revoked your privileges to drive alone upon your return on July 15th, it was based on your June 12th positive tox screen for a felony substance. In consultation with Mr. Coolwater, we knew that we had to be sure you were not a chronic user of illegal substances, hence the subsequent random tox screens on July 17th, 27th, and August 21st, 22nd. We also need to make sure you are not an occasional user of such substances, which cannot be based solely on tox screens, but comes more from the trust that is built in living together day-to-day. We won't repeat here the legal consequences we have discussed in the event of an accident and/or possession.

We expected the initial suspension to last about a month, subject to receiving your "epiphany" letter (August 26th), that you'd have several clean tox screens, and that trust would be rebuilt. While your letter spoke volumes to mom, it is clear that we need to make sure your future socializing allows you to enjoy your friends in an environment without illegal substances. Based on the sabotaged tox screen sample on August 21st, we do not have all clean screens. And the level of trust is probably worse than before you went away.

To speak to the trust in specifics:

- *your sleepover on Aug 4th, where your friend left "trashed"*

- *exactly where you were with Audrey the evening of August 18th*

- *trying to prevent investigation, by force, when asked for your cell phone on August 19th, and discovery of urine in your room the previous evening*

- *discovery of alcohol in a "Gatorade Ice" bottle in your backpack on August 21st*

- *refusal to comply when asked to check your purse on August 21st, which resulted in a call to 9-1-1, and discovery of a drug baggie from your purse*

- *your disposal of alcohol on the basement carpet on August 24th*

- *a number of unsettling cell phone call patterns, including lying about the identities of callers*

Clearly there have been many delightful times with you this summer, like the college/Aunt Hattie trip, and the Italian dinner for your sister. There have been some major positives: finishing both pre-calculus classes, tackling your AP coursework, resuming cross country, taking your sister to the airport, seeing you bake, and clean the car and your room. But we cannot lose sight of the seriousness of driving. Even if you had had a clean tox screen in June, the events of recent weeks would have led us to suspend your driving privileges.

As you and Dr. DeSantos have discussed, it is important that you take responsibility for your actions as part of a pattern, and not isolated incidents. In general, your pattern has been to go no more than a few months between serious incidents. The last few weeks have been exceptionally dismal as far as visible incidents. We need to establish a pattern of trustworthy behavior, in terms of substances and honesty.

Because of the erosion of trust in the last few weeks, working back requires more time and more transparency. We therefore will reconsider resuming driving privileges on a limited basis in six weeks, or October 8th. The inconveniences (to all of us) are more than outweighed by having confidence that you will be truly safe to drive. The prerequisites that will be considered include but are not limited to:

- *additional random urine and/or blood and/or hair test(s). Sabotage is failure.*

- *random property searches (including purse, backpack, cell phone). No drama. Any attempt to sabotage these will be considered a failed tox screen.*

- *building "trust points" which we will document as a way of reinforcing constructive behavior and discouraging destructive*

- *cell phone bills that do not raise suspicion*

- *general feelings of trustworthiness and honesty, including that you are being totally straight with us in disclosing your whereabouts, especially when with friends.*

As mentioned, we want to feel that we can see you off in a car confident that you are fit to drive, and will go where you have told us, and not go where you haven't told us, especially in a deceptive way (go back to March and the deception involving the movies with your sister, whereby you returned with Vicodin in your purse and another drug baggie in your room). You would be surprised at how often you might be seen by people acquainted with our family. Closer to regaining driving privileges, we will outline a specific list of expectations and consequences concerning the actual driving so we are all on the same page.

Amy, we truly wish we could be trusting you now to drive alone (we will continue to allow you to drive with us present to maintain your skills). It would be a lot easier for all of us. So let's start fresh and use these next few weeks to establish the type of trust that will give us all the relationship we want, not just for senior year, but the rest of our lives. We are here to help.

In the wee hours on Monday, I entered in my diary, "Summer time is over and it doesn't get easier.... Wrote summary for Dr. Herowitz. Realize: what could go on the BVMP wire re: the August 4th sleepover? Want to be able to look at recent weeks without being sick to my stomach."

Amy replied to our email with a letter:

Dear Mom and Dad,

I read over your letter about driving privileges and I found it relatively sensible. I realize that I've made some mistakes over the past few weeks and I understand that I must pay the consequences. I do, however, have a few suggestions and changes to the "plan" that I'd like you to consider.

First of all, I'd like to talk about the proposed 6 week driving suspension period. As Dr. DeSantos would say, we approach situations involving trust completely differently. I look at most punishments as moving too slowly, while you see them as moving way too quickly. I'm not trying to ask for my driving privileges back right away, because I agree that I do need time to rebuild the trust necessary to regain your confidence when I'm behind the wheel. Believe me, I don't want you guys to have to worry every time I take the car out, and I think waiting a few weeks in exchange for your trust is definitely a fair trade off. I would, however, like to ask you guys to shorten the suspension time to 3 weeks. I think 21 days is a long enough period in which to establish a healthy level of trust, assuming I don't have any more major slip-ups. As you mentioned, getting my license back would also provide ease with regard to transportation; I am, for the second time, looking forward to a point where I don't have to pester you for rides to the mall or to meet up with friends. Let me try to prove my progress and if you're not convinced after 3 weeks you can re-extend the time period. Feel free to talk this over with Dr. DeSantos or Mr. Coolwater.

I have no problem with the proposed property searches because I no longer have anything to hide. I would like to ask that you refrain from reading my diaries and personal notes, or I will stop writing them. I also understand your suspicions about potential drug use on my part. I can honestly say I'm [sic] have not used any recreational substances recently, nor do I have the desire to use in the future. To prove this to you, I will agree to random tox-screens, but I'd ask you to stick with urine tests. And no, I'm not asking for this because I want to 'cheat' the system because, whether you believe me or not, I have never used previously bottled urine for my tests. I just feel like blood and hair tests are too invasive. If it makes you feel more comfortable, I know there are systems where a nurse or supervisor actually stands in the room while the subject is taking a urine test to prevent fraud, and I'd be willing to do something like that.

Other than those two points, your proposal sounds fair. Please think about what I've written.

Lots of love,

Amy

The opening faculty meeting was on Monday morning, August 28th. Dr. DeSantos left a voicemail that Amy was anxious to enjoy the last few days of summer, and was also trying to hold things together; he hoped for better with the start of school.

At 8:00 p.m., my husband and I had our first meeting with Dr. Herowitz. We needed help. Should we be looking for colleges or rehab? Amy admitted to use but not abuse, and she claimed she no longer desired to use in the future. But what else could she say? What was the diagnosis/prognosis? What interventions were appropriate and what would be effective? Was there any adult to whom she didn't lie? What about Amy's first therapist, Ms. Firther, indicating a "characterologic" label a few years ago? We were concerned about the clandestine social life Amy had developed, and my worst fear was whether she might be dealing. After all, her favorite movie was *Catch Me If You Can*. How could we encourage her into a positive social scene? Audrey was leaving BVMP senior year for her local public high school. We had one last chance to move Amy, too, but she seemed to be looking forward to senior year, especially to AP biology with the teacher she'd had sophomore year. But perhaps her social/substance connections would be easier to continue from BVMP, so she wasn't pushing to change schools.

After twenty-five minutes of taking the history, having rejected my carefully compiled written summary, Dr. Herowitz gave his global view. Amy was a "gifted pain," he said, an oppositional kid (defiant, tough, smart, gaming the system), and a "Saturday Night Adventurer." The evidence was not horrible, but the tox screens were extending the game without helping much. He asserted it was best when a kid says, "Check me." He felt the biggest danger for her was Hepatitis C and AIDS. By bringing illegal substances home, she had abrogated her right to privacy. The family therapy piece was to enable letting go, he explained, "To play the hand you have, not the one you wish you had." He felt she needed to see Dr. DeSantos more frequently than every other week, saying, "Every week she needs a surrogate brain." He spoke of wellness dorms at colleges.

Amy met with Dr. Herowitz the following day. I made the note, "Talk in car home. Never H + why." I'm guessing that means we talked about never taking heroin and why, but I can't recall if it was me warning her to never take it, or her telling me she had never used it to assuage my fears.

BVMP classes resumed on August 30th, and Amy was taking AP biology and calculus; honors English, physics, and French; and religion. I wrote, "DREADING next summer." We sparred over her uniform skirt which was probably rolled up too high. She didn't bring a running bra, so she couldn't run at cross country practice—not exactly good role-modeling as co-captain of the team. She and I became stressed about changes in evening plans involving dinner; my appointment with my therapist, Dr. Sporsy; the BVMP athletes' meeting; and buying school supplies.

Amy remained in the waiting room during my meeting with Dr. Sporsy. He had spoken with our first daughter's counselor, Dr. Hischolor, the colleague who had recommended him. Dr. Sporsy asserted that teens always lie, especially where drugs are concerned. He reinforced that I was doing the right things and I should not feel overly vigilant. He said not to buy into Amy's story about "trying to clean out" the alcohol from her room, even though I wanted to believe her and not ignite her temper. Besides, at least four other times she had used the alibi of "old" substances. He asserted that she was going to drink the alcohol and she needed to admit that dumping it on the carpet was "horse sh--." She needed to stop treating my husband and me "like morons" and start owning up to the truth; if she was a big enough girl to use, she was big enough to admit to the use. He claimed she was a senior coming up with explanations that were junior high league. She was showing a "ridiculous immaturity" about being caught. Where there's smoke, there's fire, he said, and she was caught enough times with a smoking gun, yet she was acting as if she were the victim of rumor.

He went on to say that, while the words in her letter were very nice, she needed to stop "the cr--" and stop trying to humiliate us with middle school explanations. He added that I needed to be more hard-nosed and not held hostage in the relationship. He suggested saying, "Stop talking to and insulting me unless you talk turkey. There are no negotiations until you tell me the truth." He questioned whether her "forgetting" to sign in at the hospital was potentially a violation of policy/law, and whether she actually needed a cell phone. He also said that if she were using heroin, I would know it. I should have asked, "How would I?"

I spoke with Amy's psychologist, Dr. DeSantos, that evening. Similar to how Dr. Sporsy had said there were consequences for creating a culture where people exaggerated and Amy was the target, Dr. DeSantos was trying to get her to understand how the world worked. He emphasized the need for her to think before she acted, take more responsibility, not screw up, and to see how not having freedoms was the result of her behaviors. She needed to respect the house rules so we could function as a family. He still believed the school year would be better because of the structure.

I then raised the question of rehab as I considered the terrifying possibility of whether Amy could be addicted. Dr. DeSantos shared that in Amy's view she was using very little and not using heroin or ecstasy. He admitted the struggle from the clinical end. She could be lying and had a bigger problem that she was not ready to admit. But even if he believed there were a bigger problem, she was not ready for a program. He really believed that her use was minimal and, based on what she said, a treatment program was not indicated. He was telling her to stop making bad choices about drugs and alcohol, and he suggested we let her call more of the shots. He saw her as still walking a line and wanting to do well in her senior year. He was on her case about motivation. He told her, "Don't do well to get what you want; do well because it's the right thing to do." He and I also talked about her resuming driving. He suggested a three- to six-week trial with consequences if she messed up.

That night, my husband heard a 3:00 a.m. call, but when he checked Amy's cell phone, he saw no record. Did she erase it? The next day, Amy was at practice until 5:00 p.m., went to her boyfriend, Lonny's, at 5:30, and I collected her at 10:30 p.m.

On Friday, September 1st, BVMP had no classes because of Labor Day weekend, but Amy had practice at 7:30 a.m. Later that day, my husband, Amy, and I had our first family session with psychiatrist Dr. Herowitz. The doctor reiterated what he said when my husband and I met him on August 24th, namely that the shape of the plan depended on the willingness of the patient to engage. He asserted that the central issue was Amy, Mom, and Dad being together, and the broader issue was the three of us "living on separate planets." As parents we had anxiety about Amy's behavior, he observed, and we were trying to take heroic actions. He was not really convinced that drugs were a major issue, claiming,

"The lab lies much less than people." In retrospect, I'm appalled how such a credentialed specialist could be so naïve about how users fudge urine tests. He said the theme of Amy fooling around with drugs was undeniable, though she could deny it. He noted that Amy was oppositional but did not have the earmark of a career criminal, and his biggest worry was for her personal safety from putting herself in harm's way. He diagnosed her as having an "addiction to moderate risk taking." He said her judgments were not the greatest and that she had to grow up. He emphasized that, as parents, we couldn't stop risky experiments, and he used the "sand in the hand" control analogy. He indicted me for really being on Amy's case, with the ratio of my negatives to positives directed at her about 25:1. I found these numbers interesting and wondered to myself how he reached *that* conclusion.

Dr. Herowitz went on to say that Amy had to accept consequences. After all, she was the school vice president of Students Against Destructive Decisions (SADD), which my husband and I believed reflected her knowledge of right from wrong and wanting a behavioral foot planted more firmly on the "right" side. The doctor articulated the tension of parents wanting to know what was going on, and children not wanting to let them know. Apparently, Amy had conveyed to him that therapists were the ones to turn to when in trouble, although he felt the better answer was "parents." Dr. Herowitz opined that the urine in Amy's purse was "weird" and to back off from drug testing, a major difference in approach from Dr. Sporsy. He talked about being supportive versus controlling, that we needed to keep talking and understand how the three of us solved problems, and to agree on the ongoing family behavior, expectations, and responsibilities. He warned that Amy was not invulnerable, and the question was how to reverse the mutual distrust. Parents needed consistent trustworthy behavior over a period of time. We talked about Amy's pattern of the "accordion" of crises in between longer periods of calm. He then started talking neuroscience and how drug use rewires the brain. As the session ended, we agreed to meet in about a month. Amy, my husband, and I departed for lunch at a local restaurant that his parents had loved.

I spoke with Amy's psychiatrist, Dr. Adderoth, that afternoon. He asserted that her impulsivity was greater than her judgment. He agreed with Dr. Herowitz's "no tox screen" approach and said she was clean. I wondered to myself how he could be so sure.

That night, Amy asked to go out with Audrey, who was no longer at BVMP. When I said no, but countered that Audrey could come to our house instead, Amy dropped the idea. On Saturday, my husband took Amy to cross country, and I collected her at the diner across from school. My husband took her to the hospital to volunteer. At church on Sunday, I blurted out to a friend how we were feeling the aftershocks of all the pain from our summer. Amy went into the city with Lonny. I left a message for Dr. DeSantos: I was encouraged that Amy went willingly to Dr. Herowitz on Tuesday, and to the ninety-minute family session on Friday. I relayed that Dr. Adderoth said she had self-tapered off her antidepressant when she was at the biology program. She still had about twenty-three Adderall capsules, which I would administer and watch her take. I also left messages for the psychotherapist and substance abuse counselor, Mr. Coolwater, and Dr. Herowitz, impressed with how willing and engaged Amy seemed to be, and seeing a big difference in the school year. I collected Amy at 8:05. I jotted in my diary that my relationship with my husband felt trashed by Amy.

On Labor Day, I left a message for Dr. Sporsy that we'd had more than a week with no crises, but I was concerned about the contradictory guidance we were receiving from professionals. I was dismayed about my runner's identity; I'd run three marathons in the last year, and now I was barely training. Audrey came by in the evening and the girls investigated colleges online.

School resumed on Tuesday, September 5th, and I wondered if Amy was spacey or tired that night. My husband and I discussed our sessions with Dr. Herowitz, and it seemed that I was being identified as the one with the problem. The next day I observed, "Amy volcano re: BVMP in car. I kept quiet." In retrospect, I wonder if such eruptions were related to her using, while for years we had been rationalizing them to teenage mood swings. We had discussed our different expectations about when she went out. I wanted to know in advance where she was going. She wanted to check in with me along the way, citing how she didn't always know where she'd be going, and "plans change." On September 7th, during my break, she convinced me to go buy a birthday cake for her beloved chemistry teacher.

On Friday, we learned that our 1991 used car failed inspection and would need to be replaced, so we started car shopping. Amy and I were having disputes about where she was hanging out with Lonny. On Saturday, our family hosted our second annual pasta party. My husband took Amy to cross country, and I picked her up, then dropped her off at the hospital to volunteer. During the party, I drove her to babysitting at 7:15, and I was supposed to collect her around 11:00. She called at quarter of, saying the parents were running late. I was suspicious. I was concerned that "stuff" was going on, and around midnight I checked her cell phone voicemails and made cryptic notes of concerning messages from the summer. I felt caught in a dilemma: Dr. Herowitz said to talk about mutual distrust, but we *did* talk. And the basis for mistrust continued to play out. I noted that she had not yet asked for Adderall.

On September 10th, I drove our son to the airport for his last year of college and cried the whole way home, asking myself if we were losing Amy. I was a wreck. Amy did homework all day and did not go to the hospital volunteer award ceremony, to Mass, or to see Lonny. On Monday, we drove to school together. I drove her to babysitting at 5:30, and the family returned her at 10:30. I spoke with Mrs. Guicona, Amy's guidance counselor, about Amy's self-esteem, college choices, and my concerns about her making new friends now that Audrey had left BVMP.

On Tuesday, I was hyperventilating from stress. I asked Amy why her summer boyfriend, Calvin, was still calling, and she became *really* defensive, snapping, "I know not to answer my cell phone." We went to look at cars, then to our favorite Mexican restaurant and talked about colleges. On Wednesday at noon, she lit into me about my control of her Adderall. I heard from her friend Liza's mom, and we commiserated that it was so hard to tell what was really going on, but she had no reason to believe that Liza made up anything about the August sleepover. I showed up for a Dr. Sporsy appointment, ready to talk about my daily crying, constant emotional pain, and not knowing what the truth was, and, if I couldn't know, how to deal with it. I was concerned about Amy's anger, and I suspected that Lonny was a stoner. I was stunned when he said my appointment was in fact the next day.

So a day later we discussed how this time of Amy's life was supposed to be "prideful" for me, seeing her emerge as a young adult, capping her high school achievements, heading to college. As long as I had serious doubts about her truthfulness, he said that my husband and I should be extremely cautious and deal with Amy's freedom and privileges on a day-to-day basis. I might add that this mode of operation was exhausting compared to what "normal" family life should be. He reassured me that I wasn't overreacting because not everyone's daughter did what Amy did. She needed me on her tail as an alter ego. Once she was eighteen I didn't have to do anything, because that's what the criminal justice system was for, although I screamed inside "not in *my* family." His enervation in talking about Amy's behavior seemed to serve a need for him to vent, but it wasn't helping me make changes.

On the 15th, I was told that police in BVMP's town needed "probable cause" to do anything about Calvin, and he had a right to pick up someone at school. Thus Calvin's right to be on BVMP property was legally more protected than keeping teenage girls safe from a dealer. "What a country," I sighed. I also listened to a voicemail from Lonny on the 4th, alluding to some very disturbing incidents, including reference to Amy being with heroin dealers and worse. My heart sank and my stomach turned. While Amy said she was done with Calvin, I would never know what they had really done that summer, and Lonny's intimations scared me.

On Friday, I typed one of Amy's papers and we went grocery shopping. I felt some hostility since she waited until I had finished before she started shopping for her items. I tried to confront (not ambush) her with my concerns about her sexual activity, leaving practice early, and her plans for the weekend. I left a message with Dr. DeSantos that I needed to talk about the continuing concerns.

Another Car Mishap

On the 16th, Amy volunteered at the hospital from 9:00 until 1:00. She drove to the city with Audrey, and in the evening went with Lonny for ice cream. She drove our 1991 car over a curb and blew out a tire, causing enough damage to render it un-drivable and its resale value zero. I was angry because she hadn't called me right when it happened. I later learned from her rehab notes that she had been driving under an influence, which would explain the delay.

I also contacted Mr. Longwood, to whom Mr. Coolwater had referred us. He ran a support group for couples who had children with drug issues and thought we might find it helpful. The group met monthly for ninety minutes, and he was facilitating it "pro bono" as a "didactic experience." My husband and I attended on the 19th, and I found it "kind of depressing." The children of the other parents were forty-nine, thirty-eight, and twenty-four, while Amy was only seventeen. We talked about fabrication being part of the disease, thus the need for an "All Points Bulletin" to family members to put them on alert for enabling and risk. The *modus operandi* (m.o.) had to be "guilty until proven innocent." This m.o. was not how I grew up, and not how I wanted to live. I was particularly anxious about what this m.o. would mean in practical terms when dealing with my beloved elderly friends and relatives. I felt they would be so disappointed to learn that my daughter was "one of those." And the thought that she could steal from them was perhaps my biggest fear and dread, since I had put so much of myself into building trusting relationships.

I also called one of my doctors to say that I thought I needed a short course of antidepressants. I was breaking down daily and feeling "the black ice of post-traumatic stress" and didn't want to slip on it.

On Wednesday, September 20th, when I was picking up our replacement car, Aunt Hattie's nephew, a friend since my early teens, called to say that Aunt Hattie had died. Amy told me when I returned home. Her newest friend, Maurann, who was also one of my former students, was at our house for the first time. On the 21st, I was concerned about how Amy looked. On Friday, she and I had a "cargument." She thought that if the 2005 car we were buying was replacing the 1991 model, she should drive the new one and not the 1998 mini-van.

I flew to Aunt Hattie's memorial service and stayed with Tara, my best friend from childhood, who reiterated that "Amy will do what she's going to do." My concern was how to not enable, perhaps the first time I used that word.

The book *Celebrate Recovery*, by J. Baker and R. Warren, states, "Enabling is doing for others what they need to do for themselves. It is reacting to a person in such a way to shield him or her from experiencing the full impact of the consequences of their behavior. Enabling behavior is different from helping in that it permits or allows the person to be irresponsible." As the eldest of four siblings and someone who took great pride in being personally and professionally responsible, I could be vulnerable to enabling others. It is only since Amy died that I have learned about the real nuts and bolts of enabling from my weekly Nar-Anon meetings, a twelve-step based support group for those whose loved ones are addicted to narcotics.

I had another long talk with Dr. DeSantos on Sunday evening. He and Amy perceived that the last three weeks had been good, perhaps the best since March. He wanted to see Amy taking positive risks on college which seemed to cause her frustration. He observed that when she was not walking the "using/not using" game, she stuck around better people. She told him she wanted her father and me off her back, but she did not seem as convinced that she needed to change things because it was "the right thing to do," as opposed to getting what she wanted.

Dr. DeSantos and I compared the various approaches to drug testing, including what my husband and I would do if the tests were dirty, and the fact that Amy could extend the "clean screen" game. There was "just to make sure" testing, not due to suspicion. Yet another approach was once-a-month testing to stay on top of the situation. Some practitioners espoused that it was better if the child told us she was using, or if we knew she was. Barraged by all the conflicting professional opinions, we never pursued regular *or* random testing.

Looking ahead, Dr. DeSantos hoped that Amy would display her maturity the next summer, rather than use the months after high school graduation as a "last chance to go wild." He wanted to see her in a good college next September. He asserted, "She certainly won't tell us if she did heroin." He said that her relationship with Calvin "started as a deception she was bound to get caught in." That night, I looked up the arrest log from a nearby newspaper; Calvin had recently been arrested for "operating a motor vehicle under influence of liquor, failing to stay in marked lane, possession of hypodermic syringe, illegal possession of heroin." I was shaken, but not surprised. My daughter had spent so much of her summer with a person of this caliber and we had allowed him in our house. I felt violated. We also learned of a family whose daughter in college had been taken to the ER having passed out from alcohol poisoning. The parents learned two weeks after the fact when the ambulance bill arrived because, due to privacy laws, the hospital could not call them.

After reviewing with my doctor on the 25th about the toll that Amy's situation was taking on me, we agreed that I should take a course of antidepressants. I also called Mr. Coolwater and told him we'd tried the group, but that my big concern was Amy crossing the line from cocaine to heroin and hoping we'd made effective interventions. We also learned that Amy had done "something" on another family's computer when we were visiting them. When confronted, she told us she had been printing maps. However, what she had done put the husband's job at risk since he telecommuted for a major company and his computer usage was monitored. The wife was concerned about Amy's brazenness, while Amy insisted she was innocent.

We had an "intense" three-way meeting with Dr. Herowitz on the 26th. My husband was feeling hurt, and I was feeling "mind-f---ed." While we were not in the middle of a crisis, Dr. Herowitz reiterated that Amy's risky behaviors would be proportional to the tightness of parental controls, and less risky behaviors would be proportional to parental understanding. He urged us to worry less and enjoy more, and claimed that my anxieties and Amy's risk-taking were related. So basically he was saying that if I just eased up, despite Amy's drug history, calm would prevail. She had to trust us enough to not lie. He felt we were at a safety crossroads, and he reiterated the danger that seventy-eight percent of those who shared needles to inject drugs were infected with Hepatitis C. My husband seemed more freaked out after the $400 ninety-minute session than before. The seemingly contradictory messages we were receiving were overwhelming.

I was grateful that my antidepressant already seemed to be working, because sometimes the effects can take six weeks to "kick in." I was less anxious, not weepy, and felt as if I were in a "six-foot instead of a ten-foot-deep pool." (I stopped the meds a few months later, when I didn't feel constantly in crisis and disliked some of the side effects.) On the 28th, Amy and I had our second college discussion dinner at our favorite Italian café.

On September 30th, I was able to use my recent years of pain to help coach a buddy whose son had started experimenting. The next day, our son turned twenty-two, and Amy mentioned that I should burn the blue notebook, the one in which I kept my detailed notes about her incidents since her positive tox screen for cocaine. We also received a phone message whose caller ID was a state boot camp and I didn't know what that was. I returned the call the next day and was asked by the automated attendant for a PIN number followed by the pound key. Since I did not have this information, I still had no clue about the source of the call.

My husband and I had our second parent meeting with Dr. Herowitz on October 2nd. Topics ranged from where the marriage was to whether Amy was ingesting enough protein. He thought her lying bordered on despair and panic, and that she felt weak and powerless in our presence. He relayed that she believed her back was to the wall, and she didn't enjoy it. She was in a "prisoner's dilemma" that was causing poor judgment. But he felt that Amy was not a "runaway locomotive" and was not sure she needed to be looking to me as much as she did. He felt she was programmed with our values so we didn't have to worry about her moral grounding. He asked about our respective responses to her wild behavior. For me it was "new news" because I hadn't seen anything like it in my family of origin. Dr. Herowitz recommended the quid pro quo of backing off as she took more responsibility.

On October 5th, Amy and I stopped at a bakery on the way to school to pick up a birthday cake for her French teacher. That evening, Amy had not done her chores, but she still met Audrey at a local coffee shop; I saw them after I attended a school open house nearby. On the 6th, despite the antidepressant, I felt "like crap." I was crying at my therapy appointment for the first time since starting the meds, mostly about Amy's cell phone messages. Dr. Sporsy again provided me with wonderful rhetoric for telling Amy how her cell phone was our property and I needed a very good explanation about what I was hearing. Also, he said that parents needed to stick together because teens banked on them being disconnected. But nothing seemed to change.

On October 7th, I flew to my hometown for my relatives' fiftieth anniversary. We had another call from the state boot camp, and a collect call from Calvin, which my husband answered but did not accept. I left a message for Dr. Sporsy, saying, "Who needs soap operas when you can have a daily installment of 'life with Amy …' Stay tuned for her b.s. answer." At least twenty-four hours had transpired without incident. But perhaps my attempts at humor were ill-placed, as was my "11:00 p.m. news" quip a few weeks prior, at a time when I should have been far more serious about what was really going on. On the 8th, I noted, "Another Amy incident. Sigh."

The next day, we had our third three-way meeting with Dr. Herowitz. The assessment of the "family therapeutic trial" was that Amy was taking more responsibility and my husband and I had become less investigative. Dr. Herowitz emphasized that while a culture of lying and misrepresentation ruined everything, we needed to believe the actions, not words, so we were not so driven to disprove what was being said. In retrospect, the fact that addicts also lie by their actions torpedoes this theory. I heard from Dr. DeSantos that he had told Amy we'd find out if Calvin had called the house. In fact, Calvin was receiving incarceration and treatment at the state boot camp. Now we knew. Was there not some ethical code that practitioners who treat minors should inform parents if their child was involved with a criminal?

On Tuesday, October 10th, I had nothing to note. But the next day Amy had senior privilege for the first time, meaning she could arrive at school starting second period if she had no first period class and leave after sixth period if she had no seventh period class. She brought me carrot cake. After school, I collected her at her track meet, and her coach was extolling her running talents. On Friday, she stayed home with a headache and practiced SAT problems that evening. She took the SATs on Saturday, and slept at Maurann's house on Sunday, apparently up until 3:00 a.m. On Monday, she was asleep at 6:00 p.m., and my husband and I went to Mr. Longwood's group. On the 17th, I had my fifty-sixth session with Dr. Sporsy, and he reinforced that having data was my style.

By October 21st, I was "so much less anxious," and I even wrote on the 27th, "the calm is nice," and on the 29th, "enjoying normal." We met Dr. Herowitz on October 30th for our fourth family session despite Amy's protestations of heavy homework. I have no notes from the session because I was probably trying this new and unnatural "laid back" approach that Dr. Herowitz seemed to think would help. Although Amy loved Halloween, her intense school schedule made it impossible for her to prioritize decorating. We didn't even have pumpkins! I let Amy stay home on November 1st, though she came to school for cross country practice and detention.

We appeared to have a few uneventful weeks until November 13th, when Mrs. Guicona informed me of another rumor about Amy, but I'd only jotted "health concern Hepatitis B HIV." The notes from my November 16th session with Dr. Sporsy mentioned "a lighter strategy" and words such as, "You know how I feel about any smoking. These are our values, and I hope yours, too." On the 21st, my husband and I attended Mr. Longwood's group again.

During Thanksgiving weekend, Amy worked on college essays, and that Sunday my husband found an empty vodka bottle and beer cans in her sister's closet. Amy owned up to them being hers. I was "VERY angry," harbored intense resentment, and was too agitated to sleep (and I considered myself to have insomnia if it took me more than ten seconds to drop off). On the 28th, one of the school administrators reported finding Amy in the elementary school bathroom after school, alleging she was "looking for me." That explanation sounded thin even to me. On November 30th, I had a stress-induced migraine. I had met with Dr. Sporsy, who provided more rhetoric of outrage to use with Amy (to no avail). He also said something about alcohol being a "lubricant" for lines of cocaine.

I checked in with Dr. DeSantos on December 3rd, who mentioned the pattern of drug-related deaths from a nearby high school in recent years. Yet Amy seemed to have had a really good three months. His sessions with her focused on preparing for college and making good choices, and being smart for herself, not for him or Mom. He noted one nearby college policy on drugs: first violation is counseling; second, you're out.

On December 4th, we had our fifth family session with Dr. Herowitz, but my notes were minimal and cryptic. On the 6th, Amy was forty minutes late for school but I have no record of the reason.

Altercation with Nancy

On December 8th, I saw Amy in the school office around 9:10, and forty minutes later I was pulled in by the principal and dean. Amy and her classmate, Nancy, had a fight after the Immaculate Conception Mass, its roots allegedly in a comment Amy made to her about Calvin during the service. Later, next to the senior lockers, we were told that Nancy started hitting Amy, knocking her to the floor, but Amy had the presence of mind to not fight back, which probably prevented her from being expelled. Amy had to sign a behavioral contract; Nancy was suspended.

On December 12th, I received another message from a student informant, though I can't remember the content. On the 14th, the dean told me that she had seen Amy "inappropriately smiling." Amy had been looking "funny" to me that week, and I was tempted to drug test her. By the 19th, things were "feeling good" with Amy again. For Christmas, she gave me the audio book *Marley and Me*. On New Year's Eve, all three children went to the city for First Night, one of those "prideful moments" that Dr. Sporsy had told me I should be having.

Amy Turns Eighteen, and Another Car Accident Under the Influence

On January 17th, we had our sixth three-way meeting with Dr. Herowitz; my only note says "frustrating." Amy turned eighteen on the 20th, and I knew that legally we were now in a different ballgame and healthcare privacy laws shut me out. On Friday, January 26th, she had her wisdom teeth extracted. It never crossed my mind to question the pain medications she was prescribed.

That Friday night, on February 2nd, my husband was away, snow was falling, and Amy had a car accident; in a notebook entry I found after she died she wrote that she had been high at the time. I had strongly urged that she stay in; she disagreed but later admitted I had been right. Most importantly, nobody was injured, and neither she nor the man she rear-ended required medical attention. While the back of his van was merely scratched, the front of our new car was crumpled and the frame was damaged, and we weren't sure if it would be our fifth totaled vehicle since 1992.

On the evening of February 12th, I retrieved Amy from an indoor track meet in the city. She had missed qualifying for states by two seconds. I don't recall exactly which event it was, and I seem to remember she was a tad disappointed. On the 15th, I found a drug baggie but can't recall what substance I suspected or whether I confronted her or mentioned it to the counselors.

College Applications and Decisions

Amy filed her college applications without visiting any of her final list of eight, geographically spanning schools in Colorado, Missouri, Nebraska, New York, Tennessee, Texas, and Vermont. We visited the college in San Antonio during February vacation when she was deferred, and we stopped to see her sister on the way back. Our seventh and last three-way meeting with Dr. Herowitz was on February 28th. We talked about the upcoming summer and Amy also mentioned that she had talked with Calvin's mom, which displeased me. On March 6th, I was concerned about Amy's sleeping patterns and asked if she was using. I don't recall her reply, but it was probably denial.

Amy was accepted by St. Louis University (SLU) and was even awarded some scholarship money, so we went to the admitted students weekend on March 23rd. Our flight was six hours late, so we missed our planned visit with a BVMP valedictorian who was a SLU senior. I was pleased when Amy chose SLU; I was relieved that she had not been admitted to one particular school having heard it had one of the worst cocaine problems in the country. I also knew of another school's drug reputation, perhaps exacerbated by its location. We needed the environment to be in Amy's favor.

On March 28th, I expressed my skepticism when I wrote, "Amy and Audrey to Italian restaurant after library—I hope." A few days later, I jotted some concerns about Amy falling asleep while studying and wondering how she spent her job earnings from the previous year. While Amy had been hanging around a lot with Lonny, I noticed four calls in the phone bill involving Calvin, but I can't recall if he was still incarcerated.

On April 5th, Dr. DeSantos shared that Amy had made a pact with him not to use while finishing senior year. During Easter break, Amy invited me out to breakfast before her appointment to start a new round of physical therapy for her stress fracture. She was late, and we only had time for carry-out food. Then we arrived at the office only to find her MD's orders had expired. I thought to myself how I had been hijacked by Amy again, a pattern I wouldn't miss when she'd be in college. Another such example was collecting her after a track meet. We were at different athletic complexes of the school, and it took us an hour to find each other, even with cell phones, dashing my plans to run seven miles that afternoon.

Amy accompanied me to my hometown for Easter, and her brother and sister flew in so we could celebrate my dad's eighty-fifth birthday. April vacation was off to a rough start as I wrote, "I despise family life. I have so much to offer, or so I thought, and it's been a huge f---ing letdown. Why does Amy keep body spray in the car? Change my name to wallet." I was also feeling rage that others knew things about Amy that I didn't, but those observations by and large were not shared, making me feel deprived further of knowing what was going on in her life.

My husband and I had our last session with Dr. Herowitz on April 26th. I told him that life with Amy was like Chinese water torture. I had a litany of continued minor rule violations. He commented on how her immaturity and emotions were leading the decision-making process. I had made a chart to summarize my view of Amy's future:

Trustworthiness / Behavior	Honest	Dishonest
High-performing	Ideal	The second worst
Low-performing	The second best	The worst

How could we best encourage the ideal, and prevent the worst? I sadly realized that I was now willing to settle for second best.

Our homeowner's insurance company announced they would exclude Amy in our umbrella policy due to her driving record, necessitating a very expensive rider from a company that insured high risk. The new car was in the shop for about five weeks, so Amy and I had to share the old mini-van a lot. On May 1st, I learned about another accident that Amy had two days prior and noticed that I was burned out.

The physics and calculus teacher reported that Amy wasn't doing her work. Amy asked to take a mental health day, and I said no way. The following day at school the secretary asked me for permission to dismiss her, and I said no. Amy said she had a stomachache, but her eyes were dilated, and the substitute nurse did not have a flashlight to check any further; she was concerned about a rumor that Amy had used ecstasy. Amy slept in the nurse's office for the first three periods. I was feeling in a free-fall again and called Dr. Herowitz, who told me I smelled burning but there was no fire. Our son and first daughter told me they thought I was micromanaging. In my May 10th meeting with Dr. Sporsy, he again had a slew of arguments to use with Amy, but nothing was changing.

The End of High School

Amy's last day of classes was May 11th. She failed fourth quarter English and AP biology but passed for the year, so she could still graduate. My brother was invited to say the baccalaureate Mass, and my parents came into town for that service as well as for graduation. Amy attended three proms. On Thursday, June 7th, she flew with my husband to our son's college graduation, and I followed on Friday after classes. On graduation morning, Amy wanted to go to her favorite bakery for the must-have chocolate croissants and iced coffee she had enjoyed during the summer biology program. So amid the thousands of people funneling into the courtyard, I simply told her "fine" and took my place in our block of twelve seats. I managed to stay mellow as I watched her smile her way to her seat as the ceremony began.

Amy's first incident of the summer was a late-afternoon drama involving Lonny, the car, lying, and poor judgment. Writing about those hours would be my last entry in the "blue notebook" for two and a half years. However, on a more positive note, Amy started drum lessons, and one of the music teachers at BVMP loaned her acoustic drum set to Amy for the summer. As musically talented as Amy was, I was still amazed at how quickly she progressed on a percussion instrument, and I even enjoyed listening to her practice. I was pleased that she asked me about teaching her piano during

the summer, though we never made that happen. I finally returned her rental oboe as drums became her new musical passion.

Amy was offered a job at a bagel shop on May 23rd, the second time she'd landed employment based on being a customer in whom the owners saw a potential employee. She was working about thirty hours per week and would proudly leave the house wearing her company T-shirts and visor. I also ran her babysitting ad in the town newspaper. As she requested, I waited until after graduation, but then she was furious that I'd run it at all. "How much do you want me to work this summer?" she yelled one day. My reply was simply, "How much spending money do you want to have when you get to college?" She referred the numerous overflow jobs to her friends.

The "SLU 101" orientation was on July 9th and 10th. My husband drove Amy and me to catch our 4:30 p.m. flight. He was going to take us to public transportation, and Amy insisted she was *not* deliberately late to force a drive all the way to the airport. Once at the hotel, Amy aggressively scoured the local restaurant delivery menus, but tiredness prevailed and we were asleep by 10:00 p.m. On Monday morning, Amy checked into her residence hall, leaving most of her belongings in our hotel room, which meant logistically *I* would have to schlep them on Tuesday rather than *her*. We had separate activities most of the day. While she had come to SLU as an engineering major, she switched immediately to business and was making friends. We parted ways at the airport on Tuesday. She was flying back home and would be driving with Audrey to Quebec for a music festival.

The Quebec Festival

We learned about the festival from Audrey's French tutor, who had taken groups of students before, and who claimed it was an extremely civilized event and would be a great experience for the girls. My husband and I were uneasy. I told Amy I'd probably feel more comfortable once she had a year of college street-smarts under her belt. I wasn't thrilled about two eighteen-year-old females driving alone to Canada.

But we decided to let her go. Of all the different summer travel they had schemed at one time or another (including Mexico, Florida, the Netherlands, and a cruise), this venue seemed the most tame and included the educational component of using their French. They'd be staying in youth hostels with a curfew. Taking the train or bus put them at risk of missing curfew, and flights were too expensive. The harm we feared could just as easily happen here. They'd drive during the day and Audrey's dad would let them use his GPS. They'd have cell phones, AAA, and I secured maps. As some of my running buddies advised, sometimes you have to say yes.

I was actually glad they went. They recapped their long conversation about travel with a woman from Singapore who was also staying in the hostel. Their account reminded me how important it is to experience other parts of the world, especially at their age, and the good examples our au pairs set that way. I really encouraged Amy to study abroad at least once, and after she died I found a "study abroad" list she compiled, covering six continents.

Amy left on July 30th to visit our friends in Hawaii. She missed her connection and had to spend the night in Las Vegas. I was actually grateful she'd had the Quebec experience to boost her ability to travel independently.

The relatively smooth summer would not last forever. On August 12th, I smelled perfume in the garage and found a pipe in the car that smelled of marijuana. But our family was hosting company from out of town and I don't recall confronting Amy, although I noted the incident with a "☹" in my diary.

The biggest drama pre-SLU departure was about bed linens. We'd procrastinated, couldn't find the extra-long size in the local stores, and had to buy the sheets online and have them express-shipped to our house to take in the suitcases. At least this stress was not life-threatening.

20 N. Grand Blvd.
Busch Student Center, 313
St. Louis, MO 63103
Phone 314-977-7326
Fax 317-977-2196
www.slu.edu

Six

September 2007, St. Louis University: effort and independence

I accompanied Amy to SLU during the hottest days of the summer. She made friends rapidly and was sweet-talking people into favors, such as asking the lobby attendant in her dorm if she could leave her case of bottled waters at the front desk and take it upstairs to her room later. I made a point to distinctly remember how I left her as I drove away, putting down the passenger window and yelling to her, "Don't forget your waters."

The empty nest had arrived. My husband and I celebrated with champagne on the 25th, and the next day I wrote, "I'm liking it." When mothers of Amy's friends pined about how they dreaded their daughters leaving, I was saying that I could hardly wait. On the 28th, we said goodbye to Mr. Longwood's didactic group since Amy seemed to have stabilized. I was grateful that we weren't in the situation of someone else in the group whose young adult son was unemployed and living at home smoking too much marijuana. And I couldn't believe another couple's horror story of a boyfriend injecting his girlfriend in the back with heroin as she slept after she'd been clean for almost a year. We felt we were finally on a more fortunate path. And from all reports Amy was working hard.

I was able to train for my sixth marathon on October 14th. I had entrusted my training plan to an email coach who had never run a marathon and who, despite coaching college students, was probably not the right fit for a woman in her fifties. My Achilles tendon sustained a serious overuse injury and I performed poorly in the race. My primary outlet for stress—running—was compromised, and I spent months seeking a diagnosis and treatment that I trusted.

My husband attended the SLU Parents' weekend. He and Amy did some sightseeing and shopping and attended the symphony, courtesy of tickets from her percussion professor. Amy came home for fall break from the 19th through 23rd. Every call home from her was positive, including one at 12:30 a.m., exuberantly wanting to talk to zonked-out dad about whether he'd seen the end of the Red Sox game. She was already talking about an apartment for sophomore year, though I told her "no" when she asked about having a car. I was impressed by her decision to drop out of the sorority rush. As she put it, "As much as I know I could make a lot of good friends, I know that college is supposed to be about meeting all kinds of different people, and I'm afraid sorority life could be a bit limiting." She took the train to visit her sister at college and flew home for Thanksgiving.

By the end of first semester, Amy switched her major to nursing. She said she wanted to have a well-paying job upon graduation and had expressed interest in health professions during high school. I was pleased because she finally seemed to be owning her capabilities in math and science. For Christmas, she gave me a "SLU Mom" sweatshirt. One of the gifts we bought her was a brick for the new piazza at her beloved Tulips store in our town center that was inscribed with "WARMED UP SESAME BAGEL W/ CREAM CHEESE ♥ AMY 07." She had always called in this breakfast order during high school as Tulips did not have a toaster yet. She was thrilled when the brick was laid that spring. I now often meet people on the piazza for coffee and show them Amy's brick.

I'm staggered at the toll the year 2007 wrought. The word "exhausted" appeared almost daily in my diary, reflecting lack of enough hours of sleep although actually sleeping was rarely a problem. Rereading the details reveals constant emotional exhaustion and pain, as well as the physical manifestations of the stress when Amy was home, especially in my gut. And it is only in retrospect that I see how many times my husband had gone to the ER.

My new year started with a migraine so severe that I had to ask my husband to stay home from work and take me to the doctor, where I received injections. Fortunately they were effective, and the next evening we took Amy, still home for Christmas break, for Japanese food. On January 9th, I took Amy to a presentation at Harvard Business School (HBS) on "Why Football Matters to Women in Business and How to Survive the Playoffs and the Super Bowl." It was given by a classmate, my friend who hadn't seen Amy in about fifteen years. It felt really special when Amy attentively listened to me ramble on with all sorts of stories and memories as we drove to the city and walked the campus, where she hadn't been since age three. I had been longing for this type of interaction, savored every moment of it, and hoped for more to come. On January 15th, I started Mandarin classes, a long-term dream I actually had the energy to pursue since I was only teaching five classes, as opposed to six during the previous two years.

Departure Drama as Amy Turns Nineteen

The rest of Amy's vacation went smoothly until the day she left. She wanted to be home for her nineteenth birthday, went out with her friends on January 19th, had dinner with us on the 20th, and chose a 4:45 p.m. flight on the 21st (Martin Luther King, Jr. Day) in time to resume classes on the 22nd. I suggested leaving at 2:15 to catch the 3:00 bus so she'd be at the airport with more than an hour to spare. She pleaded for more bonding time and I caved, which meant we had to leave by 2:45 for the airport. When we finally left at 3:05, I'd listened to the traffic reports and no delays were reported, but I knew we were cutting it close. We missed the next two reports, and when we heard the next one, we were already stuck in traffic, too late to enter the carpool lane.

Amy took the "it's all good" approach to discount my words of experience that baggage had to be checked at least forty-five minutes prior to departure. We arrived curbside at 4:20, and she assured me I should just leave; any problem was hers and not mine, and she was sure the airline could get her out that night. I did not follow my instinct to park, and headed home, only to receive her call eleven miles later that the airline couldn't fly her out until 6:00 a.m. I told her to call my husband to make sure he could drive her the next morning and headed back to the airport, not happy to have lost two additional hours on my day off, though grateful I wasn't stuck in more traffic. She was frustrated because, even though the aircraft was still boarding when she arrived, she couldn't fly because her bags missed the time cutoff.

She was emotionally disoriented to be heading home since she'd said her goodbyes, and her SLU friends had been planning to celebrate her birthday that night. She met up with a friend that evening, although I'd hoped she'd make good on her intent to clean our mini-van. The alarm rang at 4:00 a.m. Her bags weren't quite balanced. Airlines now strictly enforced the fifty-pound weight restriction, and one suitcase had been overweight on Monday afternoon. In my sleepy state, I said some things to Amy that I probably would have said in a dream but not if fully awake; I later apologized. She made her flight and caught up with the professor whose class she missed on Tuesday morning.

I had a "nice talk" with her on the 25th, when she decided to drop English and start Spanish, then switched to French. On the 28th, she actually asked me for running advice, and on the 29th, I made reservations for her to come back and visit Boston College (BC). Amy told us she really missed living in our area and wanted to transfer. I wasn't thrilled with the idea for a variety of reasons: A local college would be more expensive, she would probably not be awarded scholarship money, she was away from the bad influences near home, and I wasn't sure how much had to do with her relationship with her new friend, Oliver. So I was adamant that she only apply to schools that were academically at least as strong as SLU, which she actually did. On the 30th we had a three-way call with my mother. I wrote with delight in my diary, "What a joy!"

Amy came home again for the long Valentine's Day weekend, which went smoothly. My husband visited her for a day en route home from a conference. Her ten-day spring break visit also went smoothly. She and I made cupcakes. A friend from SLU visited. Unfortunately, we also had some rather frustrating dealings with city court about a train ticket citation. Apparently she could be detained at airport security since she owed the city of St. Louis a fine.

The New Boyfriend, Oliver

After break, Amy visited her sister at college again. I visited her at SLU for a day in April. Upon returning home, I found myself missing her. I hired her now-boyfriend, Oliver, for the first time to do yard work for me on the 27th. I can't recall if Amy told me directly, or if I had to learn from another source, that she had met him during Christmas vacation at a party hosted by his younger brother. Apparently, they started dating in March. I was concerned when I saw that her phone bill showed one-to-two hour calls with him almost every night.

She applied to BC, where only about ten percent of transfer applicants are admitted. When she received a "wait list" decision, I urged her to ask why. She was told that her high school grades had been lackluster, and they wanted to see another semester of consistency in college.

Amy flew in to join us for our first daughter's college graduation dinner on Friday, May 9th, since one of her final exams conflicted with the actual ceremony. I remember thinking during the ceremony, "Two children graduated from college; one more to go." I felt prideful as I watched Amy bound into the restaurant, looking poised in her brown denim jacket and flowing brown hair. She spent that night with her sister, and I flew back to SLU with her in the morning. On Sunday, we had a Mother's Day breakfast with one of her friends. Amy seemed to be happy and making good friends. Maybe the maturing effect we had hoped for in college was taking root. I flew home with two suitcases of her belongings.

Amy flew home on Monday, and Oliver's grandmother actually collected her at the airport. While it was a convenience for me given the pressures at work, I regret that I didn't assert my parental prerogative to pick up my daughter. I realized I was starting to give Oliver's family too much power. During the next few days, we had a dinner with Amy's best friend from BVMP, Audrey, and my husband found reasonably priced NBA playoff tickets and took Amy. She and Oliver went to a local pond, then with his grandmother to ballroom dancing lessons. Amy, Oliver, my husband, and I went out to dinner. On Sunday, she really wanted to make her dad a Father's Day dinner, and did.

In June, I concluded six and a half years of teaching at BVMP and was about to start a new job at an alternative Catholic high school (ACHS), serving students who normally would not be able to afford a private, Catholic, college prep education. ACHS was affordable because students worked one day a week at an entry-level, white collar job, earning the majority of their tuition. As an administrator in the work program, I would be able to combine my decades of business experience and my love of working with high school students.

On the 13th, Amy's eyes looked odd to me, and I worried if she might be using again.

In between my old and new jobs, I was scheduled for surgery on my Achilles injury. The decision did not come easily after months of conflicting medical advice. I knew that if I didn't have the operation, I wouldn't be running again. Yet even with surgery I would be sidelined for at least six months and a full recovery was not a shoo-in. On Friday, June 20th, Amy drove me to the surgical center. I was disappointed that she didn't stay during the procedure and went to meet Audrey for breakfast. But she drove me home, and I napped most of the day, realizing the extent of my new limited mobility. I was in a post-op stupor most of Saturday and on Sunday stopped taking the Percosets (the surgeon prescribed thirty!). I felt some nurturing when Amy changed my dressing.

But overall I was feeling overwhelmed on all fronts. My dad had just had a mini-stroke and was making frequent trips to the ER, and I lived five hundred miles away. Our first daughter was a thousand miles away, and she and I were having lengthy conversations as she vented her post-graduation frustrations, including how her application to teach in Japan continued to be delayed. I was recovering from surgery and the upcoming physical therapy felt uncertain, both in terms of how I would fit it into my schedule and whether it would be effective. And Amy. On Monday, she received calls from a prison (we believe from her ex-boyfriend, Calvin). I searched on Google and to my great dismay found Oliver's arrest record. I once again felt her "kick 'em when they're down" pattern when she pushed back at times when she could have been supportive. So on Tuesday, June 24th, I emailed the ACHS president and said I would volunteer the first month of my new job because I had some developments on the homefront that could result in some interruptions.

Suboxone . . . and Shooting Heroin?

I don't recall exactly how, but I learned that a psychiatrist near SLU had pre-scribed Amy the opiate inhibitor Suboxone in March, about the time she and Oliver started dating. Perhaps it was when she gave me the prescription co-pay receipts for reimbursement, or maybe I discovered one. When I questioned her on the 24th, she insisted the medication was to help her with her unspeci-fied "cravings," and thus it was a non-standard "secondary" use of the drug. I searched on the Web and then contacted psychiatrists Drs. Adderoth and Herowitz, as well as Amy's psychologist, Dr. DeSantos. They all concluded there was no reason to prescribe the drug other than for opiate addiction. This inquiry process reminded me of when I pursued the probability of false positives on the cocaine tox screen when Amy insisted the results were wrong. She later admitted she started experimenting with prescription painkillers during her first semester at SLU, including OxyContin, about ten times. I wonder now if the Suboxone prescription was a way for her to pay for other drugs, as a month's prescription cost close to $400, but our insurance co-pay was only $25, so she could sell them to buy other drugs. The night of Amy's funeral, we learned that she had apparently faked the symptoms to be given the prescription.

In my notes on the 25th, I wrote, "Feel like the bad dream is worse than before. I can deal with bad news. The lying and denial are crazy-making." I reached out to several people, including my priest brother, Mr. Longwood, and Tara, my best friend from childhood. I spoke with Dr. DeSantos for more than twenty minutes. He said the positive was that Amy knew how to get out of a relationship, citing how she was no longer with Calvin. He was hoping Oliver was a "summer fling." He didn't have a complete handle yet on why she was attracted to guys who struggled. He conjectured that it was some kind of messiah complex. He told Amy she was a fantasy for Oliver: very bright, attending a good school, had good grades, a good family, not to mention that she was strikingly beautiful. These guys were shocked that they ended up with her. He reflected that she couldn't walk both lines forever, and she walked the line too close and hadn't bottomed out. The question was why she worked so hard to make her life so difficult, making risky choices that threatened everything else she'd tried to do.

He continued that the previous summer she was excited about college and ready to go, but summers were more difficult, and this year the familiarity was winning out. As we knew, "She's so bright it's a curse." Obviously, we couldn't stop her from making bad choices, but we could ask her what she thought. But Amy repeatedly demonstrated her controlling side, saying "I'm gonna do what I'm gonna do and you can't stop me." Some of that was a maturity issue, yet Dr. DeSantos saw her working harder to get her life together.

Sometime in the midst of all this post-operative tumult, I was lying on the couch in a fair amount of discomfort when another student informant called me. She warned me to definitely keep an eye on Amy, and confided that Amy was injecting heroin and spent nights at Oliver's house. He was really bad news, she said, and his family had had a lot of trouble with the law. Rumor was that the family was selling from their house, and someone had died of an overdose in their basement. (Later, officials said yes to overdoses, no death.) The informant had heard that at SLU Amy became friends with a few of the wrong people and disassociated with them, but she was sniffing heroin. Oliver had injected in the past, and was furious with Amy for injecting. Amy told the informant she was stopping, but the pattern was Amy being into the heroin, then Suboxone, then relapsing, a yo-yo. She said that Amy had picked up drugs in Canalboro with Oliver. Curiously, whenever I referred to marijuana as "dope," Amy became very agitated. I have since learned that while "dope" used to be slang for marijuana, now it means heroin.

Speaking with one of my husband's relatives on the 26th was the first time I heard that when someone decides to quit using, they need to get rid of the old playmates. This person suggested I pay a visit to Oliver's mom. I didn't. I just didn't know what to do anymore. I only wish I had been in my Nar-Anon group back then.

I abstracted what I was learning into a little script for Amy. "Based on what we've been hearing from professionals, Suboxone is prescribed for only one reason: abuse of opiates. No one is telling us any differently. If your doctor can, great, otherwise we assume it's for opiates. There are real dangers of hanging with this crowd, and even if you're not participating, consider the opportunity cost." Great ideas, but they wouldn't make a difference.

On the 27th, I told Amy that I was *so* psyched about my new job. On the way home, I stopped to talk with the town police chief but did not find him to be of much help. While he commiserated about how bad heroin was in our area, he said he couldn't tell me more about Oliver and his family for "confidentiality" reasons. When I saw him at Amy's funeral, I couldn't help but think that if not for "confidentiality" in so many spheres, my daughter might still be alive.

I worked from home until July 1st, and then Amy sometimes drove me to and from work until I was able to drive myself on the 7th. On the 4th of July weekend, I flew to the wedding of one of my BVMP colleagues and, when Amy collected me, we went out for Mexican food and talked about someone I was close to as a child, who as an adult had become involved with an addict and the tragic road that relationship took. Our first daughter visited from the 7th through 10th. During that time, all the comings and goings made me note, "I miss the empty nest."

On the 9th, I returned home to a house with no girls, no dog, and no note. The girls weren't answering my phone calls. It ended up that Amy and Oliver took River to a local pond despite our first daughter's protestations, incurring a ticket because dogs weren't allowed. But rules didn't apply to Amy; I'm not sure she ever paid the ticket because I found the citation among her papers after she died. Driving home, I was thinking about how much more gratifying work was than family life, especially given the students with whom I was now working. I was upset on the 10th due to the disarray of the house. Amy and Oliver did some work at the house for us, and on the 18th, I went shopping with Amy to buy myself shirts that met the ACHS dress code.

On July 20th, Amy told me she was spending the night at her high school friend Maurann's. But when Amy was late coming home and I called the house, I learned from the brother, then Maurann, that Amy had *not* been there. I felt badly because, once again, Amy had used a friend as a "human shield." Maurann's mother proceeded to tell me what a bad influence Amy was on her daughter, and what she'd heard about Amy's drug life. It was painful to hear, and, worse, I found myself having to agree with the mother on many counts. Yet I felt no empathy or sympathy coming from her. And my migraines were returning.

On the 21st, I talked with Dr. DeSantos, who affirmed that kids lie about their whereabouts all the time with their cell phones. Even if Amy was doing better now, he said, her reputation had a lot of baggage and history. His prognosis seemed a little more dire than a month ago. He forewarned, "One of these times, she's going to have a lot of trouble pulling away. Her functional level is so much higher than these guys she's hanging with." He mentioned that Oliver didn't want Amy talking with him; Dr. DeSantos knew Oliver from high school. Fortunately, Amy was still coming to her appointments and calling Dr. DeSantos. He said he'd much rather she stay out of town for college, and thought that at SLU she had a little better chance, and she should consider graduate school near home instead of transferring as an undergrad. He also said, "Even if she needed it, she wouldn't go to rehab."

....

As I write this book two years later, that red flag seems staggering, and I think I underreacted. I'm not sure it was denial as much as hope that things would work out, which maybe is a kind of denial.

In late July, our son and I went to my hometown for what would be the last family reunion with my dad and all his siblings and their spouses, and most cousins and their children. On Sunday morning, the 27th, my husband called from the ER, where he was admitted for a severe headache. Amy and Oliver attended my husband's family's annual cookout without him.

Amy took a chemistry class May 27th through July 27th. Between the lab and lecture, she was at the university from 3:00 p.m. until 10:00 p.m., two or three nights a week, and was enjoying it. She continued to work at the bagel store and babysit. She was finding it tough to save money since we were having her buy some of her own gasoline. But even at $4 a gallon, I now wonder how much of her earnings were going to drugs. On August 13th, I questioned whether Amy's being "nicey" was "sincere or another scheme." Yet, when my husband was visiting our first daughter before she left for Japan, Amy slept with me on his side of the bed. I saw that as a hopeful sign of her wanting the safety of home amid the danger she was in.

Starting Sophomore Year

On Friday, August 22nd, my husband, Amy, and I enjoyed a going-away dinner. I flew with her back to SLU on Saturday with virtually no drama, and all four of her suitcases made weight. But every trip had to have a special Amy moment, and this time she spilled half a bag of popcorn all over the airport gate area carpet. She was assigned a single room in a Greek dorm, although she was not in a sorority. She had convinced Residence Life that she needed a single due to her electronic drum practicing, despite headphones. She left her laptop in my hotel room so I could do some work, and I was sickened by some screensaver pictures of her and Oliver in bed. I wondered what I should do. I decided to not confront her directly, but continued general discussions about healthy relationships.

I talked again with Dr. DeSantos on September 4th. He knew Amy could be done with guys, sounding more confident than he had in July. He was pleased she had stayed in touch during the summer, but he noticed how she was still drawn to risky characters, still walking the line (hoping less so), and had low expectations. He felt there was always the "potential for her to delve into the dark side." He wondered if she would ever date a guy she couldn't manipulate. Yet she had her "big heart" and "so much potential." He'd told her it was "so easy to lead a crappy life," and how good self-esteem and maturity would take her the farthest. He urged her to think long and hard about her rationale for transferring and to consider instead a junior year abroad.

Early in the semester, we were notified that Amy had been caught by the campus police smoking marijuana behind her dorm. Of course she minimized the incident and was determined to fight the $100 fine, which after a year she ended up paying. We also learned how one of her grade school friends was having a serious drug problem. We found beer cans in the basement on September 20th; when I asked her about it the next day, she admitted with a surly "yes Mom" that they were hers.

Meanwhile, she found a part-time job at a sub shop which lasted briefly, then changed to waitressing at a restaurant chain. I sensed increasing strain between her need for money and her work/study balance. I kept telling her that if she could justify the need for more money we could consider increasing her allowance, but she never gave me the numbers. My husband visited her in October, and she came home later in the month for fall break, and this year she carved a pumpkin. She and I saw the movie *The Secret Life of Bees* together, and my husband joined us for Mexican food.

Oliver had transferred from the community college to Canalboro University, and I offered to tutor him in math. It seemed to be a good sign that he was pursuing his education, and Amy convinced us he was trying to pull his life together. And I understand that everyone needs a second chance at some point or another. I met his grandmother, who picked him up since he did not have his license. We learned later he'd lost it for driving under the influence. I was not pleased to learn that he visited Amy again at SLU, and I suspected she had paid for his plane ticket.

On November 17th, my husband and I met Oliver's mother and brothers when we either dropped her off or picked her up at his house. His mother, who also happened to be close friends with Calvin's mom, effused, "We *love* Amy." And who wouldn't? Oliver, sometimes assisted by his younger brother, formed my leaf raking crew, and the lawn never looked better going into winter. It was what we *didn't* see that never looked worse. Amy flew home for what would be our last Thanksgiving with her, and she'd bought cheese for an appetizer tray. While I expected our kids would be home for

Thanksgiving their first year of college, I figured anything after that was a bonus. I remember savoring the fact that she wanted to be with us. We enjoyed visiting with BVMP friends during the long weekend.

Early in December, Amy received an acceptance into a rigorous nearby undergrad program, with assurances she could transfer into the nursing program in September. But on December 9th, she received an acceptance into the BC nursing program and would start classes on January 14th. I was incredibly proud that she reapplied despite being wait-listed for the fall and that she was starting to own her capabilities and aspirations. Her BVMP class valedictorian had matriculated at BC, a school to which Amy would never have been accepted straight after high school. The website claimed that only fifteen percent of transfer students were admitted, though I was hoping that her acceptance was due to what would be "normal" attrition and not due to a casualty of the tanking economy. Her SLU friends were devastated that she was transferring. I had mixed feelings. Life had been easier with her away at SLU, but maybe having her local wouldn't be so bad.

Leaving St. Louis

I flew to St. Louis to help move Amy out, and we had coffee with her dear friend, Patrick, whom she had convinced to change his major to nursing. She was always impatient with me for not being able to keep straight the names of her friends, so it was great to finally be putting faces to names. Who could have fathomed that, a year later, this young man would be one of Amy's pallbearers?

Moving her out of SLU was quintessential Amy drama, including the fact that she would not let me finish packing her room while she took her last final. My suspicion was that she didn't want me to find evidence of drugs. She tried to reassure me, "It looks worse than it is." But between walking overflow belongings across campus to friends who could use them and closing over-full suitcases, we were sweating to make our target departure time as the snowfall accelerated. Several suitcases exceeded the weight limit and our flight was canceled due to weather. We spent the night in a hotel. I was incredibly puzzled when I awoke at 4:00 a.m. and the door to our room was wide open. I never heard Amy come in, and she claims she'd closed it. Nothing had been taken, except my peace of imagination, given how hard she had pushed for a downtown hotel to be closer to her friends. Fortunately, we were able to fly out the next morning, made an earlier connecting flight, and I headed to work for the afternoon as Amy napped.

The Friday before Christmas, a severe storm was forecast for the afternoon, and snowflakes started right on schedule. Amy did not want to believe the reports about the storm and stopped at Oliver's house after doing some shopping. By then the snowfall was one to two inches an hour. My husband and I told her to just stay there overnight because we felt it was no longer safe for her to venture home, and we hoped that going forward she'd heed warnings more seriously. In retrospect, this was the one time I felt I'd given up on her. I will never know if that time enabled her drug use, and I'm ashamed that I bought her "staying on the couch" line. I truly regret not insisting that she very carefully drive the five miles home.

On Saturday, Amy went into the city with my husband for some last-minute Christmas shopping. On Sunday evening, she wanted to visit a friend on the other side of town. I wanted her home by 10:00 p.m. since I had work in the morning. She called at 10:03 to say she was leaving, had the car shoveled out by 10:26, and upon arrival home, the twelve inches of driveway accumulation proved even too much for the four-wheel drive. I did not know when our plow would come, so we felt we had no choice but to shovel ourselves. The plow arrived around 11:30, then became stuck, and the driver had to call a back-up. By then Amy was yapping, "You should have just let me stay at my friend's longer and then the plow would have come." I collapsed into bed around 12:30 to imbibe four precious hours of sleep.

On Monday, Amy went to BC and brought home a booklet about nursing graduate school. Talking with her about those possibilities was exciting and gave me cause for optimism. On Christmas Eve, she brought Oliver to the midnight church services. Christmas morning, after our family opened presents, she went to his house to make him crepes before joining the rest of our family at her relatives' home.

On Saturday, the 27th, my husband, Amy, and I awoke at 2:45 a.m. and were en route to the airport by 3:21. I dropped them at 4:01 for their 6:00 flight to New York. They made their 9:50 connection to Tokyo to visit our first daughter, who was quite disturbed by how much time Amy spent video chatting with Oliver instead of focusing on her.

About a year later, in talking with Patrick and another SLU friend on the night of Amy's funeral, they told us how her motives for moving back closer to home were one hundred percent Oliver, and not to believe otherwise. This disclosure was tough because she had written such an eloquent essay on November 8th:

BC Transfer Essay

In the fifteen months since I started college I have learned more about myself than I did through my entire high school career. In this new state of self-awareness, I have begun to realize the changes I must make so that I can achieve what I truly want out of my remaining years in college. While I have grown immeasurably from experiences at my current school, Saint Louis University (SLU), I have concluded that my personal goals and needs would be better fulfilled elsewhere.

One of the greatest transformations since becoming a college student is my attitude toward academics. I've abandoned the laid back, procrastinating approach I previously took toward my schoolwork to embrace my newfound desire for knowledge. The academic success I have achieved thus far reflects my efforts to learn as much as possible while I still have the resources to do so. Unfortunately, as academic achievement has become increasingly important to me, I have noticed the large percentage of my SLU peers to whom school is nothing but an obstacle that they look to overcome by the quickest and most simple means. This lack of academic enthusiasm, characteristic of many of my peers, has become a growing—and increasingly gnawing—issue for me as the school year has progressed, and I've realized that my intellectual interests would be better fostered at a more academically rigorous institution. Although my teachers and parents kept telling me that through the years, it has me taken [sic] until now to actually believe it myself.

While going through my initial college search process during high school, I was convinced that the only way to prove my independence involved creating a large geographical distance between my new school and my home. Moving half way across the country certainly increased my independence and responsibilities, however, I have since developed a longing to live in Massachusetts again and explore areas I failed to appreciate while living at home. While I've made a point to discover much of St. Louis, I've come to realize details about Boston that I previously took for granted, such as the higher quality public transportation system (yes, the MBTA), the cultural diversity and the urban development—not to mention the scope of the medical resources for clinical education. Seeing the intellectual growth in several of my friends who chose to stay local for college has sparked my realization that personal effort, regardless of one's distance from home, is the key to gaining independence. I have decided that I want nothing more than to spend the remainder of my college years in the city I once tried to leave behind, only now with a greater appreciation for all that Boston has to offer.

My first three semesters at SLU have introduced me to the Jesuit mission, an aspect of the school I have come to love. The Jesuit mission promotes education of the whole, encouraging students to achieve success in every part of their lives. I feel that, while some institutions overemphasize the importance of the future and finding a job, SLU focuses more on helping its students grow into well-rounded, mature individuals. SLU also promotes the Jesuit tradition of service to others by offering thousands of service opportunities for students each year. My personal dedication to community service, which developed as a result of several volunteer service projects in high school, meshes perfectly with the Jesuit mission to serve, and I enjoy being part of a community that shares my enthusiasm in helping others. As the Jesuit influence has unexpectedly become an important part of my life over the past fifteen months, I've decided that I would like to continue my education at an institution that upholds similar values.

My decision to apply to Boston College once again, after being waitlisted as a transfer applicant for the fall semester, comes as a surprise to many of the people I encounter. I, however, do not see my experience last year as deterrence but rather as encouragement to now work even harder at proving my eligibility for admission into BC's competitive nursing program. As my academic and extracurricular achievements continue to grow in number, I hope that my hard work in college will soon overshadow my less than perfect high school record, thus representing the great personal changes I've accomplished during this period of time. I look forward to embracing each and every challenge that a BC environment would provide for me, and experiencing the benefits of an academic community I could once never have dreamed of joining.

Looking back at the past year, I am shocked by the progress I have made since my initial college application process. I realize that the self-knowledge I now hold was the missing element in my original college decision. As a matured woman with a much stronger sense of identity, and belief in my capabilities and aspirations, I have approached my third (and, hopefully, final) college search process knowing exactly what I do and do not want. Throughout the next three years I want to be pushed to be the absolute best I can in all aspects of life. The several reasons I would like to transfer back home stretch beyond the various factors I am able to objectively identify. I do not know if it's the excitement I experience whenever I see a Red Sox hat, or the strangeness I feel around non-Bostonians who actually pronounce their R's, but I have realized that for the remainder of my college years I belong nowhere else than "down by river" at Boston College.

I was so proud of the strides Amy had made in her first three semesters of college, and had I been an admissions officer, I would have been convinced by her essay. Wouldn't you have been, too?

Amy returned from Japan on January 5th, and soon after we hired her boyfriend, Oliver, to paint one of our bathrooms. I arranged for Amy to live off campus in a house with five other BC girls, and on Tuesday the 13th, she and Oliver drove our mini-van into the city to begin her move-in. My husband and I met them for a burrito dinner, then I drove the mini-van back, accompanied by Oliver. I was pleasantly surprised that he and I were able to carry on a conversation the entire way. Amy emailed me her first reaction to the rental house, "I'm a little unhappy with the room. The dresser is broken, there's no bed, the whole house is filthy...looks like a lot of parties go down here. But we'll see how it goes!" She was already happier with the academics and culture at BC. She insisted on buying a double bed, citing the ability to sprawl out her materials when studying. I suspected it was due to Oliver spending the night.

The transition appeared to go smoothly. Within a few weeks, she was talking about potentially doing her master's right away, possibly to become a certified nurse anesthetist. I was encouraged. But while this career would draw on her excellent math and science skills, I learned from her rehab notes that she had growing concerns about the temptation of access to serious drugs.

On January 15th, I had an evening event at HBS, after which I made my first trip to Amy's house from there, a ten-minute drive. We went out for coffee and watched TV footage of the US Airways flight that Captain Sullenberger and crew successfully ditched in the Hudson after a bird strike took out both engines. I thought how if your plane is going down, you want a seasoned pilot with judgment, but our society doesn't always want to pay for expertise. (Less than a month later, I flew to my hometown the day after Continental 3407 crashed, with its distracted forty-four-year-old pilot and sick twenty-four-year-old copilot.) I wondered if Sullenberger-caliber professionals were helping Amy. I've since learned that "Sully" credited the landing with teamwork and following practiced procedures. That approach might have helped save Amy, too.

On January 20th, Amy's twentieth birthday, I bought her some cakes on the way home from work. My event that evening at HBS was canceled, then plans became complicated because—here comes the drama—Amy needed to pick up the mattress she bought on Craigslist, grocery shop, and eat dinner. My husband and I arrived at her house around 7:15, drove the five miles to retrieve the mattress, and he had to figure out how to work the straps he borrowed to secure the unwieldy object atop the mini-van.

We drove back to her house and unloaded the mattress. Thankfully, the woman's son would bring the box spring and frame when they had the moving truck on Saturday. Amy and I grocery shopped while my husband found a gas station and tried to finalize birthday dinner plans with our son. The restaurant Amy originally selected would be closed by 9:00 p.m., so our son found a place in the next town. After finding a parking spot in between snow banks, we discovered it only served take-out. By then, everyone was up to their eyeballs in stress, but at least Amy could snack on some of the groceries. We ended up back near the grocery store at an Indian restaurant where our son and his girlfriend joined us. By the time I was writing in my diary that night, I was weary but jubilant about both the presidential inauguration and "no more teenagers!"

On Saturday, January 24th, my husband collected Amy from the subway and the next morning I drove her back to BC, something I couldn't do if she were still at SLU. On Tuesday, I had a "nice talk" with her. After an HBS event on Thursday, I took her grocery shopping and to dinner. On Super Bowl Sunday, she took public transportation to her brother's apartment to watch the game with him. The son of Tara, my best friend from childhood, who grew up like an older cousin to my children, joined the party. Knowing they were together made me feel that parenthood did have its occasional reward. On February 7th, Amy, my husband, and I saw *Slumdog Millionaire*, the last movie we would watch together. The next day, my husband drove her back to BC, again a perk of proximity. On my birthday, I attended a workshop at HBS, then went to Amy's where she had made me a truly special birthday card with the best present she could have given me: two photographs from our visit with my elderly women friends during our San Antonio visit two years ago. We ate dinner at a tacqueria, braving the city snow banks.

The day after Valentine's, my husband picked me up at the airport after my birthday trip to my hometown, and we joined Amy for dinner. The day after President's Day, I had coffee and "a nice conversation" with Amy, then dropped her at the library. On Thursday, the 19th, Amy flew back to SLU for Mardi Gras. Thank goodness her flight home on Sunday was delayed or she would have missed it. Despite the city's public transportation, she asked for a ride back to BC so she could be on time for a pathophysiology test review session. I agreed to drive despite the severe weather alert because I wanted to take advantage of the bonding time. Road conditions were worsening; I was grateful to have so many miles of tunnels leaving the airport. Amy hadn't had dinner, so we stopped at a sub shop near her house. She also had to stop at a pharmacy. My drive home was the second worst winter weather I'd driven in. Was I conned by Amy to run her around, or just being a good mom?

On February 23rd, the house landlord started questioning the legitimacy of Amy's subletting. It was always something! Amy was mostly home for spring break in March which was really pleasant, but she baked a lot, so I needed to be careful to not gain weight. My husband and I took her up on her suggestion to go out for a Japanese dinner, having developed the philosophy that if your child asks you to do something good together with them, you say yes. We had pizza together on the 13th, then dim sum (Chinese breakfast) the next day. I drove her back to her house on Sunday via the neighborhood where my husband and I first lived when we were married, and we talked about my life at her age.

On March 21st, Amy and Oliver joined us for our parish's annual murder mystery. My husband played crooner "Dream Martin." Our eighty-one-year-old pastor made a cameo appearance as singer "Fig Newton," donning a brown shag wig and a bright green polyester pantsuit, belting out "Danke Schön." That performance touched Amy in some way, because for the rest of her life she'd bound into a room singing "Danke Schön, mommy Danke Schön..." The next morning, I drove her back to BC, first stopping so she could buy breakfast, then taking her grocery shopping. On March 24th, after an HBS event, I collected her and we went to the pharmacy, then for sushi and ice cream. I did not make note of any red flags during all these simple encounters.

On March 25th, the drama began concerning Amy's apartment search for junior year, but it was nice to be on the sidelines and not actually in the middle of the proceedings. On the 27th, I went to a lecture at BC with four people from ACHS. Amy joined us, and she was very impatient about returning to her house. Oliver, whose driver's license had been reinstated, joined us late for dinner at Amy's favorite sushi restaurant. I started to sense tension between them. The season of Lent began, and I decided I would take better care of myself, which would include one piece of chocolate and a glass of red wine at bedtime.

On April 6th, I collected Amy after her appointment with Dr. Buprine, the local psychiatrist prescribing her Suboxone, then we went to the pharmacy and grocery store. Amy accompanied me to my hometown for my annual Easter trip. I appreciated that she joined me for most of the rituals, including having our photo taken next to the giant Easter egg at the botanical gardens. Mid-month, she walked with me and the dog we were watching, and she and Oliver, with a new car, helped (he more than her) with the annual brush burning in the back yard.

I spent the first week of May in Japan visiting our first daughter. In Kyoto, I bought the special green tea cake that Amy had requested. I was reminded of pleasant travel times with the children and the pangs I sometimes felt leaving them. I wrote, "As Amy pushes for the family to take a vacation, I can feel why. Unfortunately, my ACHS job is not conducive, but having made the Japan trip, perhaps I'll be more creative, even long weekends. It's a shame that our first daughter returns during ACHS summer training. But if I can sufficiently plan ahead, maybe there's hope." We had not taken a family vacation since the summer of 2003, around the time Amy started using marijuana. I wish I had said yes to this major request of Amy's and not just all the smaller ones.

I returned from Japan shortly before midnight on Mother's Day. Amy greeted me with her signature dessert: three layers of chocolate cake, with chocolate mousse in between, slathered in mocha mascarpone frosting, a whopping five-hundred-fifty calories per slice. We sat around the kitchen table eating in the wee minutes of the new day. Mid-month, she and I cleaned her sister's room in anticipation of her return from Japan.

On Tuesday, May 26th, my husband and I started reviewing Amy's apartment lease. On Friday night, we took her to a Mexican restaurant she hadn't been to since before England. On Sunday, I was the graduation speaker at BVMP, and I was pleased that Amy came, as were her many friends in that class.

Moving In and Picking Up

Monday, June 1st, was moving day for Amy. One of her apartment mates, Ramona, was home overseas, and her wire transfer did not come through. I received several calls from Amy late in the afternoon and during ACHS running club about these last-minute payment problems. Amy and her other apartment mate, Sandra, agreed to cover Ramona's first month's rent and security deposit, but I had to call the payment in on my Visa card when I returned to school. On the drive home, I received a call that the rental company could not take personal checks until after the first month, so when I arrived home I had to make another Visa payment since the checks

I'd written for Amy wouldn't work. Amy was finally able to move in late Monday. The drama could have been much worse, and I was happy to help in that way, while her friends helped her move her belongings.

On June 7th, Amy and I started out on a run. She did a three-miler, and I did five. On the 11th, Amy took our futon from England to her apartment. I appreciated her moving things out. I had planned to piggyback my first visit to her apartment with an HBS event that night, but the event was canceled so my visit was delayed. One thing I had *not* done was to request that, as cosigner of her lease, I also be given a set of keys to her apartment. Perhaps I would have used them to make random checks on her living situation, or perhaps not.

On Friday, June 12th, Amy announced that she'd found a great Craigslist deal on a flat-screen TV, something she'd wanted since early high school. She could now buy it with her earnings, not mine. After work on Friday, June 19th, I had tea with Amy, and then headed to the airport to fly to California for a long overdue visit with friends. I flew the red-eye home on Sunday night, went to work, left early, and Amy collected my husband from the train and brought home a pizza. I felt like I'd had an emotional IV given the tension at work surrounding the firing of my boss and the resulting prospect of not being able to take more than a day of summer vacation.

Thursday, June 25th, the day Michael Jackson died, was the annual strawberry festival in town. Amy brought Oliver and his grandmother. I enjoyed meeting her and felt empathy for what she had endured with her daughter and grandsons. The town Old Home Day was that weekend, an annual festival that included a pancake breakfast, parade, activities for kids, art show, and road races. I was struck by a comment that Amy emailed me on the 24th, saying, "I'm really looking forward to the strawberry festival and Old Home Day events this weekend! It's great that our town has kept those traditions going, especially in these tough economic times." I made my post-surgery race debut in the five-mile run, then Amy and Oliver ran the one-mile event. Arriving home, I was touched that my husband had picked up our medals: she and I both finished first in our age groups.

My husband and I headed over to dim sum with his friend, Dan, and his family and other friends. Amy joined us, and Dan convinced her to visit them again in Hawaii later in the summer. After, my husband and I picked up my glasses, which were actually new lenses in Amy's old frames.

On Sunday, Amy and I grocery shopped. I attended an event at HBS on Monday, then met our son for coffee. I'd hoped to visit Amy's apartment, but she wouldn't be back until even later. Even so, I realized I now had the luxury of being able to visit two of my children in the city. Amy joined us for dinner on July 3rd, and she and her brother headed separately into the city for fireworks on the 4th.

On July 8th, my husband, Amy, and Oliver went to a Red Sox game. I returned from a trip to my hometown on July 12th, and wrote in my diary, "Caught up with Amy," though I did not elaborate on the where or how of this simple act. On the 15th, I finally saw her apartment and told her it was going to be the best location she would ever have, never expecting it to be the last. We also bought what would be her last pair of running shoes. On the 19th, Amy baked her tempting seven-layer bars. On the 24th, my husband and I went to our condo, and Amy and Oliver drove out to join us. They opted to eat at Amy's favorite steak house, while my husband and I ate at a restaurant owned by my pastry chef friend and her husband. (During the week before detox, Amy had mused about an internship with this friend the following summer given her love of baking. I was non-committal. How could I even think about asking our friend knowing that Amy was a heroin addict?)

In late July, Amy started a three-week intensive microbiology course at BC. On the first test, she earned 108, and on the second "only" 104. She finished the course with an A. She loved it, declaring that she might want to take more science courses, extolling the quality of undergraduate teaching at BC. My husband and I looked at each other and reached the terrifyingly false conclusion that she couldn't be messing up *that* badly if she could pull these grades at BC. Amy also began a job as a care attendant for a woman in her early nineties near campus.

On Sunday, August 2nd, my husband and Amy went to his family's annual cookout while I stayed home to work. On Thursday, the 6th, they attended the Paul McCartney concert at Fenway Park. Despite Amy's encouragement, I did not go because of needing the evening hours to work from home since it was ACHS crunch time. Amy told me I missed a great performance as the former Beatle was on stage nonstop for two and a half hours, the crowd was really into it, and the weather was perfect. Her BVMP friend, Sherryl, remembers Amy talking about how much father-daughter fun she had with my husband, and how she updated her Facebook status with "Sir Paul has still got it!"

On Friday, my husband, Amy, and I went to our favorite Japanese restaurant for his birthday, and she made him her signature dessert. On Saturday, we celebrated by going out to dinner with our son and his girlfriend. Amy and Oliver joined us, and I sensed a difference between them. He was more withdrawn and barely communicative. Mid-meal, we received phone confirmation that our first daughter had landed in her college town from Tokyo. On Sunday, Amy and I finished preparing her sister's room for her visit home.

Warning Signs

Our first daughter came home on August 14th, and was seeing a completely different side of Oliver. She was deeply disturbed by his temper and the way he talked to Amy. Yet my husband and I had only seen his polite, clean-cut, "Hello Mr. Caruso, Hello Ms. Weiksnar" side. Someone in town even commented, "He treats her like a queen." That day, the big news story in the town weekly newspaper was how Oliver's younger brother had been arrested for a series of housebreaks in our town. Amy was almost maniacal in grabbing the paper from me.

On August 16th, while my husband was on a business trip, I enjoyed going out for dim sum with my two daughters for the first time in more than a year. Five days later, the evening before Amy left to visit our friends in Honolulu for ten days, my husband, both daughters, Oliver, and I had a going away dinner at a Mexican restaurant. Earlier in the summer, Amy had started to talk to me about wanting to go off Suboxone. She admitted she had been seeing a drug counselor, Mr. Goodruco, was having trouble self-tapering, and she hinted she might have to go to detox. After Amy died, I found in a locked file on her iBook an excruciating account revealing that one of her motivations for the Hawaii trip was an attempt at self-detox:

> **8/22** *Sick sick sick sick sick sick sick.. that's what I am. Plane to Hawaii- 6hrs of dope sickness.*

> **8/26** *That was just about one of the worst time periods of my life. I didn't think the sickness would come so full force but I guess considering the amount of heroin I was shooting (at least a 70 bag at least 5 days a week for at least a few weeks before Hawaii), going down to nothing would torture my body into multi-symptoms of confusion and withdrawal. It started in about 2 hours into my flight from Pheonix (sic) to Hawaii and I think I may have taken a Suboxone too soon because in about 20 minutes my body turned from feeling slightly off to full fledged kicks, cold flashes and desperation. Looking back, I never want to go through that ever ever ever again, but I am so scared that I'll return to Boston and get right back into dope. Even today, Wednesday, my cravings are extremely heavy.*

Day 1 (Saturday 8/22)- no fun, I'm done.
Day 2- feelin (sic) like poo and a little blue, don't know what to do
Day 3- WHY ME???
Day 4- still craving more
Day 5 (today, Wednesday)- will I get through this alive?

Reasons to stay clean:
-Money in my bank account
-Salvage things with Oliver
-Make my family proud instead of tolerant of me
-Give Mr. Goodruco some faith in me
-Have normal relationships with my roommates and others at BC
-Won't need to miss fall semester for rehab

Earlier in August, Amy had stopped at the convenience store where her close friend from middle school, Byron, was working. Amy was known to stop by his house in the wee hours, calling from the driveway to tell him they had to go to the International House of Pancakes (IHOP) even though he was already asleep. But this time, Byron sensed a very different Amy. They started talking, and when Oliver walked in, she mouthed silently to Byron, "call me," turning around to leave with Oliver, a look of panic in her eyes. Byron knew that something was terribly wrong in the relationship, and that was the last time he saw Amy alive.

Junior Year and Clinicals

On Sunday, September 6th, I noted that our first daughter and Amy's best friend from BVMP, Audrey, went to a local pond. Someone must have shared some concerns with me, as I wrote, "How serious are Amy's issues?" The next evening my husband, the girls, and I had dinner at our favorite Italian restaurant, then took Amy to BC to start classes the day after Labor Day. She was now planning to graduate

AMELIA
CARUSO
STUDENT NURSE

in four and a half years so she could double major in psychology. I wrote, "While I kind of miss taking her to SLU, there is something to be said for having her local!"

Two days later, I talked with Amy for about an hour, and even longer with our first daughter. I wish I remembered specifics, because the conversations were about growing suspicions of Amy's serious problems. Amy and I continued the Suboxone conversation through the fall. While I did not notice any change in her physical appearance, she felt like a side effect of Suboxone was living "in a bubble" and did not want that. She also kept mentioning how she needed to break up with Oliver. She seemed to realize that she was not going to be able to solve the problems in his family and was tiring of their dynamics. One day when she and I were walking the dog together, I tried to reassure her that while breaking up could be very difficult, there were many resources that could help, and her father and I were prepared to support her in whatever way was necessary, including restraining orders or moving her out of state. In hopes of encouraging her, I told her about someone I knew who, in her early twenties, broke up with the love of her life because of his drug issues.

On September 10th, following an HBS event, I collected Amy to bring her home for the weekend and our annual family pasta party. She once again made her signature dessert. Oliver came to the dinner and seemed even more withdrawn, which felt beyond awkward given how I knew Amy was trying to break up with him. We took what would be our last family photo.

On September 20th, I cooked fingerling potatoes from the town farmers market, which Amy loved. Two days later, I emailed her a playlist of songs she was going to download to my iPod. She also started her nursing clinical rotations in the medical/surgical unit of a major teaching hospital. I called her at 5:00 a.m. on Tuesdays so she could be up in time to take public transportation downtown for a 7:00 a.m. start. We denied her request to borrow our car for this purpose.

During the weekend of October 3rd, Amy bummed a ride home, then drove our mini-van back to BC. My husband and I were in my hometown for a wedding. Our son and his girlfriend collected us from the airport on Sunday, and we all met Amy at her favorite sushi restaurant for dinner. I then drove her grocery shopping where her predicted ten-minute trip only extended to twenty, and I drove the mini-van home. She came home the following weekend when my husband and I went to our condo. Looking back, I question whether Amy's trips home were to score drugs locally. She had also started asking about buying a smart phone, and I argued that she couldn't afford it, and she stopped asking, which was unusual given her typical persistence. I wonder if she had wanted the phone to facilitate her drug lifestyle.

On Monday, October 12th, when I came home from school and went to do laundry, I found a hypodermic syringe in Amy's white wicker clothes hamper. I was panic-stricken. I called several 1-800 hotlines and the ER, trying to find an answer I probably already knew. Talking with a pharmacist, he was sorry to agree that it probably meant heroin. I eventually asked Amy, who claimed the needle had belonged to Oliver's brother. She explained that she and Oliver found it when they were cleaning out the brother's room after the burglaries, and she was going to take it to BC where she could safely dispose of it. I so very much wanted to believe this explanation.

On Tuesday, I attended an HBS presentation after work, and then met up with Amy for dinner. My husband left for a conference on Thursday morning, leaving the car at the subway terminal for Amy to retrieve later. On Friday, the 16th, she came home again and the next morning she and I attended the last town farmers market of the year, and the annual harvest fair. I reflected, "She really seems to appreciate some of the town amenities and traditions." We bought lunch at the fair, including the best homemade apple pie. On October 21st, I attended senior night for the BVMP cross country team and caught up with the athletic director, Ms. Dirath. Our conversation included how well Amy finally seemed to be doing.

A few days later, I attended another HBS event and visited Amy after. My husband and I saw Amy briefly on Halloween. Much to her chagrin, we hadn't decorated or bought candy for trick-or-treaters. She was planning to make a "balloon boy" costume out of two Mylar® blankets I still had from marathons. Later, she talked about having attended haunted houses. When we cleaned out her apartment after she died, I found the blankets, with no evidence they had ever been made into a costume.

On November 1st, I wrote, "Amy high when home yesterday: red eyes, slow eating, indecision?" She was sitting across from me at the kitchen table, nodding off as she was eating a tuna sub, and did not seem able to answer the questions I asked her. Standing in front of her next to the dishwasher, looking into her eyes, I asked if she was high, and of course she denied it. I was not angry, but deeply concerned that I didn't seem to be connecting with her. I drove her back to BC the night of November 2nd, and we talked of her struggle trying to taper off Suboxone and how she may need to go to rehab. To take care of myself, I signed up for swimming lessons, and on the 5th, I began working out with a caring and enthusiastic personal trainer who was my student during my first semester at BVMP.

On November 10th, Amy told me that she would be scheduling an appointment for me to meet with her and Mr. Goodruco. Then all week, she kept telling me we'd talk that weekend, but in her inimitable style, the conversation never happened.

Meeting with the Drug Counselor

My diary entry on Monday, November 16th, was, "I am the mother of a heroin addict." I'd left work at 1:55 and picked Amy up at her job, finally meeting the nonagenarian woman whom she assisted. We parked on the street and met Mr. Goodruco at 3:00 p.m. in a building where the painted cinderblock walls reminded me of being back at my Catholic elementary school. I was expecting a discussion about rehab, but after a brief prompt by Mr. Goodruco, Amy opened the meeting by looking me in the eye and saying with a weak smile, "I'm a heroin addict." I uttered a profanity and slammed my keys on the table. Mr. Goodruco sat stoically at the end to my right, and Amy sat slightly nervously at the end to my left. I had been totally blindsided that Amy had progressed to the end of the abstainer-experimenter-user-abuser-addict spectrum.

Mr. Goodruco reminded me how addiction is a disease and Amy had it. Once someone injects heroin, they are considered an addict. When I asked about the Suboxone, he educated me that it allows a lapse during which the addict can use heroin. Initially, the Food and Drug Administration allowed it to be prescribed without adjunct counseling, but that had changed. He believed that Suboxone induced a "false confidence" and that abstinence from all drugs was the answer. He told me that lying is part and parcel of addiction and not to take Amy's deceptions personally. The biggest lying was the addict to herself.

He clarified that rehab is more than detox. He recommended that we send Amy to the Triangle facility ninety minutes away, which took private insurance. "She'll be glad she's there," he assured me. (Note: Triangle is the umbrella name of the facility that includes the Triangle detox unit, the Rhombus rehab facility, and the all-women Circle Center residential program.)

I pulled out paper and a pen, and began taking notes despite Amy's objections. I questioned whether she could finish her semester. She offered that she could with Cs and Ds, but she wanted to earn As and Bs, so she would take a leave of absence. Mr. Goodruco reiterated that I had to change the focus from thinking about academics to her getting well. She could not return to school until she was ready, and BC would not tolerate a relapse. He had a lot of confidence she could do it and reassured us that she hadn't lost anything: She was healthy, young, and able to pull it together. He reflected that Amy hadn't really been able to be a BC student yet and would be on top of her game when she was back. He had referred numerous people to Triangle, and he said of the "A+" Rhombus rehab facility that he never knew anyone who left not thinking it was the greatest thing they did. He would try to set up an admission by Thursday; he had connections.

I anxiously, if awkwardly, walked back to the car with Amy. Despite the gravity of what had just transpired, my dominant feeling was gratitude that the car hadn't been towed. I drove Amy the few blocks to pick up the mini-van she had parked near her work, having driven it in during the weekend. She and I drove home separately, despite my preference that we go together. She had an appointment with psychiatrist Dr. Buprine, and while I offered to accompany her, she declined. She said she would tell him about the detox/rehab decision. On her way home, she bought needles from a Broton pharmacy at 5:18; I learned of this purchase a few weeks later when I found the receipt in her bedroom.

Once home, I called Tara, and talked with our first daughter's counselor, Dr. Hischolor, who offered that Amy had fallen in with a bad crowd and it appeared she was reaching out for help. I can't remember when and how I broke the news to my husband.

I was awake at 2:00 a.m. on Tuesday, November 17th. "The bad dream is reality," I wrote in my moment of deepest desperation.

In the morning, I missed the exit on my way to work. I kept my office door closed much of the day as I made personal calls. I spoke with psychotherapist and substance abuse counselor Mr. Coolwater, who recommended a different rehab facility. He said that Amy would have to reprogram how she dealt with stress, discomfort, and irritation. He added, "If she does it right, she'll never have to do it again. She hasn't even begun her adult life. She just messed up her teen years, which most people do." I also spoke with Dr. Herowitz. He agreed that we finally had a "major, major" diagnosis and he had had "good luck" with Triangle. I must have made some comment about how we were encouraged about all the factors in her favor, including how bright she was. He said he never doubted Amy's intelligence, but in a way that I was starting to realize that intelligence was a moot point in dealing with this disease. That afternoon, Amy went to a dentist appointment and found out she needed a root canal.

I cried a lot on the drive home but still went to work out with my trainer. Once home, I was saddened to learn that my husband's late mother's best friend, someone we'd visited often, had died in August. I had a long, wide-ranging talk with Amy that evening. She expressed her outrage at how Suboxone and OxyContin are made by the same pharmaceutical company, which is not true, but I understood her intimation about the conflicts in the pharmaceutical industry. We'd had several talks about how she was ready to break up with Oliver and was finding it difficult; I kept offering sources of support. My mind couldn't help but get ahead of itself on the irrelevancy of wondering whether Amy would be "relegated" to relationships with other addicts (hopefully in recovery), and the complications that could ensue. At 9:17 p.m. she sent my husband and me an email:

From: Amelia Caruso <carusoad@bc.edu>

Subject: books

Hi Mom and Dad,

At my last appointment, Dr. [Pedreia] recommended a book pair, "Beautiful Boy" and "Tweak." One is written by a father (David Sheff) and the other by his son (Nic Sheff), who struggled with a meth addiction. Anyways, she and I think reading these books might help us understand each others perspectives and behaviors a bit. Here are the links on amazon if you're interested:

http://www.amazon.com/Beautiful-Boy-Fathers-Journey-Addiction/dp/0618683356

http://www.amazon.com/Tweak-Growing-Methamphetamines-Nic-Sheff/dp/1416972196/ref=pd_bxgy_b_img_b

Thanks again for all your support and understanding through this process. I know the last 24 hours have been extremely tough on the whole family and I'm so overwhelmed with guilt :(It hurts me sooo bad to see the disappointed looks in your eyes and to see you crying, but I'm just glad the lies are over and everything is out in the open now. I think this process might really change my relationship with you guys, for the better. I promise to put everything I have towards my recovery and I'm really looking forward to going on this journey.

Love always,

Amy

After she died, I found notes she must have been writing for a nursing class that references a psychology class she was taking during the fall semester. I painfully transcribed them when I visited my hometown in February of 2010:

Onset: I continued my prescription for about a week until there were no more pills, but when the prescription had run out I felt an abnormal emptiness that I had never previously encountered. Later that year, after suffering injuries from a ski accident, I was prescribed a month long supply of Oxycodone and this time when I stopped using my prescription these empty feelings were accompanied by a slew of flu like symptoms which I would later recognize as withdrawal.

Progression: Before my two medical interventions I had never been the type to experiment with drugs or alcohol, but the harsh contrast from constant exposure to a strong narcotic to nothing at all propelled me to actively seek out more, and before I knew it my opiate problem had escalated to the point where I was using almost every day.

Now, in writing this essay I am of course concerned about the implications of admitting my slip into such a lowly esteemed sector of society, that of the drug addict, but as I stress about the opinions of those who read this, I also realize the importance of expressing this difficult part of my journey and, in a way, lifting it from my chest.

As I learned in Stress and Behavior, having one or two "soft addictions" can be healthy but by summer my opiate addiction was the opposite of soft and would soon alter my life in drastic ways.

I feel that details regarding the extent of my addiction are trivial compared to the stresses that resulted, so for the purpose of this essay I will merely state that my addiction was out of control. It pains me just to recall the (disrespect) for my absent values, constant lying and neglect of relationships to name only a few. I did both to sustain and protect my drug use. Every day seemed a new obstacle as I struggled to find sources of money, and met with some of the sickest people I have ever met, and face the painful physically torturous pains of withdrawal, all the while trying to live a superficially "normal" life, concealing my habit from those closest to me.

Many people who have not themselves experienced drug addiction wonder why addicts wasn't [sic] able to "just quit." Believe it or not, this was a question that constantly haunted me as I dealt with the shame and embarrassment of not being able to control my own actions and probably one of the factors preventing me from coming forth with my problem and asking for help. One common perception is that drug abuse depends on individual choice and any desperate person who allowed themselves to fall into such a circumstance would be considered weak and unambitious, the scum of society for not successfully climbing out.

Sinking ship

Self esteem

Self care

Social Life

Stress of recovery

Fall so fast it's terrifying

Rapidly accum.can my ??? my ??

....

Amy's self-awareness and pain in this essay astounds and devastates me.
Yet I will never be able to know the extent of poetic license. For example,
I did not know of any ski accident for which Oxycodone was prescribed.
She also wrote on a bright green, three-inch square sticky note, in red ink,
"sometimes I want to apologize to the girl I was 10 years ago…for not
becoming the girl she dreamed of being 10 years from then." She includes
a small diagram, the first box labeled "baby pic" and the second unde-
cipherable. This note seems to be from the same time period as the essay
above. Sadly, the ink on this note bled during a water spill on my desk.

On Wednesday, November 18th, during my evening walk with River, I
talked with our first daughter from her college town for seventy-five minutes about our new family reality. She was shattered. I also told our son, who
did not seem to take the news as hard, probably because he had not been
as close to Amy and had not experienced what our first daughter had seen
firsthand over the summer. Amy's psychologist, Dr. DeSantos, and I talked
for about fifteen minutes. We discussed how we never learned why Amy
was into so many substances, and also the need for her to find a practitioner
after rehab whom she wouldn't be able to manipulate. He raised the specter
that because Amy liked him so much—for example, she usually brought
him a dessert when she came to her session—she might not be telling him
everything for fear of disappointing him. So he thought that he might not
be the most effective resource at this time but would always be there for us.

I also called a friend who had enrolled her son in a wilderness school.
She spoke about "one day at a time" and how you have to learn from the
inevitable setbacks in the rehab process. Amy had the first half of her root
canal. I was "feeling hopeful much of the day." I noted the timing coincidence of commitment to my personal training, a fitness rehab of sorts, and
Amy's decision about drug rehab. I thought back to two years earlier when I
was wondering whether we should have been looking for colleges or rehab.

On Thursday, I spoke with Mr. Goodruco about the insurance negotiations in paying for Amy's treatment and possibly a different rehab facility
after detox. He still felt Rhombus was best. He shared that Amy was more
than a little scared, and infinitely more malleable. Amy had her intake
phone interview with Triangle, so now it was a matter of negotiating the
start date. Mr. Goodruco said he could see the relationship with Oliver
"fading all by itself" and that Amy "has been working on it" and was
more motivated to break up. He proffered that Oliver was a good kid but
needed to focus on his demons full time.

I also spoke with Triangle. Amy's admission was scheduled for 9:00 a.m. on Saturday, which was ironically five years to the day from the Saturday before Thanksgiving when she'd been hospitalized briefly in tenth grade and we had felt we were in freefall given the rumors of her substance use but had no handholds. She would be in detox for six days. She needed to bring a picture ID and insurance card. She should bring alcohol-free toiletries and no money. My husband and I would sign three pieces of paper and wouldn't stay long. We would know the name of her detox counselor on Monday. There would be no visiting in detox, but we could see her once a week in rehab. The representative could offer no percentages on success.

I cried while driving from work to my fitness session. I could barely hold back the tears as "Amie" played on the radio while I pumped iron, the same song that inspired me to name my daughter Amy. To add to the stress, my new boss was furious because someone on the Board of Directors wanted to micromanage our department by having us log every phone call. That night, my husband and I called one of his relatives who lived near Triangle, hoping she might be able to give us the local scoop on the facility. She hadn't heard much but knew that, "If Amy is serious about getting clean, she *has* to let go of the 'friends.'"

Amy asked to have Mexican dinner with us on Friday. She claimed to have wrapped up all loose ends at BC and cleaned up her apartment. On the way home from work I received a call: A van driver could not find the workplace of a student. Once home, I logged on to Google Maps and enlisted the help of a bilingual teacher on the landline to help navigate the pickup. Resolving that problem chewed up more than half an hour when I really wanted to be focusing on the family matters at hand.

My husband, Amy, and I had a lovely dinner, but she did spend a long time in the bathroom before meeting us at our table, a pattern many had observed. Was she shooting up? In retrospect, I wondered whether I should have barged in on her at any of the times she had been in the bathroom for what seemed like too long. But to what end? After the meal, she announced that she was going to hang out with "friends" and be home by 10:30, which seemed reasonable to my husband and me. I called her before we went to bed around 10:45, and she impatiently revised her estimate to 12:30. She returned at 2:30, and then pulled an all-nighter on what would be her last night in her bedroom at home.

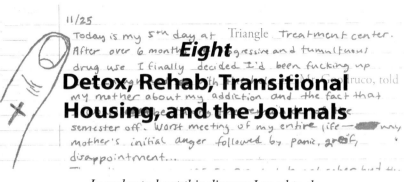

Eight

Detox, Rehab, Transitional Housing, and the Journals

*In order to beat this disease I need to do
one crucial thing: outsmart myself.*

Many books have been written along the lines of "your child's first day of school." However, I didn't even bother to look for one about "your child's first day in detox."

My husband, Amy, and I left the house uneventfully around 7:00 a.m. on Saturday, November 21ˢᵗ, stopping first at Tulips, the store in our town center. It was the opening day of their expanded premises, and Amy, groomed impeccably as usual, greeted the beloved owners in her usual exuberant fashion. In reply to "how's it going," she mentioned the upcoming end of the semester, but not a word about where we were headed after making our purchases. Fortuitously, one of the owner's sons was also on-site. He had sold Amy her daily breakfast during high school for $2.29 with a twinkle in his eye, no matter what she ordered. They bantered about meeting up when the semester ended.

Since I was unable to attend my 8:00 a.m. running group, our eighty-year-old leader read the birthday poem I wrote for one of our members turning sixty. We drove the ninety minutes toward Triangle, and since we were slightly ahead of schedule, we stopped for coffee at a Dunkin' Donuts®, just like we had five years ago that day en route to City Pediatrics Hospital when we took fifteen-year-old Amy to the ER. This time, Amy spent what seemed like a long time in the bathroom.

Once at the facility, my husband and I signed a few pieces of paper accepting financial responsibility. The staff was gentle and the proceedings were very matter-of-fact. It was difficult and awkward for me to watch a middle-aged man whose family was trying to have him admitted for alcohol detox. They were rejected for lack of proper insurance, and perhaps I felt a little guilty because our family had acceptable coverage.

Amy's Drug History Documented

Amy stated in her inpatient screening form that she "started on Oxy when I was 17 years old … tried it about 10x … snorting oxy went away to college and started on oxy again and this led to heroin." Yet her bio-social assessment three days later records the age of first use of her primary drug of addiction, heroin, as 17, and her secondary drug, cocaine, as 15. The record finally put into one place her history with substances:

	Ever used (Y/N)	Date last used	Frequency of use in past 6 months	Injection Use Y/N
Alcohol	Y	?	Rarely	N
Cocaine	Y	11-19-09	3-5 x week	Y
Crack Cocaine	N			
Marijuana/ Hash	Y	11-19-09	Occasionally	N
Heroin	Y	11-20-09	Daily	Y
OxyContin	Y	1 month ago	Rarely	Y
Other Opiates	Y	?	Occasionally	N
Benzodiazepines	Y	2 mos. ago	Rarely	N
Barbiturates	N			
Methamphetamine	Y	One time (age 16)	0	N
Amphetamines	Y(Rx)			

To answer the question "What is the longest period of sobriety/clean time that you have had in the past five years," "10 months" is recorded, but crossed out with the word "error" by her rehab counselor Mr. Robichaud and replaced with "3 months." To the question "How has your addiction affected your family and those close to you," she answered, "recently very upset, 'it's just killing my mother.'" The clinical summary noted, "Amy's level of insight re: the need for personal change(s) is minimal. Patient seems to be underestimating the severity of disease state." The box for "very high relapse risk" was checked "high."

As we were waiting for Amy to enter the unit, she said she needed to make a phone call and stepped outside. She also used the restroom.

We watched Amy walk through the double doors into the unit around 9:10, entrusting her life to the healthcare providers we hadn't met in a setting we hadn't seen. Saying good-bye was not as wrenching as I'd expected, it simply felt like we were taking the right step. We later verified on the phone bill that the call she made was to her boyfriend Oliver. Also her medical records state that she told Triangle she last used about 9:00 a.m. that morning, so it had to be either when we stopped for coffee, when she used the bathroom in the lobby, or when she called Oliver. We never imagined she was that desperate, that sick.

Upon leaving Triangle, my husband and I drove straight to a "meet and greet" at the dog care home where River would be staying when we traveled to my hometown for Christmas. We stopped at a deli to pick up brownies to take to our dinner hosts that night. I dropped my husband at his voice recital rehearsal, came home, and updated our son. He and I drove separately to the recital so I could stop at the shoe store. Several friends and relatives attended the performance, but we said nothing about what we'd done that morning since we really didn't have a communication plan. After the recital, my husband and I stopped at the drugstore to buy Amy a phone card, sighing at the variety of unsatisfactory options. We regrouped at home, and then drove to a dinner with my start-up's co-founders and their wives. While we said not a word about Amy's situation, spending time with these people was the best thing I could have done that evening as we shared rich stories from some great years together at work. It was close to midnight when he and I began our forty-five minute drive home, ending one of the most emotionally exhausting days of our lives.

On Sunday, we hired some RPHS football players to rake our leaves; we would no longer be using Oliver or his brother for that job. I found another syringe receipt. Amy called shortly thereafter, talked about coming home for Thanksgiving and denied anything about the syringe. I talked with psychiatrist Dr. Buprine, who was shocked to hear that she had gone to detox. She hadn't told him on Monday as she had promised. Amy's psychiatrist, Dr. Adderoth, returned my call. He wished us the best, stating that Triangle was a "decent place," but said everyone gets religion and asked rhetorically if she would keep faith or lose it along the way. He reiterated, "If she's determined to use, she'll use, but if she decides to stay clean, she'll need resources." He gave us the name of a psychiatrist closer to BC.

When I straightened up Amy's bedroom that evening, I began to realize how much she had fallen apart. She had never unpacked her suitcase from when she returned from SLU almost a year prior. I found letters from her professors about being late with her clinical reports in October and failing her history class. This cleaning made it easier to find the items she would ask me to bring her during treatment. But little did I know that this exercise would make it less difficult to begin dealing with all her belongings after she died.

Our first daughter called us that night. Amy had phoned her, wanting her to convince my husband and me to choose an alternate rehab, and saying that she could get a ride home for Thanksgiving. We talked with a Triangle nurse around 10:00 p.m., who said Amy was "into" the detox. The nurse claimed that Amy "really does want it and is willing to go the length." I wondered if she had read Amy's bio-social assessment.

The Monday before Thanksgiving, I talked again with substance abuse counselor Mr. Goodruco. He described heroin injection as "the lowest of the low," the "bottom of the pile" of addiction. He introduced me to the saying that if an addict's lips are moving, they're lying. The fact that Amy couldn't sustain her performance was what addiction was, and her using minutes before entering treatment was proof of how far she had gone. He also cautioned that treatment was not fun, but neither was what she was doing. No matter where she went she would complain, he warned, but I didn't have to address the complaints. I should direct her to talk with her counselor or with him. He emphasized that the recovery was not related to how she felt: how she *thought* was the issue. That fact kept me wondering how it could be humanly possible to change six years of entrenched behavior in a nine-week program.

Mr. Goodruco had observed how Amy was used to getting her way and not used to hearing "no." Even if she had to be underhanded, she would find a way around any impediments. He told me that we needed to picture her as if she were hospitalized for a physical problem, connected to IVs and machines at one of the major teaching hospitals. He said it would be okay to clean her apartment, but we might find drug paraphernalia like needles and burn spoons, which we should throw away. He also said that once you take the drugs out of the picture, there was no reason for her to be with Oliver. He suggested we check out some Al-Anon meetings because we might have to try six or eight to find the one(s) that really worked for us. (Al-Anon meetings are twelve-step support groups for those whose loved one has an alcohol or drug problem. The addict would attend an Alcoholics Anonymous (A.A.) meeting.)

I spoke to Ms. Decelle, Amy's detox counselor, from the town library parking lot that night. She found Amy very forthcoming and cooperative, but whether that would be long lasting remained to be seen. They had had a few individual chats, and she said, "I told Amy point-blank that the

Our friend Giuliana raised the question, "Can one generalize to say that high-performing addicts are much further in their progression of the disease than is recognized by the mental health professionals?" Perhaps the analogy is how by the time some cancers are detected, it's too late to effectively treat them. Why was the severity of Amy's disease only being caught after more than five years of progressive serious-

ness? Her increasing ability to keep it hidden? The apparent lengthening of time between incidents, until her crash and burn in the fall of 2009? As Craig Nekken writes in *The Addictive Personality*, "Long before anyone suspects or knows there is a problem, many changes will have taken place deep within the addict" (p. 19).

boyfriend needed to go." Amy was medically stable without significant withdrawal symptoms. Ms. Decelle then talked about addiction as a family disease, and that we should seek some Al-Anon meetings. She raised the specter of Amy having a borderline personality disorder, and she questioned what came first—the disordered behavior patterns or the drugs.

Amy called at 5:38 that evening, and did very little complaining; however, I wish I'd made notes of that conversation, indeed *every* conversation from during her treatment. I could see from her October 31st bank statement (our accounts were still linked) that her spending had gone out of control in the month leading up to detox. She had even stopped tanning, perhaps prioritizing money for drugs. I had not questioned Amy about her pattern of coming home every weekend, but I was becoming a little suspicious of all the rides she claimed she was bumming. She had mentioned her friend Lily and a BC classmate. After she died, I questioned them: They had each driven her only once.

I spoke with Mr. Goodruco on Tuesday, who was not pleased to hear the borderline personality label being used after three days in detox. That reaction brought back memories for me of my nursing professor friend Gail's reaction to the "characterologic" label posited by Amy's first therapist, Ms. Firther. He said he never met an addict who didn't look like a borderline; they acted that way because it took a lot of work to lead a double life. I was experiencing again how even among seasoned professionals, disagreements reigned. I felt "in the middle." He and I spoke about Amy's status at BC, and it sounded like she would not be eligible to return until the summer. However, Mr. Goodruco encouraged me using data on the prognosis for nurses in recovery.

I made financial arrangements with Triangle for Amy's move to rehab on Friday. I questioned Ms. Decelle about Amy making a phone call from an unauthorized number (hail caller ID) and an unauthorized cash withdrawal (hail electronic banking linked accounts). I faxed some of Amy's history to Ms. Decelle. I could have faxed more, but she said that I should just bring the rest later, which never happened with Amy moving to rehab. I felt like my years of documenting Amy's illness were being minimized, despite how useful I thought the history would be.

Mr. Goodruco continued to liaise with the nursing school about Amy's return. While she might attend the night school in the spring, he confirmed that she definitely would not be allowed to return to the nursing program until the summer at the earliest. I began to worry about what she would do in the spring. But BC would adjust her fall tuition toward her first semester back, an unexpected generosity for which I was deeply grateful. We talked a little about her aftercare and how she would be fragile coming out of rehab and might need a transitional setting like the all-women's Circle Center. But it was "way too soon to know" and depended on how she responded, how committed she was, and how strong she would be. But so far she was doing well, although he noted that charm and lies often went together.

Mr. Goodruco also guessed that probably a half to a third of those on Suboxone sold it to buy heroin since the two drugs could be used interchangeably. A pill goes for $15, he explained, and cost the seller virtually nothing if insurance had paid, and $15 could buy three to five bags of heroin.

I was grateful that ACHS had only a half day the Wednesday before Thanksgiving. Mr. Goodruco called me with the update that Amy would be eligible to return to BC in the summer and that she should contact her dean when able. This dean saw a lot of potential in Amy, having worked with her as a transfer student, and she liked her a lot. I also received confirmation that Amy would move to Rhombus on Friday morning. That evening my husband and I watched the movie *28 Days* about the Sandra Bullock character who went to rehab for alcohol. Amy had also written her first journal entry from detox, which I found later in March:

11/25

Today is my 5th day at Triangle Treatment center. After over 6 months of progressive and tumultuous drug use I finally decided I'd been fucking up long enough and, with the help of Mr. Goodruco, told my mother about my addiction and the fact that I would not be taking the remainder of the semester off. Worst meeting of my entire life — my mother's initial anger followed by panic, grief, disappointment...

The entire week I was so excited to get sober but, then again, I had the drug in my system at the present time, not realizing the difficult work I would soon face...

I've had several great discussions with people here and a few have asked me whether or not I'm serious about getting sober. They ask, how bad do I "want it"? I'm on day 4 of protocol (aka suboxone administration) and I must say that at times, my cravings are unbearable. Some people here talked about not being "done" with their drug of choice (especially in the case of opiates), and I wonder if I'm one of those patients. I wonder if the whole reason I'm doing the 30 day program isn't to lower my tolerance or gain my mothers trust back. That's my "disease" talking.

I know how much I want and need my sober life back. I know the real Amy is inside me somewhere and I need to get her back before my life turns to complete shit. But am I willing to do the work? I'm one lazy son of a bitch and I'm going to need constant reminder of my misery in order to heal.

—Until Later—

....

Thinking back, it is striking to read her perception of my reaction at the BC meeting because I don't recall panic. To read the tension in her about her commitment to rehab is heartbreaking, as well as her concern about gaining my trust back. And I never would have called her lazy. Why did she?

On Thanksgiving morning, I started out with my running group, but then turned back after less than a mile because I was feeling so devastated about Amy. I can't even remember who among my husband's relatives at dinner knew then about where Amy was. We had limited communication with Amy that day. I was incredibly frustrated that we couldn't reach a human through the Triangle switchboard. When we finally talked, she mentioned the A.A. aftercare standard of "ninety meetings in ninety days," how there were "good and bad people in detox," and how we "caught her in time." It was a short conversation because she was being called to a meeting.

Moving to Rehab

Amy moved to Rhombus rehab on Friday, November 27th, and I learned about the family visitation program. Typically, only two family members were allowed, but the staff at Rhombus said our first daughter, who was home for Thanksgiving, could join us. We would hear from Amy's aftercare counselor soon and her primary rehab counselor in the new week, someone who specialized in young people with opiate addiction. Amy called us late afternoon, explaining the bank card charges I'd questioned: quarters for laundry, A.A. books, and postcards. It was her first day off Suboxone. She sounded more subdued than usual. We heard nothing from or about her on Saturday, but we had been led to expect that communication wouldn't be daily.

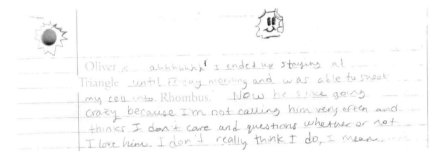

Oliver is ahhhhhh! I ended up staying at Triangle until Friday morning and was able to sneak my cell into Rhombus. Now he is like going crazy because I'm not calling him very often and thinks I don't care and questions whether or not I love him. I don't really think I do, I mean...

On Sunday, November 29th, my husband, our first daughter, River, and I drove to Rhombus for the first family visiting day. Arriving at the check-in desk, we had to sign in and agree to confidentiality. The facility felt casual and comfortable, not creepy. The staff was welcoming and professional. They inspected the items we brought for Amy. She'd called that morning to request, among other things, her black Nike zip-up jacket, jeans, Express® sweatpants, long sleeved shirts, T-shirts, socks, spandex running pants, and running bras. We also needed to pick up a prescription for her, and she wanted us to sneak in candy, which we declined to do.

Amy walked us into the cafeteria, and I felt unsure about how to acknowledge other residents and families sitting at the small round tables. At 1:00 the residents had a group meeting, and my husband, our first daughter, and

I went to the family session. The gathering time was awkward. It would have been interesting for someone to take a picture and update it a month later: the parents of the young man who would hang himself within the month, the husband and preteen daughter of the woman who would become one of Amy's closest friends and inspirations, the friends of a professional whose alcoholism would relapse within days of leaving rehab, the girlfriend of the young man who would be diagnosed with Hepatitis C, the parent and sibling of the girl who would discover Amy overdosed in the bathroom.

The session focused on signs and symptoms we saw in the addict, then in their loved ones. The more traits we added to the lists, the more they overlapped: changes in sleep, appetite, hygiene, and interests, as well as the emotions of fear, helplessness, frustration, and a sense of loss. I was struck by how both lying and a double life were common to the addict and the loved ones. Given how I wasn't sharing Amy's illness with most people, by not telling the whole truth wasn't I, too, living a double life?

We addressed post-rehab practicalities, such as making sure the living quarters to where they returned were cleaned out of any alcohol or drugs, and that the addict attend ninety meetings in ninety days. We were also told to think of rehab as a gift and Rhombus as providing a safe environment.

We went over the 4 "Cs" for families, something reinforced in Al-Anon and Nar-Anon:

- We did not CAUSE the addiction. The addict *will* thank us for supporting rehab.
- We can't CONTROL the addiction. We *can* encourage the addict to get everything they can from rehab. It's a once-in-a-lifetime experience that many don't want to leave, and they want to return. (After all, the alternatives to being in rehab are jail, institutions, or death.) We were not told anything about relapse rates, just the acronym Sobriety Lost Its Priority, and that people can be "sectioned" by the courts for mandated help.
- We can't CURE. Addiction is a fatal disease that can kill people (but this statement didn't resonate, given all the positive indicators we heard in Amy's case).
- We have to COMMUNICATE. We would meet with the addict and their counselors.

We were told that alcohol lowers inhibitions and therefore can return addicts to their drug of choice, so they could never drink in safety. (I committed to abstain from alcohol in solidarity, at least through Amy's treatment.) We were urged to keep expectations low and acceptance high. If the 2:30 to 4:00 p.m. visit with our loved one wasn't going well, we could leave. If we heard complaints, we should listen but not argue. With Christmas coming, the residents would be safe at Rhombus, missing the holidays one time to enjoy them the rest of their lives. We were cautioned to notify all medical providers that our addict was in recovery, and they should not receive any mood-altering prescriptions.

We met Amy back in the cafeteria, and then my husband and I gave our daughters time alone while we walked River. Our first daughter was impressed at how Amy drew a diagram of how her life could take two directions: upward or downward. Amy slipped us a note as we left, written in pink marker on her quintessential pink construction paper, folded into ninths:

11/29/09

Dear Mom, Dad

Thanks so much for coming to visit me today. I'm still feeling sort of crappy and the "comfort medications" only make me tired, so I apologize for not being more upbeat. Things should be much better by the next time I see you all I hope everything is going okay back home — it hurts me to see the disappointment and sadness in your eyes ‿ I just want you to know that I'm constantly missing and thinking of you but, more importantly, I'm doing a lot of introspection, and taking in all that Triangle has to offer. I feel like I'm already at a much better place (mentally) than I was and, although I have much more work to do, I have a positive outlook regarding the future. I could not have asked for a more supportive family and I truly, from the bottom of my heart, appreciate all that you continue to do for me. I am in the right hands — these guys seem to know what they're talking about! So just keep sending your prayers and blessings and I'll continue doing the work I need to be doing here. I love you all so so much and I am incredibly grateful for your love + effort. Please don't hesitate to bring anything up with me if you want to talk!

I love you all ‿y much!

♡ Amy

....

I was encouraged by her confidence in the staff and her willingness to be open. However, my husband noted after reading this manuscript that, "So many times we wanted to believe we were turning a corner, because she was saying all the right things. But addiction can make someone say the right things, so they can get enough freedom to find more drugs. I still wonder how many of the sentiments in her beautiful letters were real, and how much was an effort to put us at ease. With Amy so divided, I have to think: some of each."

On Monday, after putting our first daughter on the airport bus to return to her college town, I attended my first Al-Anon meeting. I wasn't sure it was the right one for me. We did not hear from Amy on Tuesday, but in talking with an aftercare counselor, she acknowledged the devastation that addiction wreaks on families and recommended individual counseling for our first daughter given how shattered she was about what was happening to her little sister. Amy's counselor would be away until Wednesday. I still questioned why Amy turned to drugs, even wondering if she had experienced an earlier trauma. For most kids, "life sucks" was the reason. Was self-esteem the root cause of her addictive behaviors? Why had there been issues with her separating from Oliver? Could he be a threat to her, or to our family?

We heard from her for about thirty seconds that day, but she journaled:

Rhombus Rehab   Day 5 ⇒ Days clean: 11 .

I don't know what I want. All I know is that I'm
sick of acting like a hypocrit and leading a double life.
I have this boyfriend who I tell I love just about
every 5 minutes but I tell all my friends and family
that I don't want anything to do with him. Truthfully,
I know that it's just about over between Oliver and
I - he just doesn't stimulate me intellectually,
emotionally, sexually... I mean a year and a half of
faking it?   How much can I take, really? Haha,
but on a more serious note, I'm scared shitless of
being alone and without somebody to talk to every
time I'm happy, sad, desperate, crazy... I'm terrified of
facing the world without him by my side. That,
however, gives me all the more reason to break up with
him after the separation that rehab will provide. Now that
I'm sober, I see absolutely no value in being with him.
I now understand why he didn't push me to go
to treatment - why he even helped me get drugs when
he knew how addicted I was - heroin was the shield
over my eyes - the glue that kept Oliver and I
together for 6 months longer than I ever should
have been with him. And worst of all, I've spent
the last year and a half focusing all my

AC ♡ ?

Topic for Robichaud
↳ self ♡

energies on Oliver instead of Myself. I really need to work on introspection and self love because I honestly can't go 2 minutes without feeling insecure, out of place, obligated... Is it possible that I'm 20 years old and still haven't figured out who I am? Seriously, I know that my favorite color is purple, I love chocolate and the drums, but even the things I love can change based on who I'm talking to. I'm a people pleasing, unsure, inconfident young woman - the worst type of being. And this is only getting worse by my actions → the fact that I'm a nursing student shooting heroin in the hospital bathroom, the fact that I'm dating a guy I absolutely loathe... I need to grow up and face all these internal battles that have been suppressed from 2 straight years of opiate use. But I'm scared shitless and I don't know if I can do it. My body's aching for any type of drug to take me away from the reality I'll soon need to face. I've already devised a plan to get drugs both when I leave here and during my stay (through an "appointment") - how sick is that? I sure have a lot of shit to figure out. I'm still completely numb to emotion - can't cry, can't laugh... NUMB. I spoke to the shrink here and about 2 minutes into the conversation he goes "less than 50% of opiate addicts survive the disease" "More than likely, you will die from it" ♪ I survive! can you believe that? he kept rambling about the % of people staying (clean - even half of opiate addict die as a direct consequence of use) blah - scary stuff but the weirdest thing is,

it didn't scare me. I'm still so numbed by the drugs that I can't even take something like that seriously. Ay yai yai ... I need to get better ♥ Amy

We had no idea she was in such pain with such ambivalence. It certainly didn't come up in my first conversation with Amy's rehab counselor, Mr. Robichaud, on the 3rd. He said she was "in a really good place, where she belongs" and was owning that she was a heroin addict and had it "pretty bad." He encouraged her to be honest with us, and she agreed to do so; however, there was no need to share the "gory details." He said he thought she liked him and they were forming a good therapeutic alliance. He thought that if she did all the work and produced, she could be home the day before Christmas, although they hadn't even approached aftercare.

I poked around online and read the August 17, 1999 Salon.com articles by Seth Mnookin, "Harvard and Heroin," and Wendy Mnookin, "My Son the Heroin Addict." I needed to know that we weren't the only well-educated family to have a child with this disease. We did not hear from Amy that day, but she journaled:

12/3/09

Day 6 off Suboxone completed. Starting to feel better. One significant thing today—I was moved from the room I was staying in (a double with a private bathroom) because according to the staff, Marta and I "need some space." I don't know what that's all about because me and her weren't even that close. I mean, we talked about our relationships and other stuff and got along just fine. My initial reaction was that Marta asked for me to be moved and that thought is still prying at the back of my mind—she didn't react very strongly when I mentioned the room change in women's group and even went as far as to say "oh well I have fun by myself anyways." Then she's just been M. I. A. all night. It's so hard to read this girl, but why am I focusing my energies on her anyways? Maybe this move is for the best....
I can't tell if it's my self esteem beating me down or if Marta is just acting weird. I have a feeling both our low self-esteems contribute to the awkwardness between us (ever since I figured out she likes girls I haven't been able to strike up conversation or even look in her direction w/out feeling awkward). I think it's fear of rejection and wondering about each other's opinions that's caused the slow, nervous beginnings. Agh I'm so confused tho b/c we had such a good conversation the other night for like 4 hours.

Wow...see, this is why it might be a good idea to separate us. I obv. care too much about being liked and not enough about my sobriety...more on her later…I'm just terrified b/c this girl Claire I met at detox comes to Rhombus tomorrow and I'm scared those 2 will branch out leaving me alone. Oh well, I need to let go of these anxieties and just let fate handle it. AAGH. Feeling emotionally absent—numb. I don't know if this is because of the heroin, the withdrawals, or maybe the fact that I haven't been focusing? Or Maybe I've just forgotten how to experience feelings. Either way, I'm at a total emotionall (sic) plateau. _____ (the only _____ dude here) told me to look at it as a "balance" instead of numbness, and to appreciate my mood swing absence. It's all about how you look at it …

> *Till later,*
>
>   *Amy*

....

Reading this entry now, it is agonizing to read how, in addition to the conflicted feelings about her drug use, the close quarters of rehab introduced its overlay of sexual tension. And Amy, whom everyone loved, was terrified about whether she'd be liked. Her insight about self-esteem shows how that issue was still following her since being diagnosed six years prior.

Amy called on Friday, and I wrote in my notes that she sounded "good, strong, committed." But she was telling her journal so much that she wasn't telling us or her counselors.

Saturday was a blur, and on Sunday, December 6th, my husband and I decided to "mix it up" on our trip to visit Amy. We had River stay at dog care since we learned we weren't supposed to bring pets to Rhombus even if we left them in the car. Of course Amy thought we were being ridiculous about following that rule, insisting that everyone else brought dogs. We did a little Christmas shopping, then stopped for lunch at a quaint local diner. Then we attended the second family session, which focused on relapse and recovery.

During the session, we learned that addiction's job was to divide, conquer, and distract. For the first time, we heard that only one-third in rehab were sober a year later, and two-thirds needed a repeat of an inpatient program. Insight and intellect, they told us, do not necessarily equate to successful recovery and change.

In the hour with Amy that followed, she seemed "a bit reserved," alleged that I was trying to be too controlling, and said in the earshot of the counselors something about smuggling in chocolate. She was still talking about being discharged on Christmas Eve.

On Monday, I was feeling "tired and irritable, too much to do." I mailed Amy the socks I forgot to bring her the day before; she did not call. My husband and I attended our first Nar-Anon meeting, which seemed to meet our needs.

Amy journaled:

12-7-09

Out of Marta's room into a single, then moved back into the room w/ this girl Claire (not the girl I thought but wicked sweet). Lots of thoughts still revolve around a certain someone here. She was asking Oliver why I switched too! Mixed signals. HIV and Hep C tests came back negative! _____ got Hep tho ☹

Night,

Amy

....

I was struck by the exclamation point about the test results because, as a nursing student, Amy was well aware of the disease risks she faced. But her "double life" caused her to take risks despite her knowledge.

Tuesday brought the specter of a snow day on Wednesday. Amy started writing in her brown journal:

"But though they may be parted, there is still a chance that they will see … there will be an answer, Let It Be"

—The Beatles

12-8-09

I feel like the drugs have taken over my soul. What happened to the strong, motivated young woman I was last spring? The impending doom sets in as I realize my disease has never been this bad. Thinking back to the near end of my "sober" 10-½ months, I remember fiening [sic] for a fix to change pace from the Suboxone monotony, but because I was nearly finished with school for the year I told myself to wait. I can't help but think that this run up was planned and expected, but I have no idea when I planned to stop. Maybe before fall semester? Maybe never … Drugs have been my plan, my sole coping skills, for 6 years now. At the beginning of this last run I still had my head on straight. I had the aftertaste of sobriety reminding me that I didn't need to live the way I was. I truly thought I would only use for a short period, then get back to my normal life. But as the use increased, my control quickly diminished, and, once into the "chronic" stage of my addiction, I lost sight of what was most important to me. I stand today as heroin's puppet, feeling as if every fiber in my being is dull, responding only to the stimulation of potential drug use. The disease has a stronghold—a white-knuckled fist, fingernails, ripping through my skin, prying deeper and deeper into my body. I wonder what I can possibly do to break free from it's [sic] grasp and remember the life I used to love and show up for.

17 days clean today. Seventeen! Crazy because I know if I was out there I would have gotten high just about every day. Starting to get scared about leaving here—what I'm going to do, what my life will be like. My fear isn't big enough though. I'm scared my disease won't let me go....
....

I wish Amy could have shared this pain with someone who could have helped. But was there anybody?

I set my alarm for 4:30 a.m. so I could leave the house earlier due to inevitable complications the storm would wreak on the ACHS work program. The principal did not declare a snow day, but some students would not be able to get to school so they could go to their jobs, some employers would shut down, traffic would be snarled, and so on. By then, Amy had written:

12-9

Just finished Day 17 and am sitting in bed at 12:45 am on Dec 9ᵗʰ. Got another 23h 15 min to go. ONE DAY AT A TIME! Talking to Oliver less and plan to break up with him on Thursday. I'm terrified, but have never felt more ready

"Though they may be parted, there is still a chance that they will see, there will be an answer, Let it Be"

I need to do this now, while I still have the support of the wonderful people here. If I leave here, 1 of 3 things will happen:

1. *I'll relapse instantly and stay w/ him*

2. *I'll dump him and then relapse to deal w/ the stress*

3. *I'll stay clean but be too weak to dump him*

Most likely, I'd take option #1 real fast. So I realized the need to break things off while I'm still here, but I don't think he has any idea. The family counselor is going to come help me do it when Oliver comes here on Thursday. I have plans for him to sneak something in but he doesn't know it yet and I don't think it would be the best idea. Although, I could probably do that and have "just 1." OMGosh, please Lord save me from the grips of this disease. I keep telling myself how much things will change once I'm without Oliver. I hope it's true…

> *Amy*

It is terrifying to read the insight Amy had into her dilemma, and how her double life continued to plague her in rehab.

I talked briefly with Mr. Goodruco, who said the aftercare plan didn't have to happen for a while. He reminded me that Amy's work had only just begun, and it would be nice if Rhombus could talk her into Circle Center so she had more time away from home and could reorient her priorities. If she didn't want to go, we should try to persuade her, but not at all costs. At her age, it was tough knowing where she would fit in. Other students at her college went to twelve-step meetings, he said, and Amy was lucky: Although she was on medical leave, she would be allowed on campus because she did *not* have concomitant disciplinary issues. He added that she would be more than welcome to continue working with him as part of the aftercare.

Later that day, I left a message with Amy's aftercare counselors that we hadn't heard from Amy or Mr. Robichaud since Sunday, and it was already late Wednesday.

12-9-09

Woke up to snow and a beautiful view from the backyard. It's so gorgeous outside, and the weather is one of a million things I should appreciate today. I know I need to change my attitude but have no idea how to do it. It's sort of hard when every neuron in my brain in some way magnets to the idea of heroin.

I can't even get an ounce of information through my head without an interruption from the Heroin PSA – Am I f---ed? I can't help but think YES. I feel like everyone who has successfully quit dope has used the disgusting, desperate low of their "rock bottom" to mirror in their recovery – to not only motivate their sobriety, but to have a very high standard for which to reflect the quality of my recovery work.

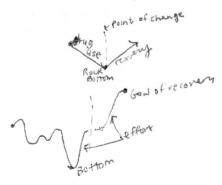

So in my mind I'm well aware of where my drug use will lead → the effect on my body and soul, the consequences on my family and my life and my future. I've been told exactly what will happen if I go out again. But just like they say, you can't scare an addict. I think there's a reason the professionals say hitting a bottom is necessary—I can imagine the dangers and the consequences all day long but if I've never lived it, if my brain can't feel or actually place me in that cardboard box on the side of the road eating out of a trash bag, then how the f--- is that supposed to scare me out of using?

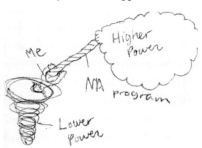

I feel like at my lowest point, I had lost money, trust, friends and school, and put just about everything on the line (I would have lost them had I been out there, right now). But I didn't actually lose some things. I always had a place to live, a meal, a lover, the support of my parents. As I look into the rearview mirror of my life, I see the

destruction, but I also see a liveable [sic] life. If I could hang out doing dope every day while still doing my thing and semi-handling sh--, then what motivation have I to live the same life without my beloved heroin, feeling all the pain and struggles of everyday life? So I know these obvious, straightforward concepts, but I can't get them all the way through my brain, through the barbed wire fence my addiction has built.

In the group I'm in right now, the counselor spoke about a girl on methadone maintenance who claimed "this sobriety thing isn't all it's cracked up to be." I'm having a hard time w/ this as well. It's like because I'm sober, everybody (including myself) expected me to suddenly wake up and "see the light." But I'm still navigating my way out of my tunnel. I just experienced a revelation regarding my progress and sobriety. So, the first step claims that your life has become unmanageable as a result of your addiction. I think I'm having a lot of trouble with this step, possibly regarding the higher nature of my bottom, but more because of the success I seemed to have with the Suboxone maintenance. For a year and a half I was able to live a normal, manageable life while every day taking an opiate. My body is used to feeding its most extreme desire all day every day, while still going to school, keeping up relationships, having money, and every- thing else. Though I was in no way <u>LIVING</u> the life I could be, I was "successfully" keeping up a habit for a long period of time. Now my disease is trying to trick me into thinking I can do the same with heroin. Until I let go of this and accept the inevitable undebatable truth, I'll <u>never</u> get clean. In order to beat this disease I need to do one crucial thing: outsmart myself.

The fact that Amy realized she had to "outsmart herself" was incred- ible. Nobody doubted her intelligence. But addiction doesn't care about your IQ.

That night, Amy called to say she'd broken up with Oliver. I lauded her. She called her sister to have her change her Facebook relationship status and password. Her sister told Amy how proud she was of her, how there were thousands of Olivers out there, but she was one in a million. Amy said, "Thanks sistah, that means a lot."

12-9-09 = My official sober date from Oliver. It's now a little past midnight and I'm still feeling the high from breaking things off. I don't know if it's because of the withdrawals or because I was just so ready, but for some reason I don't feel upset or scared by this breakup. I'm so free and no longer a possession of Oliver's. He was bawling, sobbing, begging. I felt nothing ...

I feel as if ... I lost my train of thought. PROUD OF MYSELF. That took balls, kid.

On the 10th, I spoke with Amy's aftercare counselor. She said that the team would make a recommendation that they hoped my husband and I would support, and Amy would say either yes or no. She said we were lucky to find a twelve-step meeting we liked so quickly. Amy had visited Circle Center and was not thrilled. At work, a vice president came into my group's office area to challenge one of our tracking systems. I felt like I was in a parallel universe. I only attended part of the staff Christmas lunch and forsook the Yankee Swap. I really did have a cold and was in no shape for yucking it up. When I left the office, I thought I lost my cell phone and our administrator kindly retraced my steps looking for it. It ended up being in my gym bag on the car seat next to me and didn't ring when called. I took that incident as a sign of major stress.

On Friday, I spoke with Amy's primary rehab counselor, Mr. Robichaud, whom we were told was the best person for young opiate addicts. He stated that Amy needed to go straight from rehab to transitional housing. He had been telling her this since day one and would not consider an alternative. He convinced her to tour Circle Center, and she really didn't have anything to say except that she was not going. It was the best women's program in the state, and, as part of Triangle, they would have access to her records and the aftercare workers. He didn't think an outpatient program near BC was really in the cards. He gave her difficult things to think about. He would accept a thirty-day commitment, but it would probably turn into sixty days. He emphatically stated that Circle Center would "make or break" her recovery, and "when using the amount of drugs she took, it takes a while for the brain to settle down." She wrote:

12-?

Visited Circle Center w/ Marta. The place was nice, but I'm wary about being around 30 freakin women all the time. Marta isn't too thrilled to be going on Monday. As the breakup and the lack of drugs become more of a reality, I realize how freaking scared I am to face the world. I feel as if I can't talk to anyone and I'm out of place everywhere I go. When I'm out in society I feel like this evil, two sided bitch because of my secret heroin addiction. When I'm in rehab I feel like I don't fit in w/ the junkies because I was never selling my ass or getting arrested or living in the streets. I think what it comes down to is that I can't fully commit to one thing a) because I'm so interested/see the benefits in many things and b) I'm scared I'll never be good enough if I put all my effort into 1 thing.

....

So where does a high-performing addict go for effective treatment? The counselors will say that it doesn't matter who you're with because you all have the same disease. But Amy's agony of not fitting in anywhere makes me wonder if there might have been a facility with a "better" fit.

My husband and I braved the Friday night cold to attend a "Nutcracker" performance at a local college. On Saturday, the 12th, I reviewed the year's monthly letters to develop the year's highlights for the back of our annual Christmas photo card.

I also received a call from Oliver, and he talked for more than half an hour. Amy wouldn't lie, he said, but she wasn't telling the whole truth. He claimed that when they met they were doing drugs, but they stopped, and "it was awesome" until three months ago. He didn't know what happened or how bad she was into drugs. They were fighting more and more, and he was trying to lecture her. He told her if she had urges to call him first. He tried to bring her to a few A.A. meetings, he claimed, but she wouldn't go. While he stressed they needed to be open and honest, she was doing drugs for one to two months and he had no idea. He kept asking, and she kept avoiding. She swore to him she wasn't doing anything, but when they went out people were asking, "Is your girlfriend okay?" He didn't want to believe she was using, but one day he knew she was lying, and she didn't admit how bad it was. He knew she was talking to people he didn't know about selling, and kids were calling her. He told her to stop answering the calls and erase their numbers and messages. He emphasized that dealers weren't her friends, and she didn't know what they'd do to her. He claimed that the temper our first daughter saw was his anger about Amy not cleaning up the drug paraphernalia everywhere, even when he came to see her. He told her she had to be stronger. "If only she could realize just how good her life is."

He told me he cared about her, wanted to be there for her, wanted her to get better, and really wanted her to do well. He thought her self-confidence was increasing. He said he hoped she got rid of her cravings because, "It will kill her in the end if she doesn't stop." Her use wasn't a joke, he said. She had to take it seriously, and he'd tried to tell her "a million times" how great she was in so many ways. "Every day she does drugs, life doesn't get better." He could see that when she was doing drugs she wasn't the same person at all. Half the time she was falling asleep, he said, and she would avoid telling him things, finding a way to not lie, but not telling the truth. He added that when he learned what Amy was up to, he urged her to get through the semester. Soon after that, it was clear she was not doing well and could not finish. The last two weeks before detox, she wouldn't even play catch, and she wasn't happy. The first week in treatment she asked him to bring her drugs, and she became mad when he wouldn't sneak them in. He told her he was upset that she wanted drugs more than she wanted to see him or get well.

The conversation reminded me of the saying, "There are three sides to every story: yours, mine, and the truth." While there were certainly kernels of truth in what he said (if repetitive), and he sounded sincere, others told me I was only being duped again.

On Sunday, the 13th, I wrote "tough morning, feeling all sorts of anger/upset with Amy." I must have been feeling hijacked by her again, torn by having to give up six hours on a Sunday to visit her, while feeling committed to her recovery. The family session included her that week; the topic was communication. Our son drove down from the city to join us.

While there, we received a message from Mr. Goodruco for Amy that "Circle Center is a good idea." She had left him a message the night before, and he said it sounded like she was doing real well. He wholeheartedly agreed with her going to the residential treatment house. She was already on leave from school, he noted, "So let's use the time as best we can." He suggested she consider it "grad school" for recovery, adding, "No bad will come of it." He believed she'd learn more about how to stay sober, and she needed time to solidify her recovery rather than having it tested too quickly being at home. "If you cut corners, you'll start to go backwards and relapse will be more likely."

On Monday, I was very touched that the principal agreed to reschedule our weekly team meeting so I could attend it before leaving for the meeting with Amy's counselors on Wednesday. I was also noticing how I was loving the changes to my posture as a result of my personal training, and the forty-five minute sessions with my former student felt more therapeutic than the time I'd spent with other counselors. I spoke with Mr. Goodruco and shared some of the Oliver conversation. He hoped Amy and Oliver would not reconnect. He thought she seemed to have moved on. He reaffirmed that any amount of time at Circle Center was good, but more was better. My husband and I attended our second Nar-Anon meeting, and we received affirmations about Rhombus from others whose qualifier had been there.

On Tuesday, I attended a meeting at HBS and then saw our son. Amy called and said to take no more calls from Oliver. Someone cautioned me that he was trying to play the hero. Amy wrote:

12-15-09

<u>*RESERVATIONS*</u>

- *Losing my connect and, therefore, getting strong urges to use*

- *Drinking w/ my college friends and the "party life"—esp. on my 21ˢᵗ bday*

- *I'll miss the RUSH and warm tingly "everything is okay" feeling*

- *Blunt rides w/ the homies*

- *The heroin weight loss program*

- *I'm young and might 'have another run in me'*

- *Needle addiction—fear of relapse and using a dirty needle—so why not keep some of my own around just in case?*

On Wednesday, I left work at noon, collected my husband at work, and we drove to Rhombus for a 2:30 meeting with Amy, Mr. Robichaud, and an aftercare counselor. I had summarized "the big picture" on one sheet of paper to remind me of my questions, concerns, and quotes from others. Amy was playful and positive. The proposal was for her to go to Circle Center for at least thirty days. She was intent on finishing in time for her twenty-first birthday and moving back to her apartment, enrolling in an outpatient day program, attending ninety meetings in ninety days, finding a job, and taking a night class or two. She gave no hint whatsoever about her reservations, her ambivalence, her torment.

On Thursday, I inquired about two foster dogs, enjoyed some really productive work on the strategic planning committee with the principal and dean of students, and tutored one of my former students in math. Mr. Robichaud called to announce that Amy decided to go to Circle Center, though she was thinking only thirty days despite his hope for sixty. "But half a loaf is better than none," he said. She would be able to use a local gym for a fee. We could continue our Sunday visits, but eventually she could earn passes. We would have to pay up front for thirty days, nonrefundable (though after she died they refunded her unused days without us even asking).

On Friday, the 18th, I left a message for Mr. Robichaud asking where Amy stood with Hepatitis C and HIV, and her overall prognosis, given the specifics of what was in her favor and her risk factors. He shared that the tests were negative, and his prognosis was that she had it "really bad," and this *wasn't* a phase. Don't press her for details, he suggested (as he said on December 3rd), but she was an IV addict who "got it good." Her minimum time in Circle Center should be sixty days, and that could go to six months; the standard used to be six months to a year. We would do recovery planning on Sunday, including some of the names she should stay away from, with Oliver at the top. She had deleted messages from him and his mother without listening to them. If she started heading back toward her "friends," we were to call Mr. Robichaud. She would move at 7:30 on Monday morning, be assigned a new counselor, but we would still have full access to him going forward. Later that day, I tutored again, picked up our annual Christmas chocolate order, and Amy called. I did not record any details of the conversation, perhaps because it felt like we were in a small lull from the crisis.

On Saturday, I dressed festively for my running group's annual "Jingle Run." I recited the seventieth birthday poem I wrote for one of my buddies. Writing those nineteen stanzas was a creative outlet that helped me cope with the ordeal of recent weeks. My husband and I learned that, due to an impending storm, the Sunday sessions at Rhombus were canceled; we had been planning to work on Amy's aftercare plan.

I enjoyed the "bonus" Sunday, rationalizing that we'd seen Amy on Wednesday, and we'd be seeing her in a few days on Christmas. Meanwhile, she wrote:

12-20-09

It's snowing! Beautiful, wisping [sic], white, fluffy snow. Chilling in my Room w/ my amazing roomie Claire. Good meeting tonight—I saw ___ w/ his [new hairdo] and sense of humor, ____, ____ (his glf can't have an abortion b/c she's [further along than] they thought), ____ (this sweet girl who has really reached out to me)... ____ and ____ got their 30 day keychains! My feelings about sobriety and over-all morale boost when I'm around people at NA and AA that I can talk to, even for just a minute. I need to make sure socializing and people don't make up my recovery, or become new addictions.

DON'T JUST KNOW. APPLY.

— Amy

....

Amy was just starting to taste the twelve steps.

Moving to Residential Treatment

Our first daughter came home on Monday, December 21st, and Amy moved to Circle Center. In a long conversation with Mr. Goodruco during which I took two pages of notes, he expounded that an addict has to lie because they have a completely different agenda. They lie for a living, lose track, and have to lie to take care of lies. All the ingrained patterns have to be relearned. People in residential treatment call each other out. No one is as good at telling another addict that they're full of it as another addict. Since Amy was doing drugs for so long, her maturity level had been hindered, and the longer she stayed at Circle Center, the more reinvented she was going to become. He reiterated that there was no reason to think she couldn't suc-ceed, despite the fact that she was not a college kid experimenting. She had applied all her skills, intelligence, and potential to her addiction and had become too good at it. She knew how to be the sweet, innocent college girl when you first met her, but she wasn't as wily as she thought she was. She had yet to lose a job, go to jail, or be involved in the courts, so she was not genuinely streetwise, and she was still seeing herself as "not that bad."

He also said that it was difficult to find exactly the right setting for those around twenty years old. They were too old to be with adolescents, and adults in rehab with her would tend to be protective. Amy seemed to be afraid of her father's judgment, of being cut off, but that fear was irrelevant. He had told her that staying clean was important because it was better for *herself*, not for others. She was no longer having fun, and with the right degree of treatment, a relapse would not be fun, either.

He believed Amy was motivated to obtain help, but it had taken weeks of pushing to make her more willing. When things started falling apart, she was able to do it. Suboxone was an attempt to do the right thing. He reassured me that the daughter of mine who was a good person still existed, but the addict took over. When you had cravings and you were physically ill and you knew what would stop them, it was rough to deal with. She was doing much better than others he had dealt with and she was not threatening to leave. "Everything really is pretty good." If things weren't going well, he said, we'd be hearing more from Mr. Robichaud.

The conversation then took a chilling tone as he reminded me that we were dealing with a deadly disease, and we should be worrying about Amy being alive and clean, *not* about school. Other plans were nice, but it was essential she be drug-free. School could happen when she was ready, "If she's alive to tell, rather than dead or diseased," he said. But the situation was tricky because she looked good and sounded good, but she was just as sick as someone who was bandaged and on machines. But people get better, he assured me, and she was in one of the best places.

Amy's wrote her last journal entry that night:

12-21-09

Moved to the Circle Center today with my roomie Claire. Lots of cool people here, but I was getting anxious and depressed worrying about making friends.

I'm starting to realize just how sick I am. I read a pamphlet about self-acceptance from NA that read "Because we could not accept ourselves, we expected to be rejected by others. We would not allow anyone to get close to us for fear that if they really knew us, they would also hate us."

I'm terrified of rejection because I despise myself so much. My whole life I've been trying to be or act like someone else, anyone else. Why can't I just be?

My disease is controlling 90% of the thoughts that are going through my head. It tells me that I shouldn't be here. I won't fit in. Everyone hates me. I'll never beat the cravings.

It tells me that I can't recover without reaching a rock bottom. That jail might be the turning point that sets me straight. It has me scheming about ways to make money like selling my body, dating my drug dealer, stripping, robbing houses, selling back my textbooks and other belongings. It tells me I have a whole new world of drug addiction to experience before I can really make an effort to get clean. It assures me that relapses are part of recovery.

My disease pounds self loathing and insecurity into my mind. It perpetually reminds me that I have a big nose, I'm getting fat, I'm awkward and weird. I'm never going to make it in the world.

Worst of all, it tries to convince me that I don't have a disease but am simply going through a phase. It tells me that anyone who tries heroin will become addicted, so how can I be singled out as one of these addicts. It tells me I managed to handle all my drug use before, so why can't it work with heroin?

COME ON AMY, JUST INDULGE AND PICK UP ONE MORE TIME.

NO! I've noticed my thoughts are very negative lately. I've been fantasizing about overdosing for a quick, painless death and telling myself I'd be doing everyone a favor (including myself).

I'm sick.

I'm weak.

Need Help.

But do I really want it?

— Amy (and her disease)

....

It seems like only Amy had any idea about the depth of her torment and pain. How striking that she refers to anxiety and depression, two of the diagnoses in her neuropsychological testing during ninth grade that everyone seemed to lose focus about in the ensuing years. Her references to symptoms of low self-esteem also indicate that years of psychological counseling to address that issue had ultimately failed. And while the Sheff book kept repeating the mantra "relapse is part of recovery," and the Rhombus family programs talked about the reality of multiple relapses, from nowhere did I internalize the stark probability that sometimes relapse meant death.

On Tuesday, I was feeling happy with my fitness training progress, and enjoying my increasing time on the elliptical machine. Amy and I enjoyed sharing stories about our workout progress, although she was frustrated that her sessions often ended by eating too many munchkins from Dunkin' Donuts®.

Wednesday, December 23rd, was a half day at work before Christmas vacation. I figured out the transportation for the twenty or so student job changes happening in January. I distributed our annual Christmas photo card, and my boss bounded into my office, exclaiming, "Oh my God! Your family is beautiful." I quietly thanked her, while saying to myself, "Can *you* tell which one is the heroin addict?" I bought a half-baked pizza from my favorite shop across the street so I wouldn't go through withdrawal from my daily slice, which brought a quizzical smile to the owner's face. I had my fitness assessment and learned that, since starting on November 6th, I had lost about six pounds of body fat. I had my first talk with Amy's Circle Center counselor, Ms. Underwood. She told me that a stipulation of Amy's Christmas pass was for her to attend an A.A. meeting, not call old "friends," and that I drive her both ways. She said to save discussion of Amy's August speeding ticket, which she planned to appeal in court, for our family meeting on December 31st. Our son made good on his promise to rehang the Christmas lights on the family room windows.

On Christmas Eve, I worked out at 10:30 a.m., and then delivered my family's traditional pastry to neighbors. My husband and I cut down a tree and put on one ornament, the one I'd just received from my boss. We knew Amy would be outraged that we hadn't decorated the tree, but she always spearheaded the decorating. We went to church at 11:15 p.m. for "Lessons and Carols," where my husband sang and I read as usual, followed by midnight Mass. We saw so many families together that our children had grown up with. I acutely felt Amy's absence and questioned in my diary, "Are we pariahs because of Amy?"

On Christmas Day, my husband and I left around 7:00 a.m. for Circle Center. Driving back, Amy told us how one of the young men with whom she was in rehab apparently committed suicide the week after he was released. We had sat next to him at the communications meeting less than two weeks prior. I thought back with sadness to how all of us sitting in that first family meeting were vulnerable, but never imagining that my family would be next.

We drove straight to my husband's relatives' home, where everyone hugged the usual greetings despite everyone knowing this Christmas *wasn't* usual. The annual brunch fare was comfortingly familiar, including a cinnamon bundt sour cream coffee cake, smoked salmon, and the traditional family cookies. But in observance of Amy's incipient recovery, our host had agreed to serve orange juice and tomato juice in lieu of mimosas and bloody Marys. Amy seemed so happy to be among family, although she spent much of the time on the sofa in the family room, and I thought she might be texting but didn't intervene. She later expressed appreciation at how accepting her relatives had been and how they had tried to make the day as normal as possible. The five of us drove home and opened presents. Our first daughter and my husband snapped a photo of Amy, with Christmas lights in the background. Amy's gift to us was a card with the note:

My dearest family,

This Christmas season has been unlike past holidays and unfortunately this means I wasn't able to acquire gifts for you. I wish the circumstances were different but, as you all know, I'm working hard to improve the most important thing of all: my

Warm Christmas Wishes

health. Though I have nothing material to give, I can promise to bring my love, my gratitude and (of course) my sobriety. I look forward to the time I'll be spending with you over Christmas and will surely treasure each moment we share as a family.

Thanks for all your love and support throughout these last few months. It's meant the world to me.

I LOVE YOU ALL SO MUCH!

XOXO
Amy

She also posted on Facebook at 2:11 p.m.: "Amy Caruso home for the day ~ SO grateful and blessed to be with my loved ones! merry christmas :)"

I drove her to Canalboro for her 3:00 p.m. A.A. meeting, where she told us one of her friends was speaking at the "alcathon." She asked me for $10 so she could go out for coffee. I collected her promptly at 4:30, and she was waiting for me with a small bouquet of roses from a street vendor. Our son called and wanted to have dinner in town, so we hurried to tie up administrative loose ends. I had Amy pay her electric bill from my laptop, and she made a list of the people to whom I would give the seven remaining boxes of chocolates she had ordered. Amy wanted to stop by her apartment to pick up some items, which I had planned to do with her, but we were crunched for time and agreed that our son could do so after dinner on the way back to Circle Center.

My husband, the girls, and I left around 5:20 p.m. to drive into the city, and our son walked the mile from his apartment to meet us at the restaurant for a wonderful Indian meal. Amy was delighted with her mango lassies, spiced ice cream, and chicken tikka, eschewing the onions and forking them over to her sister. She made one trip to the bathroom which was not long. My husband made a point to look at her pupils to make sure they were not constricted. I was nervous about Amy making it back to Circle Center on time. I had thought about asking the waiters to take a family photo, but I didn't have a camera and didn't assert myself to see if others had. I thought about using my cell phone, but rationalized that the quality would be too poor. According to our Visa receipt, we charged our bill at 7:09.

We all drove back to our son's apartment parking lot and said our good-byes. My last words to Amy were, "I love you, be safe." I was feeling anxious about them driving in the Miata given the weather, but our son assured me they'd be okay. I had told him he could not let Amy out of his sight when they stopped at her apartment.

I finally relaxed once I knew our son was home safely. My husband and I reflected on how well the day had gone. In fact, it felt almost too good to be true. Amy was sober, happy, and had written us that beautiful note in her Christmas card. That night, I was too fried to work on our annual charitable contributions, figuring I'd have to blitz through them on the 30th upon our return from my hometown.

Later that Christmas evening, Oliver drove to our house. He sat in his car in the driveway for several minutes and then walked to our front door. My husband observed that his gait was shaky and he stood at the front door without ringing the bell. Finally, my husband opened a window and talked to him. His voice was strange and he sounded confused and asked if Amy was at home. My husband told him that she was somewhere else and that she was getting better. Oliver said that he hoped she was "making good decisions." My husband told him that he needed to be taking care of himself. Oliver finally walked back to the car and drove away. I wish we'd called the cops; maybe they would have searched his car.

On Saturday morning, I dropped River at the dog care around 7:45, then went to my 8:00 running group. I dispatched my weekly email about the run and breakfast at 10:28. About a half hour later, my husband, our first daughter, and I departed for my hometown. We made a quick stop at his relatives' house. We bought bad pizza at a rest area at 1:34. We exited the highway at 2:25 and visited our friends whom we've known since 1981; we hadn't seen them since 2003. We had a wonderful time reconnecting with them and four of their five children, three of them the same ages as ours, and left around 4:00, hoping to reach my parents' place by 9:00 p.m.

PRIMARY HOSPITAL

CARUSO, AMELIA
DOB: 1/20/1989 F20

Complaint: Cardiac Arrest–non–traumatic
Triage Time: Sat Dec 26, 2009 16:34
Urgency: ESI 1
Bed: ED 3
Initial Vital Signs:
BP:
P:
O2 sat:

ED Attending:
ary RN:

R:
T:
Pain:

Nine

The Phone Call

My husband and I had listened to *Beautiful Boy* on our drives to and from Triangle and Nar-Anon, and as we settled in for our five hour drive west, we started listening to *Tweak*. I was at the wheel, he was in the passenger seat, and our daughter was nestled behind. At 4:36, in the middle of hearing a particularly graphic track about injecting drugs, my cell phone rang. My husband answered. It was our son, who had been called by Circle Center staff. He told us in a calm but urgent voice that Amy was found unconscious and had been transported to the ER. He was with his girlfriend and her family, and said she was throwing things into suitcases as he spoke, and as soon as he hung up they were going to jump into her dad's Jeep and begin the one hundred seventy-five mile drive to the hospital.

At 4:39 I took the next exit, hoping we could find a place to stop and talk about what to do. The only road leaving the toll booth was dark and minimally marked and felt in the middle of nowhere. I did not need this aggravation. We managed to navigate ourselves back to the toll plaza, and stopped along the side just before the booth to try and process what was happening. We had calls with Circle Center at 4:48 and 4:55 that didn't tell us much more than our son had. I was concerned about what to tell my parents, who were expecting us in a few hours, without causing them undue panic. So at 4:58 I called my second brother, then reached him a minute later on his surgeon girlfriend's cell phone, and let them know that something not good was happening. They agreed to stand by for us.

I began to wonder what kind of medical orders were on file. Had Amy signed any documents about emergency care, including possibly a Do Not Resuscitate order? I started up the car, rejoined the highway, and drove carefully in the dark, cold rain through the mountains. We knew we were at least four hours away; I'm glad I didn't know at the time that it was actually two hundred forty miles. We were not saying very much to each other. In fact, I never remember any of us trying to reassure the others with a statement like, "Everything's going to be all right."

At 5:15 my husband talked to our son, who had spoken to the hospital. The ER had been working on Amy for an hour. A woman from Circle Center called us at 5:23 with the same update, and with an upbeat lilt to her voice, told us she thought this information was good news; I somehow didn't think so, and I called my brother's girlfriend at 5:41, who affirmed my fear. Our son next called at 5:49 and said the hospital refused to give him more information over the phone, and when we called Circle Center at 5:54, they had been told the same thing, so that update sounded even worse. Here we were driving in bad weather trying to reach Amy as soon as possible, not knowing whether she was dead or alive. My parents called at 7:28 and I did not answer, but checked my voice message three minutes later. I called them when we were stopped at 7:43, first on their cell which they didn't answer, then on their landline which they did, and told them there had been a delay. At 7:48 I called my brother's girlfriend and told her we'd called my folks.

Our son and his girlfriend arrived at the hospital around 7:30. We'd asked them to call us when they arrived, then we would stop at the next rest stop and await their call upon talking with the doctor. We waited at a rest area, sitting on the high stools in the corner of a McDonald's. Despite feeling afraid to speak, I was able to articulate to my husband the reality of the moment that we didn't know whether Amy was still alive (and, if so, in what condition), whether we might be facing a "pull the plug" decision, or whether she was dead. We decided to proceed to the next rest area to inch closer to Triangle, and from there would call our son, who hopefully would have spoken with the doctors by then.

At 8:16, I pulled into the next rest area, stopped at the end of the parking lot, and we called our son from the car. He told my husband that Amy could not make it. The ER had been unable to resuscitate her after almost two hours of working on her. We staggered out of the car in utter disbelief. We walked around it in utmost disorientation, embracing and consoling each other. We had just been dealt the cruelest news of our lives and needed to absorb the shock, yet we also wanted to be at the hospital. I instructed my husband to sit in the back seat to comfort our daughter and drove to the pumps to buy gas at 8:29, wishing I'd done so at the previous rest area. After pumping $30.61 of fuel, I pulled in front of the convenience store and called my second brother and his girlfriend at 8:31. I asked them to go to my parents' apartment to deliver in person the news that Amy had died. I called my sister at 8:33, who wailed, "Oh no, not Amy!" I left a message for my first brother at 8:37, then our close friends Meyer and Giuliana, who had lost their thirteen-year-old son, Tommy, in an accident in 1996, then tried our friends whose son was at the wilderness school. As we were leaving the rest area, my first brother called back at 8:41, so I pulled over to talk with him.

It took another two hours for us to reach Triangle, with the knowledge that Amy had died. I mustered the strength to keep driving as I thought about how Meyer and Giuliana had to drive to the hospital where Tommy had been airlifted after he was struck. My husband started calling his relatives with the news, and he tried calling Anya, his friend from graduate school, at 9:36. The weather cleared a bit, and I asked my husband to drive a little so I could make some calls, and I talked with my best friend from childhood, Tara, at 9:50.

We arrived at Geotown Hospital at 10:40 and walked across the parking lot to this small community facility. Our son, his girlfriend, and Amy's rehab counselor, Mr. Robichaud, awaited us inside. Upon entering, we exchanged silent embraces. We were ushered to the ER family waiting room. I pulled out my blue notebook, my record of all the notes I'd made with all the professionals over the last six years of never knowing the extent of her drug problem, the notebook Amy hated and had wanted me to burn. How striking that only one page remained on which to make these final notes.

The first question I asked Mr. Robichaud was, "Do you think there is any chance Amy could have committed suicide?" He replied with an adamant, "No way." He described Amy as, "Too positive, too motivated, she was reaching out to others. She was focused on her future, and had the love and support of her family." He speculated that her death was probably a case of injecting as much as she had at the height of her use, her tolerance was down having detoxed, and she accidentally overdosed.

The doctor joined us, a small, middle-aged woman in her white coat carrying her clipboard. She explained that Amy had been admitted unconscious with no pulse. Between the Emergency Response Team and ER personnel, they attempted to resuscitate her for almost two hours. They were "very aggressive" and were able to generate "pulseless electrical activity" in her heart twice but could not sustain a pulse. She was pronounced dead at 6:00 p.m. We could see her body with security officers present but would not be allowed to touch her because, as an unattended death, she was a medical examiner case and would require an autopsy.

I felt I had to see her, and my husband concurred, so we were escorted to the dimly lit cool room. Amy looked very peaceful and asleep, still intubated, her substance abuse counselor Mr. Goodruco's images of being connected to IVs and machines tragically prophetic. We stood there for a few minutes, then asked whether donating her organs was possible; they said maybe. Once back in the family waiting room, we signed a form so the hospital could release her medical records to us because I didn't want to have one more thing to deal with later.

The security guard arranged for us to sleep at the nearby Holiday Inn, where they gave us two complimentary rooms. I made more calls:

11:41 talked with my parents

11:41 left a voicemail for my cousin who was close to Amy, then tried her again six minutes later

11:55 talked again with my parents

11:58 talked with Tara

12:14 a.m. tried again to reach Meyer and Giuliana

12:15 tried to reach my grad school roommate; I had been in our suite when she received the call that her father had died suddenly, and I remembered how sick to my stomach I felt when I heard her scream

12:15 tried to reach my best friend from high school

12:17 tried to reach Audrey

12:22 left a message for Amy's psychologist Dr. DeSantos (he called back at 7:36 a.m.)

12:27 called my brother's girlfriend

12:35 tried another friend in California

12:36 left a message for Mr. Goodruco (he called back at 8:42 a.m.)

12:38 left a message for Meyer and Giuliana

12:43 called my brother the priest

1:09 left a message at my workout studio that I would probably not be at my next training session

I would call others in the morning.

It was a night of fitful sleep.

Ten

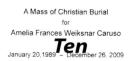

The Next Week

Our first daughter and I were up very early on Sunday, and started making more calls at 6:25. I showered and was back on the phone at 7:15. Around 9:00, the five of us had breakfast in the hotel restaurant where the service was abominably slow, and I stepped out several times to make calls. We checked out and stopped at Circle Center to meet with the staff and retrieve Amy's belongings (though they neglected to provide her phone charger or laptop, which was subsequently retrieved by the Geotown police). We received many tearful hugs from the residents with whom Amy had bonded in just a few days. The chocolates she'd brought as gifts were atop the mantle in the crowded office where we met with the staff, and in seeing this sign of my daughter's thoughtfulness, I hoped each box would make it to the recipient she intended. I must have given them to Amy on Christmas Day, and she would have taken them to Circle Center that night.

The staff explained to us what they knew so far. On Saturday morning, one of the residents notified staff that it sounded like Amy had used when she was on pass. At 9:00 a.m., staff tried to administer a drug test, with two samples "falling" in the toilet. Amy told the staff that she had used during her pass, and that she had met with her ex-boyfriend Oliver at the A.A. meeting, and he supplied her with drugs. The Circle Center staff brought Amy to Triangle for evaluation and detoxification. At 3:00 p.m., Triangle declared Amy "medically stable" and transferred her back to Circle Center. After arriving around 3:15, Amy said that she was going to take a shower. About a half hour later, Amy was found unresponsive in the shower. The staff called 9-1-1 and initiated cardiopulmonary resuscitation. At 4:10 p.m. Amy was transported by ambulance to Geotown Hospital. The staff said they found needles and packets in her clothing.

My husband and I chose to walk up to the third floor to see Amy's bedroom and the bathroom where she overdosed. When back downstairs, I pointed out to our first daughter the stained glass window on the landing that Amy had said she liked so much when we picked her up on Christmas morning. Our son loaded the black trash bags full of Amy's belongings into the Jeep. We never thought to ask for a copy of an incident report, or to request that the police be present. As would be expected in today's digital age, Amy's friends were already communicating news of her death via texts and Facebook.

We then headed to my husband's relatives' house for a short visit, and I was annoyed to be stuck briefly in football game traffic. We arrived home around 2:00 p.m. Entering the house without Amy, and knowing she would never enter it again, felt so tentative and so final. We moved the black plastic trash bags and suitcase containing her belongings into the basement. Just a year earlier, Amy had used that suitcase for the trip to Japan. My friend Trina and her husband, then Meyer and Giuliana, came to comfort us. Some of our daughter's friends came to comfort her.

Between 7:30 and 8:00 p.m., a car parked at the foot of our driveway but did not advance toward the house or turn off its lights. Feeling cautious, after several minutes we called the police. They arrived shortly and my husband could see them approach the car where they seemed to be talking with the driver. Finally, the police and the other car drove away. The town police later verified it was Oliver.

On Sunday, I logged more than one hundred calls as we talked with family, friends, colleagues, and professionals about Amy's death. I kept a yellow legal pad handy so I could write things down to keep the flurry of information straight. We knew that medication was an option if we needed help sleeping or simply making it through the day, but none of us found it necessary. At 6:54 p.m., I emailed my running group about the tragedy.

Preparing for the Services

On Monday morning, I emailed my start-up colleague. My husband, our son, and I went to the funeral home at 9:00 a.m. to make arrangements for Amy's services; our son's girlfriend stayed with our daughter and walked around the town with her. Walking from the car to the funeral home, three people from my running group saw me. They stopped, having learned of Amy's death from the email. One of them, an attorney, promised she'd deal with Amy's speeding ticket court appearance.

I thought the meeting at the funeral home would be the hardest one of my life, but it was easier than I expected, except for the inefficiencies. What should have been a one-hour meeting took more than two since the funeral director had to process much information manually instead of online. We had to choose the casket (white metal with pink trim), burial plot (near my husband's relatives), whether or not to have a limo (I said yes, my mother would appreciate it), and the holy card (*The Serenity Prayer* was the shoo-in. "God grant me the serenity to accept the things I cannot change; courage to change the things I can; and the wisdom to know the difference."). We wrote the obituaries and decided in what newspapers we wanted to run them. We left the meeting feeling good about the decisions we made and grateful that the funeral director knew how to gently keep us moving through the steps.

Once home, we chose pallbearers, all of whom graciously accepted: Amy's dear friend, Byron, from middle school, who had helped us look for our lost cat in 2000; her high school cross country coach; her friend, Patrick, from SLU; a colleague from my start-up, Gino, on whom she had her first crush when she was a toddler; and one representative each from my husband's and my side of the family.

Discovering the Journals

Brett, my colleague since 1987, and his wife, Risa, brought us lunch, and our pastor stopped by. Then, with Risa by my side, I went through the bags of Amy's belongings in the basement to find burial clothes. I could not have done this task without help. I first spotted Amy's brown leather journal. I knew I couldn't look at it then but would later. I wanted Amy buried in her favorite jeans, which she'd left on my sewing table to replace the zipper. She could have worn them as-is, but I called my start-up secretary friend to ask if she could possibly have the zipper replaced by late afternoon. She did, God bless her, despite the snow. I felt like I had honored Amy's last request of me.

We also chose the long-sleeved, blue T-shirt that our first daughter had hand-embroidered for Amy as a Christmas gift with four white paper cranes, symbolizing herself, my husband, our son, and me. We included the brown quilted vest that my husband's relatives had given her for Christmas, and her white poofy Northface® jacket. Her pink Red Sox hat would be near her head. We found a necklace chain with a cross from Iona, an island off the coast of Scotland we'd visited on a family vacation, and later Giuliana and I found some dangly earrings. While the casket would only be half open, I chose unmatched running socks, fuzzy bedroom slippers, and a pink bracelet we'd given her as a gift.

Later that afternoon, the funeral director came to collect the clothes and make-up. I emphasized that the bronzer was particularly important because Amy *always* had to have her bronzer just right. We wanted to have the wake on Tuesday and Wednesday, but her body was still with the medical examiner.

Our first daughter's friends arrived around 1:30 a.m., having driven thirty-two hours from the deep South. They were wonderfully helpful from the time they arrived through their departure on Sunday. They supported our daughter and pitched in around the house (without being asked) from mopping the floor to making soup. My running buddy from my start-up company came over in the late afternoon; I asked him to bring some single malt and we shared a wee dram. My husband and I decided we were too wiped out to attend the Nar-Anon meeting, so I called and sent our regrets, although we were scheduled to be away anyhow. We left the collection of photos for the wake pretty much up to our son and daughter, both for the collage of snapshots on poster board and the slideshow set to Beatles music. Food, flowers, love, and prayers continued to pour in. My husband and I started designing the funeral service, including connecting the choir director with my sister, who would sing one piece.

On Monday evening, after seeing more attempted calls from Oliver's cell phone, my husband decided to answer. When he spoke, the line was silent for a few seconds. Then the caller spoke and my husband recognized Oliver's voice. Oliver seemed surprised, perhaps from hearing my husband's voice on my cell phone. Oliver asked to know exactly what was going on. My husband told him that Amy had died, and he couldn't give him any more information. He told Oliver to stop calling. Oliver said that he would like to attend the wake. My husband told him that would not be a good idea. Oliver protested that he thought this wasn't fair and said that he had never given Amy "any of that stuff." My husband asked whether Oliver was in Canalboro on Friday, December 25th. Oliver admitted that he had seen Amy on Christmas but claimed that it was only to try to keep her from using. My husband told Oliver that there were reasons for him not to be at the wake, but that he was not able to share those reasons, and ended the call.

First Read of the Journals

On Monday night, I stayed up late and wrote Amy's eulogy. Around 2:00 a.m. I went downstairs to look at her brown journal. I was floored at how pained, how conflicted her writings were in the last weeks of her life. I was staggered by her last entry, and called Tara in my dismay about what I had read. I began to wonder whether Amy's death was *not* accidental, and finally went to bed at 5:30.

On Tuesday, the phones rang nonstop. It was helpful that sometimes a visitor acted as a receptionist. Sometimes I'd be on my cell phone and the landline with calls waiting at the same time. I talked with a colleague who had lost his son, born within months of Amy, at age four. Our first daughter and I met with a psychiatrist neighbor I've known for more than twenty-five years, and I showed him Amy's journal. Dr. Boyd, who works in rehab, said, "You have to find a way to have this published. I have never seen such articulate and eloquent writing by an addict about the conflict they go through in treatment." The town police came later and took Amy's phone and journal in case it might contain any evidence of what had actually happened.

My husband's grad school friend, Anya, flew in; our neighbor across the street kindly collected her from the subway and put her up for a few days. Tara arrived from Texas and rented a car. My second brother drove in from our hometown with my parents and sister, and my first brother drove up from his parish. The friends we'd seen Saturday afternoon on the drive to my hometown came to visit. A running buddy brought River back from his dog care. We were grateful for all this rallying.

BC was an unexpected source of support, including making some calls to the medical examiner's office. Amy's body was finally released mid-afternoon on Tuesday. Since I did not want to drag out the funeral until Saturday, January 2nd, that meant a one-day wake on Wednesday and a funeral on Thursday, New Year's Eve. I wanted an overnight buffer between seeing her body laid out for the first time and the wake. Fortunately, the funeral director could have everything ready for a family viewing at 8:15 p.m. on Tuesday.

Our family and Tara drove the five miles to the funeral home, located a few doors down from where my running group convenes on Saturday mornings. Amy's body looked so peaceful. The only problem was that her eyeliner was too thick. But Tara, who'd applied make-up on her as a child, gently took care of that detail. Amy had been infamous for her bottled water, so I placed one from Circle Center that had been labeled "Amy's water bottle" in the casket. Once back home, my husband and I finished designing the service since the funeral director needed the final copy of the program by 9:00 a.m. We decided on the readings with my brother, who subsequently changed the gospel and revamped the theme of his homily.

The Wake

On Wednesday morning, I was up at around 4:00 a.m. with our daughter. I could see that I was becoming tired, having trouble remembering details, and often couldn't find the phone(s). We left for the funeral home at 12:45 for the 1:00–3:30 visiting hours; people were still arriving at 3:50. We drove home for dinner, then back for the 6:00–9:00 p.m. visiting hours. Someone from Tulips had brought their signature mug for the casket. My sister's husband arrived with their three children. We estimated that more than seven hundred people came to the wake. I felt so loved, so supported. My sister made sure I stayed hydrated. I told a few people that the love-to-pain ratio was higher than one, and there was a *lot* of pain, so the love was overwhelming. The outpouring was unbelievable: family, work colleagues, my running group; Amy's teachers and classmates from her middle school, BVMP, SLU, and BC; our son's friends and colleagues, and our daughter's friends; neighbors; store owners; and professional providers. The closest I have ever felt to anything like that was running the 2004 marathon, feeling like I was being buoyed by the million spectators. A friend from my start-up who lived in the city picked up one of Amy's friends flying in from SLU, and our son's best friend from middle school picked up another SLU friend. I refined the eulogy that evening.

While going through Amy's belongings in the basement, I had come across the bag of 2009 Christmas cards she had started working on for her friends. Some were written only as far as "Dear ___," whereas others were completed with messages about meeting up in the new year. I took on the sacred task of giving them to the intended friends who came to the wake, and mailed the rest.

A few weeks later, I read *Don't Take My Grief Away*, by Doug Manning, which had been given to me by one of the ACHS employment partner supervisors. I really liked its positive portrayal of the role a good funeral director can play. I also liked the suggestion that, after the wake but before the funeral, the immediate family should meet for an hour with no interruptions, possibly at the funeral home and with a clergy person, just to talk. It's something that, had I known about then, we would have done as our family really could have used that focused time.

On New Year's Eve, we had been scheduled to meet with Ms. Underwood at Circle Center at 11:00 a.m., and then to take Amy for the second half of her root canal at 1:30, where it seems she was scheming her drug pickup. Instead, we were burying her. That morning, I brought a few other items for the casket: a belly button ring with a heart on it; the front page from the newspaper when the Red Sox won the World Series, with a photo of her beloved Jason Varitek; the half-rosary given to me by my relative for my first communion; a snip of hair from each of the four of us; and a tuft from each of the four animals. And our last Christmas photo card with a note from me.

Saying good-bye to Amy's body at the funeral home was not as wrenching as I'd expected. I was able to kiss her hard forehead and caress her cool hand for the last time. My first brother said some prayers. We had to leave the funeral home by 9:25 a.m. for the 10:00 funeral Mass. My parents, my husband, our son and his girlfriend, our daughter, and I rode in a limo.

The Funeral

The church was packed, and its capacity is more than six hundred. As we came up behind the casket to walk into the church, I realized how tragic it was that this was how my husband would last walk Amy up the aisle. I edited the start of the eulogy to include this point. Four people draped the pall: Mrs. Guicona, Amy's high school guidance counselor; Ms. Dirath, the BVMP athletic director; and one representative each from my husband's and my side of the family. Amy's twelfth-grade friend, Maurann, was also supposed to help but didn't due to some confusion.

My husband, daughter, son, his girlfriend, and I sat in the first pew on the left, along with my parents and second brother. The Mass was deeply beautiful and healing. I rejected the idea of videotaping the service as too invasive, but wish we had been able to audiotape it. Three BC priests concelebrated with my Franciscan brother, as well as our eighty-two-year-old pastor and the deacon who taught Amy for Confirmation. My brother's homily blew everyone away. During communion, as people passed by the front row, I was in awe of all those who came to the funeral on this inclement day.

Apparently, official diocesan regulations permit only one talk of remembrance, but we had four. Amy's best friend from BVMP, Audrey, delivered the "friend" eulogy, admitting the trouble the two of them had gotten into together. I was incredibly proud of how our daughter was able to deliver the paragraph she had prepared about her little sister. I did not know what our son was going to say, but his portrayal of driving Amy back to treatment on Christmas evening was exquisite. Snow started falling as I started speaking. I would not have ever imagined giving a eulogy for my child had I not seen Meyer give his for Tommy. And Meyer agreed to back me up if I couldn't get through mine. I did make it through, knowing that only I could have paid honor to Amy in that way.

We processed out of the church to the hymn, "May the Choirs of Angels." Once back in the limo, I felt like a caged animal and wanted to jump out and greet all the people who had not been at the wake and others whom I just wanted to hug. In retrospect, I should have eschewed formalities and just let myself out.

The Burial

At the cemetery, my brother abbreviated the graveside service due to the snow. Unfortunately, some people became lost and never made it. (I later suggested to the funeral director that they include the cemetery address in the program for those who use GPS, and provide direction cards for those who don't know the area.) During the service, I suddenly remembered that, in some traditions, people throw a handful of dirt on the casket, and I recalled the thud sounds as the earth hit the metal casket at Tommy's graveside service. We couldn't throw dirt, but Amy loved the snow. So in spontaneous inspiration I asked people to toss a snowball at the casket in her honor, something she would have loved. They did. I had also wanted people to leave the graveside not feeling totally morbid, so I asked our son to play the "Amie" song on a boom box. I asked people to dance in Amy's honor as they were leaving, again as she would have loved. Giuliana locked arms with me and we circled in step.

We drove back to a local inn for the reception, which my husband's relative had arranged. Close to one hundred fifty people attended. I barely had any time with my three relatives who came in from out of state. Our childhood neighbor, who moved from my hometown in 1971, came with his wife and two of their four children. We met our son's future in-laws for the first time. We had an open microphone, inspired by the one at my relative's funeral, which my second brother kindly videotaped. Having all those recorded stories about Amy is an incredible comfort.

As the snow kept falling, Tara left to catch her flight to Texas and one of my husband's relatives left to catch his plane to the West Coast. My folks returned to the hotel to rest. My family gathered at our house for dinner, then we had the Christmas present opening ritual which did not happen the evening of the 26th in my hometown. It took more than five months before I was able to put away the table top full of presents from Christmas Day and that evening, including the unopened gifts my family had planned to give Amy.

That night, I spent about three hours in a very important conversation with Amy's SLU friends. (They had stayed at Trina's house, and she took them to the airport early on Friday morning, a huge help.) Patrick shared a letter that Amy had written to him on December 7th, in which she asked forgiveness for neglecting their friendship during her autumn relapse, and to pray that she would stay clean and be able to visit for spring break. She included the haunting sentence, "Remember, life is too short (I realize that now more than ever)..."

Late on New Year's Eve, we received more tragic news: Byron's father had died suddenly that evening. They were at work together. Byron hadn't felt like going to his job that evening given that he had been Amy's pallbearer that morning, but his dad convinced him that Amy would have wanted him to. Byron turned around to see that his dad had collapsed. He began cardiopulmonary resuscitation, 9-1-1 was called, but his father could not be revived.

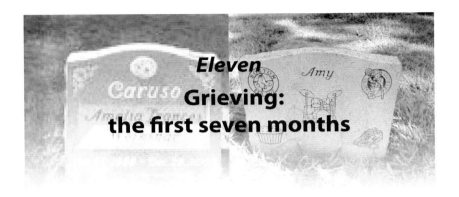

Eleven
Grieving:
the first seven months

Every person's grief journey is unique for every death. To those who say, "I cannot imagine," I want to share some of what ensued, believing here that information may be more helpful than imagination. The details show how the mundane interwove with the unfathomable, business-as-usual in parallel to life without Amy. Yet, if she were still alive, this part of the book would be the story of her recovery after Circle Center. I've chosen seven months because our former parish priest, whom I saw by coincidence on July 26th, said he believes that right around seven months is the worst point in grieving.

On Friday morning, New Year's Day, I awoke to the feeling of a geyser of sadness. It was an unpredictable eruption that I knew could happen at any time and I just let myself feel it.

My high school principal, to whom I've remained close since I graduated in 1973, came to visit at 8:30 a.m. My parents and brothers had joined us, then hit the road hoping to beat the snowstorm home along the same route my husband, daughter, and I had commenced six days earlier when Amy was last alive.

That afternoon, my husband, our daughter, and I visited his relatives. While there, I received a call from a former student. Her friend in law enforcement passed along some tidbits from his sources about Oliver; I felt a rush of encouragement because it sounded like the police were all over this case.

We had driven in two cars, and my husband stayed to spend time with his relatives. I left with our daughter, who did not want to stay any longer, and dropped her at the home of our friends Meyer and Giuliana, as I didn't want to leave her alone when I attended the annual New Year's gathering of my running group. My buddies were not afraid to comfort me or have conversations about what had happened to Amy. This acknowledgement soothed me.

On Saturday morning, my husband, our daughter, and Anya walked with my running group. Two women from the group stuck with me as I could not keep up with the regular runners. Afterward I worked out with my trainer and, feeling deeply sad on the way home, stopped at Byron's, Amy's close friend from middle school and pallbearer. Trina's husband did us the favor of taking our trash and recycling to the transfer station. We were grateful for "one less thing to do" that afternoon. Our daughter's high school counselor, Dr. Hischolor, stopped by at 6:00 p.m., offered us condolences, and then spent more than an hour with her. Giuliana and Meyer came later to check on us. I thought about how my work life must change: The pace had been unsustainable even before Amy died.

On Sunday, my husband and I went to the 11:00 Mass, and afterward we bought take-out dim sum because it would have been too painful for me to eat in the restaurant where Amy had first declared her favorite bathroom around age five. Our friend George, also a nurse and married to my nursing professor friend Gail, came at 1:30 p.m. to translate the ER records for us which had already arrived in the mail. It seemed like Amy was barely alive when she left Circle Center, and I took comfort from knowing that the hospital still took extraordinary measures. But I wanted answers that only the toxicology results could provide: What exactly had she taken and were the levels consistent with an accidental overdose?

My ACHS boss came by at 3:30, and we discussed my desire to transition to a half-time role so I could do justice both to my job and to all the practical and emotional work that follows a death. Meyer cautioned that those around me at work would forget Amy's death as time passed, though I wouldn't. About ten inches of snow fell that evening: Amy would have loved it.

On Monday, four days after burying my daughter, I returned to ACHS. At morning check-in where the students assembled before leaving for their jobs, the principal gathered the juniors at the far end of the room, told them what had happened, and provided guidance on ways of reacting. I was so relieved by his deft handling of the situation. As the students walked back across the room to head down to the vans to take them to work, every one of them gave me a hug. I could not have felt more comforted. At the weekly Monday assembly, the principal told the ninth-graders, sophomores, and seniors about Amy's death, and I spoke briefly. Students and colleagues stopped by my office the rest of the day. I felt loved and supported.

Driving home, I was seized by the trigger of remembering how often I would call Amy as I drove away from school. (A trigger is a person, place, thing, or recollection that brings back memories, in this case of a loved one, and in an addict's case, of using.) I stopped at my favorite grocery store to give the manager Amy's prayer card and a copy of her eulogy, in which I mentioned him carrying her out of his store during one of her toddler tantrums. He had seen her grow up into one of his best customers. He growled, "Damn drugs!"

That evening, my husband and I went to the Nar-Anon meeting. I felt I was among true friends who could understand as few others could, even though we had only been to a few meetings before Amy died. The next morning, our daughter came to ACHS as the principal kindly arranged for her to be a classroom volunteer. At morning check-in during prayer intentions, a student remembered our family. Indeed, prayers from every corner continued to give us strength. I noted how normal I was feeling, which seemed odd. I was finding it difficult to inform others who hadn't heard the news because we were ten days through the shock that they were hearing afresh. Much like post-September 11, 2001, I was impatient with the banality of some day-to-day trivialities and Facebook postings. I spent much of the day at work realizing how much I loved what I did, and how it would feel like another death to yank myself out suddenly.

On Wednesday, two students offered intentions for my family at check-in prayer. I was feeling pride in how good I was at my work, especially navigating the twenty job changes happening the next week. One student spoke with me at length about how drugs had touched her family. My daughter and I stopped at the Broton police on the way home to check on the progress of their investigation, but by 4:10 the detective had already gone home.

On Thursday, January 7th, I awoke angry. Amy should not have fatally overdosed in a treatment facility. We had been told the odds were in her favor as she voluntarily sought treatment, did not have a dual diagnosis (which I now question), was young, had career ambitions, had a supporting family who had not given up on her, had resources, and was in allegedly the best women's residential facility in the state.

That afternoon, I attended the reunion lunch for the first two ACHS graduating classes, and it felt good to reconnect with these students who were now in college. One of my ninth-grade boys stopped by for his daily check on me, which warmed my day. I left by 3:00 and went to an HBS program with Meyer, where we met up with our mutual friends, Brett and Risa. Afterward, Meyer helped me with the first phase of clearing out Amy's apartment. We swiftly removed her kitchen and common area items and whatever from her bedroom would fit in the back of Meyer's sport utility vehicle. I made mental note of what would remain for the final clean-out. The task was not as awful as I'd imagined, again because of help from a friend. That night, two of our daughter's college friends arrived, and it helped to share stories (until midnight!) with three of Amy's girlfriends from middle school who stopped by.

On Friday, a few of the seniors brought me cards, roses, and chocolates at check-in. I was so touched by their eloquence and sincerity. That night, my husband and I started organizing all the sympathy cards that had arrived. As we were placing them in hanging folders, the Geotown detective, for whom I'd left several messages, called back. I was fuming. Apparently, Circle Center had discarded the needles and packets. Further, 9-1-1 had not dispatched police to the scene, and neither had Circle Center called the police.

My husband and I went to my Saturday running group, and I ran with an Emergency Medical Technician (EMT) from our town and described what the detective had told me. He was incredulous. He said normally a 9-1-1 call dispatches the police in addition to the EMTs. He could not believe that needles and packets had not been collected by the EMTs as information for the ER doctors; EMTs are typically scolded if they do not bring in relevant items from the accident scene, such as bicycle helmets or pill bottles.

I started sorting some of Amy's belongings and was sad to find an empty drug baggie and instructions from syringes. Some neighbors came by to decide whether they would take the ping-pong table for their three young boys; Amy had been their favorite babysitter. At 1:00 p.m., my husband, daughter, and I attended the memorial service for Byron's dad. Our son's godfather, Frank, and his wife, Corinne, came to visit, during which we received a call from a mutual friend overseas. I also had a comforting conversation with Tanisha, Amy's first year roommate at SLU.

On Sunday morning, I paid bills and sorted some of Amy's belongings in the basement. After Mass, my husband's relatives brought their small truck to Amy's apartment. Our son and his girlfriend joined us, and we cleared everything out in an hour. Sadly, my daughter and I did find drug paraphernalia. Overall it was not as awful as I expected due to the support and doing it so quickly, like ripping off a Band-Aid. A neighbor helped us transfer the contents from the four vehicles into our basement.

Later, I talked to a high school friend who has worked in a psychiatric facility and an attorney from my running group. They offered support about how to approach investigating what happened. Despite the full day, I was frustrated that I hadn't finished my Christmas cards, written the monthly letter, or read any of the newspaper backlog, the pull of the ordinary against the unbelievable. I realized that if things had happened *as they were supposed to* my husband and I probably would have been visiting Amy at Circle Center. If all had gone according to her plan, she would have been starting her transition to sober life near BC in about ten days. Had she survived the overdose, who knows what we would be doing?

Meanwhile, we felt nurtured by all the incoming love, prayers, and support. The January 12th BVMP vs. ACHS basketball game was dedicated to Amy. Held in the BVMP gym, my daughter and I were surrounded by my former colleagues, students, and parents. Several tributes were read, and we were given flowers. I took special pride in knowing that I had taught almost every player. I thought back happily to the few times I'd seen my hoops-loving daughter play on that same court, and sad for the times she didn't want me to watch. I finished all but one of my Christmas cards by that evening.

On the morning of the 13th, I met with my BVMP principal for her insights on my situation at ACHS. I appreciated her warmth and wisdom. After school, I stopped to see Risa and watch a TV special on the opiate epidemic in our state. It was surreal to realize that my daughter was now a statistic. The next day I stopped at Tulips, where one proprietor shared that many customers had stopped by and talked about Amy's goodness.

I sent the December monthly letter on January 17th. It may have seemed crazy that I was writing one only three weeks after Amy died, but it was important to keep up meaningful rituals, and it allowed me to communicate consistently to the forty or so recipients. I had actually thought of taking my binders of letters to Amy at the December 20th family meeting, since 1996–2009 represented most of her life and I thought that the history and stories could have helped her reconnect with memories that might support her recovery. It completely slipped my mind to give them to her on Christmas Day. However, I noticed how I'd forwarded the 1996–1998 England letters to her on October 6th, which must have been upon her request: I wonder why she had asked for them.

I began my January letter by reflecting:

I started this letter Saturday evening, thinking how six weeks ago at the time we were driving to Geotown Hospital, knowing that Amy had died. It's also the second month that she's off the mailing list for this letter.

I find myself thinking: Why didn't I simply defy the order for her to attend the A.A. meeting and keep her home (her friends told me yesterday that they heard she didn't actually attend the meeting). Should she have even been allowed to have a pass or attend a meeting without an aftercare plan? And then there is the two-page list of questions we sent to the State Department of Public Health (DPH) for their investigation, including: why didn't the facility call us when she was sent back to detox? I have this image of a huge fishing net, what should have been her safety net, and the 20 or so places where it was snipped, so she fell through, a "perfect storm."

Our daughter admitted how she had the courage to ask Amy on Christmas about her reaction to the death of her rehab co-resident and whether she was feeling at risk. She is also pained because she knew that Amy was sneaking the use of her cell phone on Christmas and never told us, and I'm not sure how I would have reacted. But I am deeply curious about any text messages or voicemails that would hint as to why she would have wanted to sneak in time with her ex-boyfriend on Christmas. The town police still have her phone.

I am also reeling over how I never realized the negative depths of her relationship with her ex-boyfriend. . . . We faced the "lesser of two evils" conflict of whether to try and forbid the relationship (which probably would have polarized Amy) or accept it (without embracing it). We ran this dilemma by Amy's psychologist, Dr. DeSantos, who agreed that it was better to keep them nearby: if the ex-boyfriend were raking leaves or painting at our house, at least he and Amy wouldn't be out getting into trouble. The boy's grandmother took a similar stance: if she took her grandsons dancing with her, they wouldn't be getting into trouble . . . Amy claimed that her boredom in the relationship was contributing to her using in the fall. She admitted he wasn't the one she belonged with long term. But several people have told us that she was scared to break up. Her sister had witnessed verbal and emotional abuse, and I hope there wasn't physical abuse. Two of Amy's friends don't think so, but if he had taught her to inject, and was injecting her, how much more abusive can you get?

When asked how I'm doing, my response in the last few weeks has been "better than I would have expected." I have actually felt quite calm, my life not constantly being hijacked by Amy drama or stress. So perhaps there's a bit of relief. Which is not to say I don't miss her. She looked more like me than her two siblings did, and her personality was so much like mine. I had visions of her being a companion and resource for me into my old age, of her with a successful career and being a great mom, married to someone worthy of her. I was probably closer to her than anyone else in the family, and feel eviscerated.

I find myself wishing I had written down more of my feelings during November and December. I have copious notes of conversations with

*counselors, but didn't capture nearly enough of my riding the waves of
hope, love, anger, discouragement and resentment . . . I was remembering
how I wasn't exactly looking forward to the drive to my hometown, and
it's as though some evil scriptwriter cruelly manipulated that thought.*

That day, I also spoke with one of Amy's friends from rehab, who told me
some great stories about Amy and food, including how she was so excited
about one of the desserts that she hoarded extras and hid them behind the
milk machine in the dining room so she could have more later.

On Martin Luther King, Jr. Day I was happy that I didn't have to work. Our
neighbor from across the street stopped by with her two young children and
brought an apple pie. My daughter and I headed to a 2:00 p.m. meeting with
Amy's substance abuse counselor, Mr. Goodruco; my husband met us there.

Mr. Goodruco shared that Amy had begged him to let her tell me that
she was addicted to OxyContin, not heroin. He reiterated how Suboxone
works and described some of the dynamics with the ex-boyfriend, whom he'd
met twice. He also painted the discouraging picture of how addicts in their
early twenties are planting seeds for recovery and "testing" their relapse knowledge and not usually recovering. He said the average age for recovery is in the
thirties once they developmentally have some concept of mortality—all this
despite our November 16th meeting where he expressed "a lot of confidence"
that she could do it.

After the meeting, my husband, daughter, and I walked to the BC bookstore, which was tough. Amid all the palpable excitement of students starting a new semester, we felt the void of Amy's effervescence, and instead of
shelling out several hundred dollars for new books, I was selling back my
dead daughter's used texts. I felt impatient being in a line with administrative
delays. We stopped at the nursing school to drop off some of Amy's unsellable
books and a blood pressure kit I found among her belongings. My husband
headed home. My daughter and I went for pizza, then bought ice cream at a
shop where Amy had a loyalty card. We told the clerk about Amy and gave
him a prayer card. He remembered her and was shaken by the news. I noticed
that the Coldstone had closed. Amy always enjoyed that store, and I felt the
impulse to call and let her know, quickly realizing that I no longer could.

My daughter and I were to meet Amy's apartment-mate, Ramona, to
give her the new keys (my husband had advised the landlord to change the
locks) and to return the cable box and remote control we'd inadvertently
brought back to our house. Back in Amy's neighborhood, we decided to
mush though the slush to take her prayer card to some places where she was

a frequent customer. Several merchants remembered her as "the tall skinny girl who was always smiling." Ramona was back around 5:00 p.m., and my daughter questioned her about a sticky note she had left Amy about a "tough night." So Ramona told us more about Amy and Oliver fighting and Amy's desire to get out of the relationship as long ago as January of 2009.

My daughter and I then visited with my high school principal. We drove home past the location of the Nar-Anon meeting, and, once we were home, I decided I was too tired to head back out. Further, it was almost half an hour away and the roads were still wintry, so I called in our regrets. Instead, I enjoyed the nourishment of talking with and emailing friends, realizing the need to phase back at work so I could put higher priority on all I needed to do after Amy's death.

On Tuesday, I went to my biweekly fitness session and then voted. That evening, my husband, our daughter, and I met with Dr. DeSantos. We asked a lot of questions about Amy's personality and her ex-boyfriend. He mentioned that Oliver's high school class had five heroin overdose deaths. He also provided a statistic we'd never heard: The relapse rate on heroin among those in their early twenties is ninety-eight percent after the first rehab. Amy herself had mentioned in a December letter to a SLU friend that most twenty-something heroin addicts relapse.

On the way home, we picked up the thank-you photo cards we had printed. They came out beautifully, and I felt it would be healing to send them. The card included a photo of Amy's baptism, first communion, high school graduation, and the last photo taken of her in our house. I was grateful that before the holidays our son had honored my request to hang the Christmas lights, which appeared in the background of the last photo. I also reached the cable company about switching Amy's account to my name.

Observing Amy's Twenty-First Birthday

On Amy's birthday, my husband took the day off, and he and our daughter visited his relatives. I left work at 1:50 p.m., and the three of us visited the cemetery, once again playing the "Amie" song. We took flowers and sprinkled crumbs of her favorite white chocolate chip cookies that my parents had bought her as a Christmas gift. We had dinner at her favorite Mexican restaurant with five of her closest friends and a mom. The restaurant's tradition is to give patrons a fancy sombrero to wear on their birthday. We asked for one, set it at the head of the table, placed Amy's prayer card on it, and took pictures.

Several people ordered her favorite cheese quesadilla. Those of us over twenty-one ordered Margaritas, thinking how Amy could have been ordering her first legal drink at that dinner, though that would have been forbidden as part of her recovery. We ordered a fried ice cream in her honor, and it was delivered with nine spoons. We felt Amy's presence and know she would have approved the celebration. As we left, I gave her prayer card to the waiter, who did remember her and seemed very moved as I told her story.

On the 21st, I noted how I usually thought most about Amy in the mornings when I woke up, and for some reason whenever I was in the staff lavatory at school. Meyer and Giuliana had us as guests for dinner. They always provided the triple-crown comfort combination of their company, their cuisine, and their cozy house. With the new semester under way, we were receiving more sympathy cards from BC teachers and students. One nursing professor sent me the paper that Amy had written for her adult clinical health assessment; I was the patient she had interviewed.

It struck me how important it had been to have our daughter around as we tried different ways to support each other. I appreciated when our busy son and his girlfriend stopped by for a visit. Per the advice of a recent widower at church, I set up an Excel spreadsheet database and entered names from the guest book at Amy's wake into it, and would continue to log all the cards and gifts so I would have an accurate record for sending thank-you cards.

On Saturday morning, I awoke to the mantra, "If we can keep at least one kid from going down the wrong path, keep one kid from not pursuing their dreams, then Amy's death will not be in vain." The words didn't feel like they came from a dream, rather they were more like a message from Amy. I enjoyed my running group but was shocked to learn that the eight-year-old resident dog at River's dog care had died from a tumor in his heart. In my state of heightened sensitivity to loss, I was glad that River had come to know him from his "meet and greet" the day we took Amy to detox, the stay on the day we visited Amy at Rhombus, and during his Christmas "vacation" when Amy died.

The mother of Amy's friend, Lily, and I had lunch, reconnecting as mothers whose daughters had been best friends. I felt grateful for her support, friendship, and willingness to explore some of the past. I walked River around the block with another friend, feeling glad to have company. My daughter and I cleaned in Amy's room, but that was exhausting and could be done only in unpredictable doses.

On the 24th, I wrote my letter to ACHS, formally proposing a twenty-hour/week status. I also sent questions to the Department of Public Health that I wanted answered in its investigation of Triangle and Circle Center.

My daughter and I had coffee with my longtime friend, Lois, and then the two of them drove into the city to see a play. River and I walked with my runner friend and her dog for the first time in months. I remembered when Amy was at summer camp in Maine, when I missed her so much that it hurt, and I realized that feeling had yet to hit me since she died.

The 25th was a tough day, the month anniversary of last seeing Amy alive. Our daughter expressed, "I can't believe this is our life." I attended a good Nar-Anon meeting, but I wasn't home until well after 10:00 p.m. and had to be up at 5:00 a.m. On the 26th, I met with the ACHS president about my letter; she seemed to be open-minded. Later when driving home, I was suddenly taken aback by how I had driven Amy for the last time along the road from Broton to our town, a stretch I travel almost daily.

On the 27th, I realized that most of my memories with Amy were focused in November/December, as if going further back might start to hurt too much. I was heartened by phone calls and emails from friends who were still "checking in" on me. I'd read in the sympathy card from one class how a student had lost his nineteen-year-old brother to a stabbing when he was in middle school. When he stopped by my office, I thanked him for his disclosure, and we talked a little and shared some tears in our connection.

On Thursday, the 28th, Byron came for dinner. It felt good to share memories and go through some of Amy's belongings. He left with a number of them, including her snowboard. Lily came by with her mother, but we were less successful finding mementos for her. I reconnected with a few elementary school classmates for the first time in forty-some years on Facebook. On Friday, I called various law enforcement jurisdictions for updates; none had any.

On Saturday, the 30th, my running group celebrated the seventieth birthday of yet another member. I wrote parody lyrics to "The Twelve Days of Christmas" and my husband led the singing. I went to the bank to have notarized the document I needed to be appointed administrator of Amy's estate. This appointment would enable me to request medical records from Triangle. My husband and I went to the cemetery, but it was so cold the boom box wouldn't play the "Amie" song. It was the first day we received no sympathy cards in the mail. Someone from church forewarned that they might straggle in for months.

My husband and I hosted a dinner that we had first discussed a few days before Amy died. Brett and Risa and Meyer and Giuliana stayed for more than five hours, and it felt satisfying to be able to host after being the recipient of so much generosity in the last month. We took down the Christmas tree, but I wasn't yet able to deal with the table full of Christmas present bags.

On Sunday morning, a friend from California came for brunch with a mutual friend who lived in our town. I'd forgotten how easy it was to have people visit for a morning meal, and we shared stories about how scary it can be raising teenage daughters. Our next-door neighbors came that evening to share their condolences for about an hour. I was feeling frustrated about not writing any thank-you notes yet.

On February 1st, I awoke thinking, "I need a day off." I realized I'd been thinking about days of the week as follows:

Fridays: the too-good-to-be-true Christmas Day

Saturdays: departing for my hometown, Amy died

Sundays: the shock of the "morning after" and contacting so many people; returning home knowing she never would

Mondays: making funeral arrangements, selecting her burial clothes

Tuesdays: awaiting the release of her body from the medical examiner; the family viewing

Wednesdays: her wake

Thursdays: her funeral

After work, I drove our daughter to catch her bus to the airport. Memories flooded back from all the times I drove Amy there, and the concomitant dramas. When our daughter returned, in hugging her petite body, I couldn't help but remember hugging Amy's tall, lanky body in all her comings and goings.

On February 2nd, when I was doing "Superman" stretches at my fitness studio, the song "Amie" came on the radio. It was tough to stay composed. I remembered how it had played back in November when I was lifting weights, and once since while on the seated leg press. My trainer was so supportive, dare I say essential, to my coping with events since November. Feeling reasonably happy with my body had definitely helped me weather all the other stresses.

On Wednesday, the 3rd, my husband had dinner with some of his work buddies, and I puttered about doing work good for my soul, but I still didn't write any thank-you notes. I started missing Amy's seven layer bars and her signature dessert.

I looked forward to the luxury of my day off on Friday. I was up at 6:30 a.m., walked River, and tried to take care of various Amy administrivia. I saw my chiropractor and a career counselor about my work situation. I had the dental cleaning that was supposed to happen on December 30th, followed by a walk with a friend. I had my car headlight replaced. I called the district attorney about Circle Center, Geotown Hospital, and 9-1-1 not contacting the Geotown or state police when Amy died. The state police returned my call within an hour and the officer voiced his concerns. I received the sad verdict from Geotown Hospital that Amy had been deemed unsuitable as an organ donor. It hurt that this final act of generosity could not take place, for reasons that were not given.

Byron then visited and we made cookies in Amy's honor. We reminisced about her baking idiosyncrasies, like rinsing every cup and utensil to be sure it was free of animal hair because a visual inspection simply did not suffice. My husband went to a chess tournament while I headed to the seventieth birthday celebration for a couple in my running group. Arriving at 9:15 p.m., I wasn't sure I'd have the physical or emotional energy for a party so I planned to stay no more than an hour. Yet I was able to engage in satisfying conversations, and I left at midnight.

On Saturday, I had lunch with Maurann and another one of Amy's close high school friends, both former students. It was good to hear how they were doing, share stories about Amy, and answer some of their questions about her final descent. My husband and I then went monument shopping, and stopped by Meyer and Giuliana's home with some birthday cookies for Meyer.

I shared with Giuliana how, at the party the night before, I was asked for the first time since Amy died how many children I had. Not having anticipated this question, I was taken a bit aback. I disclosed that I had three but had just lost one. She and Meyer talked about their various approaches to answering that question, and it varied over time and according to who was asking. It occurred to me that English has some words for losing family members: "widow" and "widower," and "orphan" (though not if one has lost only one parent) but nothing for a parent who has lost a child. Perhaps that was just part of the definition of mother or father. I did notice that, in recent weeks, I had been thinking about my 1983 miscarriage and feeling like I'd lost two children, one of whom I never met but still grieved deeply, and one who brought extreme joys and aggravations for almost twenty-one years.

I was finally able to go though Amy's belongings from Circle Center while my husband was at the 11:00 Mass the next morning. Between her bedroom, apartment, and Circle Center, Amy had quite the accumulation of clothes! I found more writings which shed light on her pain and conflict.

I appreciated the non-work days when I could walk River earlier in the morning or later in the evening without a headlamp and reflective vest. I was tiring of the twenty-degree mornings, but perhaps the extended winter cold was helping to keep my grief in slow motion. I wondered whether the change in seasons would bring forth a rush of new stages.

My husband was going to watch the Super Bowl with his relatives, so after making them an apple crisp, I hoped to have quiet time to write. I started planning Amy's memorial service in my hometown. We had dinners and lunches booked with friends, and our daughter's godmother would visit us the weekend of the 27th, during which we were planning a mini-reunion of our graduate school group. That was enough to think about as we entered February.

During the next six months, I noticed the shifts in my perception of time, and life was now framed by Amy's absence, including holidays. Family and home rhythms adapted, especially for my daughter and me. She opted to remain at home and start graduate school, and I parted ways with ACHS. Relationships with extended family and friends were invariably tinged in ways that we sometimes could, and sometimes could not, talk about. I began reaching out, while still needing to close loose ends with Amy's clinicians and schools. And amid all the practical aftermaths, we had the frustrating overhang of the investigations.

Shifts in Perception of Time

After ten weeks, I had to actually count how many had elapsed since Amy's death. It was easier to think "over two months," perhaps the reverse of what happens when a mother counts a baby's age in days, then weeks, months, and finally years. Days were feeling less branded with memories of the last week of 2009. By mid-February, I was thinking about Amy a little less. A month later I realized that I had yet to be hit with a "wrecking ball" of grief and wondered if that would come. A running buddy suggested maybe not, the pieces might be smaller. Sometimes I felt like I just needed to take a day off to be sad. I'd think about Amy's definition of a "smooth day" when nothing was scheduled. It was a great, albeit elusive, concept that Giuliana always liked.

In early April, I mentally paired "months since Amy died" and "months since I left ACHS," the latter being a death of sorts, too. I found myself wondering what would have happened had she survived the overdose. Permanent incapacitation? A scare that would keep her in recovery? A return to her cycles of using and not using that would torture her and those around her for the rest of her life?

By early May, my grief pattern seemed to be little spurts of missing Amy that brought brief bursts of tears, especially when driving. But I had no "non-functional" days, or any days when I was unable to get out of bed, though I knew that could occur at any time. I had no trouble sleeping due to grief, except that first night. The outpouring of love and support from friends and family continued to buoy me.

Framed by Amy's Absence

Amy's absence had a way of keeping her present. For example, when I met my relative in my hometown in February, the coffee shop's pastry case had a chocolate "snow cake" with coconut and raspberry, something I definitely would have brought back for Amy. I did buy her favorite pizza in her honor. Sometimes I imagined "signs" from her. For example, right before Valentine's Day I made an impulse purchase of neon pink and purple daisies that reminded me of her. A few hours later, the water turned purple, presumably from the leaching dye, which made me laugh, almost as if Amy were playing a joke on us. When I attended Ash Wednesday Mass with my husband, I suddenly had this image of Amy having a grand old time with all my dear departed old women friends who had preceded her to Heaven. In the mid-March rains, I drove to a family event for one of my ACHS colleagues. When I hit a deep puddle and may have started hydroplaning, I felt like Amy had protected me.

One spring trigger was seeing the new crop of strawberries at the grocery store, knowing that I would have called Amy to ask if she wanted any. Once I accidentally speed dialed her cell phone, and the sound of her bouncy voicemail greeting pierced my heart. My husband found technology to capture incoming voicemails; he saved his and mine from Amy. On April 1st, it was tough for me to leave the HBS parking lot, because for most of the last year I would drive to visit Amy afterward, and being on the roads toward her apartment evoked a swell of pain. I took some consolation in being able to drive to see my son.

Amy and I were of similar size, and wearing some of her clothes became a kind of "comfort attire." I wore her ivory Northface® jacket a lot, her short SLU sweatpants when I worked out, and her flip flops. For my next pair of glasses I bought new lenses but used her frames. Mid-summer, I started wearing her high school ring on my favorite necklace, an idea inspired by a colleague whose infant died.

I felt a bittersweet economy when I finally balanced the bank statements from December through March because, without Amy's reimbursement transactions, it took a fraction of the time. As summer approached, my husband and our daughter were noticing how long the grass was, something Amy would have complained about for weeks. On a mid-summer bike ride with Lois, the condensation from my water bottle damaged my cell phone, which really upset me because I no longer had the last text messages I received from Amy, though I subsequently found some as "sent" messages in her phone. I also no longer had the photo of River and me on the screen that she installed with the caption, "Miss you Mom - Amy."

I made a spontaneous stop at the bagel store in Broton where Amy used to work and had an iced coffee in her honor. They had made a little shrine, taping up next to the register her prayer card, obituary, and thank-you photo card. I was so touched that they kept the assemblage up for a year. I also tried the instant coffee packets I found among her belongings, and it felt soothing that she was still introducing me to things she loved and left behind.

It really helped to be in contact with Amy's friends and teachers, but triggers continued to be unpredictable. For example, when I lectored at Mass one Sunday, I saw one of Amy's fellow middle schoolers. I screamed to myself that she was about to be a college senior, like Amy was supposed to be! I expected September would be tough, given all the memories of the academic year start-up. My husband and I came across the roster from a 1992 horse race we attended while on vacation. Amy had fallen in love with a horse named "Have a Cup." We kept the program.

I craved dreams about her. In my first, which wasn't until March, she was using the hollow temples of her sunglasses frames to hide drugs. In mid-May I awoke to a vivid dream about her injecting in her bedroom at our house. In a June dream, she was in late middle school or early high school, and we were at a mall where I pulled her aside. She admitted she had been smoking marijuana, and I recognized that she was high. This dream was striking because I don't ever remember when she admitted to using *and* I noticed it. Too many times I didn't notice, or I suspected and she denied.

May was a little tougher than April given all the "year ago" memories leading up to her move to her apartment. In July, I noticed a shift in my grief. I "flashed back" less to the week after Amy died, and instead found myself remembering what was happening a year ago that was leading up to her death. The summer of 2010 was probably my most difficult in decades (mourning Amy) and the easiest (not worrying about her).

Holidays

We had been warned about the first year of holidays. On my birthday, only three weeks after Amy's, our ever-thoughtful neighbor brought me a chocolate zucchini cake; I wondered what kind of cake Amy might have made me. As much as I'm accused of being a pack rat, I'm infinitely grateful that I saved the birthday cards she made me, especially the last one. On St.

Patrick's Day, Amy's friend Sherryl brought us some home-baked goodies, and I gave her Amy's purple stethoscope to use in her nursing studies. We looked at Amy's first notebook from Rhombus, where I found the haunting journal entry about the survival rates cited by the psychiatrist.

Easter is the most deeply rooted holiday for me, and I rarely miss spending that weekend in my hometown. We planned Amy's memorial service for Holy Saturday so we could be there for our Easter weekend rituals. Visiting the botanical gardens on Sunday was especially tough because I was there with Amy the previous year. Fortunately, we'd had a photo taken, which I used on the memorial service program. Patriot's Day is my husband's big holiday, and it was not easy for him. He, our daughter, and I attended the local Patriot Ball. Triggers of grief included watching the drummer and hearing the song "Route 66" as I remembered the postcard that Amy had sent us when she visited along that highway.

For Mother's Day, I decided to make Amy's signature dessert, the one she had waiting for me when I returned from visiting our daughter in Japan one year ago. I took some to Giuliana, a gesture of solidarity as grieving mothers. I biked to the cemetery, sprinkled some cake crumbs on the grave, and a Haiku came to me:

A mother should not
Be visiting her daughter's
Grave on Mother's Day

When I was weeding at home afterward, I received a call from Tanisha; I was blown away by her thoughtfulness and our talk was nonstop nourishment. Father's Day was difficult for my husband. He and I went to the cemetery together for the first time as just a couple. My second brother's girlfriend, whose dad died a few years ago, reminded me that Father's Day would always be tough.

We did not attend the town strawberry festival in June. It would have brought back too many memories of attending the year before with Amy, Oliver, and his grandmother. The town Old Home Day was June 26th, and our neighbor entered a pottery butter dish that Amy had made her many years ago in the art show. I volunteered at the road races since I'd sprained my ankle gardening on Memorial Day and couldn't run. The race director talked about Amy at the start of the one-mile race, including how she had run her first Old Home Day race at age five. He then had a moment of silence. I recalled how just last year Amy and I won our age groups.

Adapting as a Family

I knew it would be good for our daughter to live at home for awhile after Amy died; however, I totally underestimated how good it would be for my husband and me. Yet it was difficult to find all three of us simultaneously in the right frame of mind for conversations about our grieving. Such a topic seemed awkward to actually schedule, and almost impossible if we tried to include our son. Mid-February, upon my return from visiting my home-town, the four of us met for a snack at a bakery near his apartment, our first immediate family time since Amy had died. I felt her absence acutely, realizing there was no possibility she would bound in late, as had so often happened, imagining her long legs in snug jeans, wearing a short winter jacket, a flowing scarf grazing her hatless, long brown hair. We also passed the Indian restaurant where we had our last family dinner. I still felt pangs of regret that I didn't ask the waiter to take a photo of us. Our son came home a few weekends later and made pizzas for dinner; such visits were comforting. In mid-March, he proposed to his girlfriend, and she accepted. We were thrilled.

None of us wanted to engage in grief counseling, perhaps jaded by all the counseling during the years Amy was sick, but also not feeling a particular need. I felt affirmed when I heard a story after the 2010 Haiti earthquake that the American concept of storming in with counseling for Post Traumatic Stress can sometimes be counterproductive to recovery. Each of us felt like we were finding enough of the right support that worked for us *without* adding formal sessions onto our plates. For example, my husband was back singing in the choir and competing in a Friday night chess club. He was going to attend a math conference and visit his relatives. Yet even such supportive activities were not immune from triggers. They ate at the restaurant where we'd hosted our children's college graduation dinners, which triggered my memory of the first time I had dinner with my adult children at that same restaurant, when Amy had just turned eighteen. I remembered my feeling of motherly pride, walking behind as the three of them bantered as only siblings can, and never would again.

My daughter and I bonded over some cooking projects as a way of remembering how food was so central to Amy's being. Frying scallion pancakes in the electric pan I had bought for Amy at SLU was particularly sacred. I took consolation from eating some of the food she left behind, including chocolate-covered raisins, cherry granola bars, and the dried mangos Ramona had brought her back from Asia. Her bag of homemade cinnamon sugar lasted all summer, and I waited until a year after we had attended our last farmers market to finish the granola we'd bought then.

River comforted me when he slept across my arm, snoring, as I typed on my laptop. But in his thirteenth year, his physical decline accelerated, and I dreaded the thought of losing him so soon after Amy. When it was time to put him down, sixteen months after Amy died, I felt we had had enough time for a proper good-bye, and I could let go with fond memories.

Departure from ACHS

Amy had been on my case about the negative aspects of my job at ACHS, and tragically it took her death for me to finally confront the issues. On Friday, February 19th, my boss and I went out for lunch and agreed that I would send her another email asking for clarification of my request to go part-time given that I had not received a reply from the president for four weeks, and March 1st was a week away. My boss forwarded the email to the president, who emailed on Monday to say that she would meet with me the next day. At that meeting, the president made clear that she did not see my position as part-time, despite a restructuring plan that my boss and I had prepared that would cost the school less. Thus I submitted my resignation on my terms on Wednesday, and left at the end of the week, on the two-month anniversary of Amy's death. It was not the outcome I wanted, but I accepted that it was the president's decision, not mine. Yet leaving was another loss to grieve on top of mourning my daughter.

I fully believed in the mission of the school, really enjoyed my colleagues, and loved the students; I had even given Amy's skateboards to two of them who were boarders. I was hoping I could still remain involved in a healthy way. On March 4th, I received an email from the ACHS campus minister, asking if I would be willing to help plan and chaperone the junior retreat. I was thrilled. But when I attended a retreat planning meeting, I felt sadly awkward to be back. Although it was wonderful to give and receive such warm greetings with students and colleagues, I was "spitting nails" at how my work situation had ended. I did attend baccalaureate and graduation.

By mid-spring, I realized that I was no longer constantly exhausted, and I wondered how much my fatigue while working in schools factored into the dynamics with Amy. When at ACHS, I awoke by 5:00 and was out the door by 6:10 while my husband slept. In May, I noticed the role reversal: Now I was often still snoozing as he departed, and even took naps. I met with the career counselor to help me process my ACHS departure. I wanted to dive into researching where I might effectively "plug in" professionally to effective substance abuse prevention efforts, although investigations into Amy's case, and ensuing action, were still pending. I was feeling uncharacteristically patient, with faith the right path would emerge.

Family and Friends

Support from family came primarily through phone calls since most lived out of town. Visiting my ill relative was my first time in a hospital since the Geotown ER, but it hurt to see all the young nurses as it sunk in that Amy would never join their ranks. My relatives appreciated seeing the photo slideshow that played at Amy's wake and the "open mike" DVD from the post-funeral lunch. I visited again in August, this time driving my dear eighty-five-year-old relative to see her older sibling. I felt especially fortunate knowing I could not have made this unforgettably special road trip had I still been at ACHS during summer "crunch time."

I was blessed to have friends spanning all eras of my life, from elementary school to those I was just befriending as a result of Amy's death. By staying connected over the years, my network of support was robust when I needed it most. Amy's friends from all eras were a real lifeline to me, and I hoped to meet with more of them before their last year of college.

Friends from my corporate years came through. The support from Meyer and Giuliana never waned. I was particularly touched when they visited both Amy's and Tommy's graves (about a mile apart) and left flowers. Lois checked in every few weeks, took me to the ocean for some "rest and relaxation," helped us recover from our basement flooding, and helped us plant a kitchen garden. She, a mutual friend, and I kept our annual birthday dinner tradition at the Mexican restaurant where my husband and I ate with Amy the night before she went to detox. I remembered what hope he and I were feeling, as well as Amy's extended time in the bathroom. This mutual friend and I later had breakfast at an IHOP in Amy's honor. And the editor/designer for this book, and the sound engineer for the audiobook, were colleagues at my start-up.

Amy's death had hit my friend Gino, another pallbearer, particularly hard. He had always looked up to us as a family who seemed to be doing just about everything right. He was shattered to realize that if Amy's tragedy could happen in our family, then truly no one was immune. My husband and I enjoyed a dinner with their young family, and later I met Gino at Tulips, showed him Amy's brick, and gave him our son's and Amy's lacrosse sticks for his children.

The BVMP community was an especially important source of support. I stayed in touch with Sr. Juliann, who always kept us in prayer. One of Amy's favorite teachers was thrilled when I gave her an essay that Amy had written in praise of her teaching style. I often met former colleagues for walks and talks. Former students were an unanticipated blessing. I've met up with many and stayed in touch with even more on Facebook. I'm now much closer to one because Amy's death gave us permission to talk about the losses in our lives at a level that really mattered. I had coffee with another I'd tutored just days before Amy died, and I could tell her what I didn't feel I could share in late December. Parents of former students also reached out, which resulted in deep dialogues.

I was grateful I could make time for people who kept coming out of the closet, or should I say medicine cabinet. Several have shared that they or family members are in recovery. I met a coworker from the early 1990s to share notes on the saga with her step-teens and substances and wished I'd reached out to her when our family was in crisis.

My husband and I dined with a former colleague and his wife whose teen-age son showed warning signs of drug trouble; they sent him to a wilderness program and he had recently moved to a therapeutic boarding school. It's concerning that very little data is available on the effectiveness of these expensive and intensive programs, but this intervention for their son was working so far.

I connected with a classmate whose experience losing her daughter was so similar to mine that it was like talking to a mirror. I felt an emotional oasis in finally sharing with someone who had been through so many of the same specifics, and who had identical reactions.

I walked with someone who had contacted me based on the letters to the editor I'd written about Amy. She shared the story of her child's treatment and recovery. I kept receiving calls and notes from others in the community who wanted to confide in me about their family's turmoil.

I met a former colleague whose daughter is a recovering heroin addict, having gone undetected through high school until early college. We had no idea we were traveling such parallel paths for so many years, and she encouraged my writing and speaking efforts, especially in our demographic. She shared yet another story of a young high school student being introduced to prescription painkillers by a friend who handed out extras following wisdom teeth surgery. This student progressed to heroin: Where we live, one 80 mg. OxyContin pill goes for $80, and a bag of heroin is down to $3 to $5.

Amy's friend, Byron, came to our house often, and he helped me sort items in her room and shared stories of their middle school antics. When the weather cleared, we took our long-planned drive in Amy's honor, the twelve-mile "around the block" loop with my sunroof open, blaring the mix CD she made for my 2006 birthday, and visited her grave.

Sherryl and I met frequently, often for a meal at Amy's favorite Mexican restaurant. One of their classmates shared Amy's mantra, "If you're going to do something bad, do something double good before." While I had observed this pattern empirically, it was reassuring to hear that Amy was articulating it. This friend came up with the phrase, "an Amy moment," whenever she thought or felt something about Amy, who was one of her best Red Sox buddies. One "Amy moment" I had was being in the garage and realizing that piles of fast food packaging and mostly empty water bottles no longer spontaneously generated; I recalled the constant battle I had with her about putting her food debris into the recycling or trash.

In the spring, Ramona, my daughter, and I went around the corner from the apartment to a new frozen yogurt shop that Amy would have loved, and I had the mango flavor in her honor. Ramona told us some troubling stories that filled in more of the fall 2009 picture, including the sketchy guys Amy brought to the apartment behind closed doors. In mid-May, I met Ramona for dinner, hearing more stories, both good and unsettling. I never knew that Amy loved roller coasters, a metaphor for her life! They planned to buy a season pass to a nearby amusement park and had checked out the bus schedule so they could go every weekend. Amy apparently had one clandestine date with the good young man she told me she thought she would marry. She once spent several hours hiding in a closet with Ramona when they were at a party and needed to escape some bothersome individuals.

I am grateful for the contact with Amy's friends from treatment. My daughter and I met with Claire, who had the last known conversation with Amy and who found her overdosed in the bathroom. She generously shared a lot of details about how she saw Circle Center handle December 26th. The questions at the end of this book, "What to ask a Facility," reflect some of these details.

My daughter and I also met with one of Amy's best friends from rehab in June and shared stories. I learned that someone who knew Amy at Rhombus had relapsed. Apparently, he thought Amy was one of the people in rehab who really "got it" early on.

We learned that Oliver was in a serious car accident. The newspaper reported that the operator was driving under the influence, her baby was okay because he was strapped in a car seat, but Oliver was not wearing a seat belt. He was ejected from the car and med-flighted to the city with serious head injuries. We struggled to process this strange twist of news. When I saw the photo of the helicopter in the newspaper, I screamed to myself: My daughter never had a chance to be med-flighted when she overdosed! In May, we learned he was in physical rehab from his brain injuries. In July, we heard he was home, but he remained impaired from the car accident; his brother was still in jail after being arrested for breaking and entering while free on bail for the same charge in another town. My husband had Facebook deactivate Amy's page due to some inappropriate postings. We kept Amy's memorial page active.

Taking Care of Myself

My running group provided invaluable support; I rarely missed a Saturday convening. In 2010 we celebrated six "decade" birthdays, and as Poet Laureate, I composed original works for the celebrations, which provided a vital creative outlet for me. In mid-March, I joined a running buddy for breakfast at her favorite diner, sadly just down the street from where I dropped Amy at the A.A. meeting on Christmas afternoon.

In early spring, another buddy (the one whose birthday poem I was unable to read because my husband and I were driving Amy to detox) brought us dinner, fulfilling a promise from January. Our daughter came with me to the group and opted to walk to Amy's grave, reporting the grass on the plot was the greenest in the cemetery. The group included a stop at Amy's grave to see the newly installed headstone on the seven-month anniversary of the funeral, and that observance meant a lot to my husband and me.

I kept my tradition of volunteering at the Boston Marathon, and saw a buddy who said he would make a point to remember Amy. He wrote in his race report at mile twenty-two, "Amy carries me over the hill and down along BC." Amy and I had talked about running the marathon together some year, though she would have finished *way* ahead of me.

In the early spring, I started bicycling, often with friends. While riding with Meyer in the middle of a back road, I was overwhelmed with the feeling of how incongruous it was that his son and my daughter were both dead, yet there we were enjoying the glorious spring day. I kept going to the gym, and loved working out in whatever clothes Amy left behind that fit me. I was prioritizing my fitness, even if it did result in a sprained ankle while gardening, a broken arm from a bike mishap, and tendinitis from lifting.

Support Groups

The support of our parish was especially key for my husband as a choir and prayer group member. In February, our church's fiftieth anniversary Mass was celebrated by the bishop who was pastor where all three of our children were baptized. My husband sang, and we informed the bishop about Amy; he appreciated that we told him in person. On my first Monday not working at ACHS, I enjoyed being able to attend the 9:00 a.m. Mass. Amy had sometimes accompanied me during summer vacation.

I attended my first Grief Recovery After a Substance Passing (GRASP) meeting in March. My daughter and I attended the May meeting, but I still felt more affinity with my Nar-Anon family group. I've realized that whether our addicts are in recovery, or using, or estranged, or missing, or dead, we are all grieving.

My husband and our daughter found that the Nar-Anon group was no longer meeting their needs after Amy died. In early April, I kept thinking I'd stop going, but every time I went, I was so glad. During one meeting, I experienced a very strong emotional reaction thinking about Amy, and I received so much comfort from my friends. I started volunteering to lead meetings. A state senator who spoke at our annual meeting had already heard about Amy, and fueled my desire to plug into effective advocacy efforts.

Reaching Out

In mid-February, I emailed David Sheff, the author of *Beautiful Boy*, about how his and his son's books wove into Amy's last weeks. I was touched by his heartfelt reply. In June, I read *Understanding the High-Functioning Alcoholic*, and I connected with the author, Sarah Allen Benton. Her book intersperses research and her experience as a clinician with her journals as an alcoholic before and during recovery. As she described the patterns, starting with high school and college, I found myself checking off Amy, Amy, Amy (same disease, different drugs).

In March, I called Trina to schedule a long overdue dinner with her and her husband. I reminded her of my interest in sharing Amy's story as part of educating teens and parents. Her school was having a program on Friday morning, and she invited me as an observer. When they introduced me to the adult presenter, he asked me to join him and the two recovering seventeen-year-olds who were telling their story. We spoke to two classes. The sessions seemed to go very well, and I offered to help in future programs. Their focus on teen substance abuse prevention, including educating teachers, affirmed the calling I was starting to feel in this area.

In early April, I attended my first meeting of the Community Coalition Drug Abuse Prevention Task force in ACHS's city, furthering my fact-finding on what effective efforts I might join. In late April, I attended the Town Hall meeting sponsored by the coalition. While not well attended, I kept learning and forged new connections. Walking from my car, I happened to bump into three of my former ACHS students. We shrieked and hugged, and I realized how much I missed being with them. I also began a "Family Support of Addiction" initiative with a colleague for HBS alums.

In mid-April, I contacted a former classmate, a state representative, about the 2009 OxyContin and Heroin Commission Report. She said that we should talk. I met with her staff about pending legislation ensuing from the report, and it felt rewarding to contribute. I returned to the state house in June to lobby in support of keeping the alcohol tax, which annually generated $100 million (Amy's favorite number) for substance abuse programs.

Closure with Amy's Clinicians and Schools

I wanted to have "closing conversations" with the clinicians we had dealt with to see what we could learn from Amy's tragedy. On March 1st, I heard back from Dr. Subone, the psychiatrist near SLU who had first prescribed Suboxone to Amy. It was not clear whether Amy's story would make any difference in the way he prescribed and followed his patients. In early May, I met with my former therapist, Dr. Sporsy, to educate him more about what had happened. He shared how Amy's death had impacted him and his many patients who knew Amy. I left hoping that he could share Amy's story among his sports psychology clientele. In June, I met with psychiatrist Dr. Buprine, a wonderful man who was very concerned about what we had learned from her case. He struggled with whether he could continue to treat young females since he could not supervise their drug tests, and he told the story of how Amy once had a friend sneak into the bathroom to provide a sample.

I needed closure with Amy's high school and colleges. I still harbored affection for BVMP since leaving in June 2008. In mid-May, I attended the alumnae Mass, hoping Amy would be mentioned in the prayers (she wasn't). I felt very much at home among former colleagues at baccalaureate, and I flashed back to 2007 when my Franciscan brother had said that Mass, and Amy had received a local running club's scholarship. A few days later I met Mrs. Guicona, Amy's high school guidance counselor, for lunch before graduation. I dropped by the BVMP sports banquet on June 16th, just missing the tribute to Amy by her cross country coach and pallbearer, and the moment of silence observed by the hundreds present.

I flew to SLU in March to see Amy's friends and come to terms with all that had transpired in that environment. Arriving at the airport was almost numbing, and not seeing Amy but feeling her presence at every juncture was strange. Flashbacks to her December 2008 move out were inevitable: the Christmas carolers who annoyed me as we were trying to rebook flights; the restaurant where Amy claimed she had the worst food in the world; the baggage service office where we tried to ascertain the status of all we had moved out of Amy's dorm room; and the pay phone from where I had called my ACHS boss and left a message that had been received poorly. I found myself wishing Amy had stayed at SLU and opted for BC grad school.

I met Amy's dear friend and pallbearer, Patrick, at the coffee shop where Amy insisted that the three of us meet during my last visit. We had a much needed talk in depth and at length. A fellow nursing student of similar stature, I gave him Amy's maroon BC scrubs.

Then I met Tanisha at another favorite haunt. I had no idea how much Amy had meant to her. She told me how Amy kept her loose amid the intensity of her pre-med studies, bursting into dorm rooms to insist that the occupants join her in six-minute abs workouts, buying pizza rolls and confetti cupcake mix and frosting (but no sprinkles) at the gas station, and Amy's love of her mother's oatmeal cake. When Tanisha would return to their room after a test, she would find a little pile of candy on her desk from Amy, who created these special arrangements from her well-stocked candy drawer. Amy taught her how to bake sweet potatoes in the microwave. She reminisced about the mutual adoration between her toddler nephew and Amy. She spoke of how much Amy loved her sister.

Tanisha said that, on move-in day, by the way Amy had resolved an administrative issue over lofted beds she *knew* the two of them would be friends. She smiled as she remembered how Amy admired all of her shoes, but even when Amy dressed up, she wore flip flops. I offered Tanisha most of Amy's SLU-insignia clothing, and could not have been happier when she accepted it. Tanisha's mom then joined us, and we recalled how we had bonded when we first met in the freshmen dorm lobby, even before we knew our daughters would be roommates.

When I returned to my hotel, I had a soulful conversation with a nun I had never met in person but who had written when Amy died. I stayed in that night, decompressing, reading, writing, phoning, and integrating. On Sunday morning, I worked out at the recreation center, then ran a lap around the indoor track in Amy's honor. I was so glad that Tanisha had told me how Amy sometimes dragged her up there, although she could never keep up! Patrick treated three of Amy's friends and me to a Mexican lunch. I left a prayer card at her sophomore dorm, and then went to the student center to pay homage after all the time we'd spent there. I left a card at another coffee shop that Amy loved, and at her first-year dorm.

That afternoon, I visited the dog museum that I'd never made it to with Amy, and I met with a nun whom I hadn't seen in the forty years since high school; she had sent me a sympathy card. Another one of Amy's friends and I had dinner at her favorite chain restaurant. He ordered a grilled cheese and the sweetest possible shake in her honor. We then met some of Amy's friends in the church vestibule for the 9:00 p.m. Mass. Coincidentally, the Greek life chaplain delivered a preamble about the "forty days sober" Lenten program. His theme was about being careless or carefree versus careful. One of the petitions was directed at addiction, and Amy was remembered in the prayers.

I could not keep my eyes off a woman who looked like she could have been Amy in her mid-thirties. I realized I'd never imagined what Amy might look like as an older adult. This woman was a little heavier, but by no means overweight, and seemed sad, weighed down. I imagined Amy still struggling with her addiction, her career, her kids, and almost felt relieved that she would not be facing such a wrenching future. At the same time, I grieved the relationship with her that I had been counting on.

After the Mass I thanked the chaplain, who also said he'd seen too many deaths in his five years at SLU. I thanked the celebrant and the priest who read the intentions. We met up with Tanisha, her mom, and nephew, and went to the student center to watch the slideshow from the wake and excerpts from the "open mike" DVD, which everyone seemed to find healing. When I left on Monday morning, I felt aches and pangs at the airport as I was triggered by reminders of all the stresses when Amy and I traveled.

In contrast to SLU, I felt blessed to have BC so close to home. The memorial Mass for Amy was beautiful and well worth the wait until April 21st so most of her professors and nursing classmates could attend. My husband, son, and daughter came. I made cupcakes for the reception to follow, just as Amy would have using yellow cake mix, ready-made chocolate frosting, and sprinkles. We had good talks with so many of her professors, who all spoke about how bright she was in mind and smile, how respectful, and the unbelievable quality of her work before her final and precipitous decline. Even then she could sometimes pull off a 99 on a late clinical report. Her enthusiasm for the program included telling her professors how well they taught undergraduates.

It especially warmed my heart to finally meet her BC classmates and friends, including the young man she had told me she thought she was going to marry. The priests asked if I would speak at the upcoming annual interfaith memorial service in May; I said yes. The service was exquisite, and truly a wonderful tradition. The Liturgical Choir sang. Two priests read the names of the more than forty staff, relatives, and student (Amy) who had died in the last year, to the "Litany of the Saints" music. That song had been the only part of Amy's funeral with which I wasn't totally satisfied since the choir seemed a bit off, so the BC rendition "perfected" that "defect." So many people came up to me after, including others whose losses were related to addiction.

Being able to connect with Amy's professors has helped me tremendously. Not long after she died, one of them sent us a paper Amy had written about the disappearance and discovery of our cat in 2000. He was so impressed by what Amy had written, but unfortunately I knew the source. On October 6th, Amy had asked me to email her the story I'd written about our "lost and found" cat, and she changed curiously few of the details for her paper. I took some consolation in knowing that my writing had passed muster with a BC professor.

I met him at BC in July, which was helpful and healing for both of us. He seriously questioned what, if anything, he might have done differently. He could distinctly remember the conversations he'd had with Amy sitting in the same chair where I was seated. He shared her description of her father as a "gentle genius," and of me as a "loving workaholic." At one point he questioned whether Amy may have had some underlying, undetected brain damage that was at root of her behaviors.

I then met with the priest who was our main point of contact to thank him for all the college had done when Amy died. I saw Amy's nursing advisor and donated another medical dictionary of hers; we both choked up. I started looking into what it might cost to have a bench installed at BC in her honor, remembering the times I had picked her up on campus and she sometimes had to wait for me.

I also read *Addiction: a Disease of Choice*, a book I'd found in Amy's apartment under the foot of her bed. She and I had talked about taking this professor's class together in the spring since it was offered in the night school. The professor gave a talk about the book, which I attended with an ACHS student. I still question how he accounts for the less than fifty percent survival rate when he cites statistics on people no longer addicted once they hit age thirty. He seemed to have little emotional connection to the devastation that addiction brings to families as well as addicts. I still hope to follow up with him.

Practical Aftermaths

Around the House

In March, record rains seeped into our basement. I did not appreciate Mother Nature adding the cleanup and repairs to my grief-laden workload. When I couldn't decide what color white paint to buy for the patched walls, I chose "December Starlight" in honor of Amy. I felt like repainting the kitchen purple in her memory. Instead, we livened up the exterior shutters and door with "purple rain." Amy always complained about my overuse of beige (house, car, clothes), so I knew a vibrant shade of her favorite color would have met her approval.

Amy's Apartment

Issues related to Amy's apartment continued into the summer. One morning Ramona texted me that the cable service had been suspended. It turned out that, when the cable company changed the account name to mine, they didn't change the billing to my address, so I wasn't receiving the bills. Fortunately, dealing with the company wasn't too aggravating, and service was restored later that day. Within a month, the account issues were finally resolved, which had been a major stress for me when there were questions about where some of the equipment was. I subsequently took flowers to the cable company to thank the woman who straightened everything out.

I calculated the amount Ramona and Sandra owed for cable and electric. Despite their efforts and those by BC and the landlord, they could not find a replacement third occupant, so we continued to pay Amy's rent until the landlord came forth with a kind offer to cover part of it. Who could have imagined a death contingency when we signed the lease?

Amy's Belongings

Dealing with Amy's belongings continued to be a sacred task, primarily left to my daughter and me. We had the luxury of working in bursts when we felt like it, and taking long pauses when we didn't. In early March, she and I cleaned out Amy's white bedroom furniture and moved it to the garage. Very sadly, we found a needle under her bed; imagining her injecting at home was just awful. That weekend, a colleague from ACHS came with his truck to take the bed, dresser, and nightstand to another colleague who had three little girls. A local ministry collected her apartment bed and a garish mirror unit she picked up at some curbside, so the basement was a little clearer.

During the March rains, what belongings we hadn't given away we brought up to her bedroom. It helped to clump items together, such as all her jeans, electronics, papers, and toiletries, before deciding what to do with them. We triaged the items into "definite keepers," "decide laters," and "definite don't keeps," erring on the side of keeping since we couldn't get back anything disposed prematurely. A few items were clear throwaways, like underwear, which I bundled into a Victoria's Secret bag before placing in the trash. And cotton swabs were everywhere. I didn't know about their significance as a filter in heroin injection until after she died. It felt good to ask others if they wanted anything of hers and giving it to them.

I found some 2008 Christmas cards that Amy had started, maybe in Japan, but never mailed. I slowly sent them to the intended recipients. I also stumbled across her writing on the flap of a bright orange parking violation envelope:

My compulsion for detail and closure led me to look up the reference. A Google search yielded that the article appeared exactly four months to the day before she died. It was about an undertaker whose son died of a heroin overdose and how the father prepared his son's body for burial. This finding was almost mysterious, even eerie. I paid one of her parking tickets, and the city waived the late penalties. A nearby town waived another ticket and my running buddy lawyer friend cleared what should have been Amy's January court appearance for yet another ticket.

I took Amy's old bike for a tune-up so her sister could use it, despite the fact that Amy had used it to ride with Oliver. In April, I didn't do much with her room other than find all her BC clothes, which I took to the Mass but never did distribute among her friends.

On Holy Thursday, I dropped Amy's basketball hoop at a center for developmentally disabled adults where several ACHS students worked. I also dropped off her track coach's mittens at his gym. She told me she'd returned them to him, but I found them in her under-bed drawer when

I cleaned her room after she went to detox, never imagining then that my organizing project would be the precursor to the disposal task now at hand.

In mid-May, Sherryl and I spent about an hour going through items in Amy's room, and then I took her to the local state park for ice cream, a favorite of Amy's. The next week, Sherryl, my daughter, and I had lunch at the Mexican restaurant where my husband and I ate with Amy the night before she went to detox. We split a fried ice cream in Amy's memory. A few days later, Sherryl, my daughter, and I worked on Amy's room for several hours. At the end, we were reading her high school journals, which was very difficult. Sherryl was one of Amy's true best friends, and I believe that Amy was drawn to her by her goodness. She was also the hardest working student I ever taught, and she made me a much better teacher.

By the end of May, I was finally able to clear the table of Christmas presents. In early June, we still had so much to do in Amy's room, but I appreciated not having to rush the work. Our daughter shook her head at how many of her running clothes Amy had appropriated. By the month's end, I'd done nothing more in her room, thinking I needed to designate one day a week for that purpose and maybe enlist the help of a friend.

I couldn't bring myself to look at Amy's camera. I took her electronic drum set to be checked out prior to donating it. It all worked, but it was missing a pedal, which I later found in a laundry basket under her bedding. I subsequently donated the set to a charter school, and it has been a joy to attend recitals and see the middle-school students' progress on the instrument.

In July, my daughter and I went through Amy's clothes and gave six large bags to Big Brothers Big Sisters. Amy had been a Big Sister while at SLU and worried about the fate her twelve-year-old little sister was headed for given the family's cycle of poverty and early pregnancies.

The Headstone

Of all the things I thought I'd ever buy for Amy, a headstone wasn't one of them. My husband and I had made the initial trip to the monument store six weeks after she died. Recommended by his relative, I was not inspired. The first Monday I was not working at ACHS, I took the neon flowers to the cemetery and surveyed the headstones to garner some ideas. In mid-April, my daughter and I went to another monument store and found a slant marker for half-price because of some error when they first tried to engrave it. My daughter commented how Amy would definitely roll over in her grave knowing I would buy her headstone on sale! She and I worked on the design.

After the April 21ˢᵗ BC service, my daughter and I stopped at the monument store to resolve a challenge with some of the artwork we wanted. Shortly thereafter, I revisited the monument store where my husband and I first went just to feel sure about the choice we were making. Again, nothing inspired me, especially at double the price of our work in process.

In mid-May, Sherryl and I went to the cemetery, where the foundation was dug for the headstone. On the five-month anniversary of Amy's death, my daughter and I stopped at the cemetery, saw the poured foundation, and watered the flowers. By early June, the artwork for Amy's headstone was almost ready. I stopped at the cemetery, watered flowers, and weeded a little.

Our family approved the artwork for the headstone, which included five images etched on the back: a Red Sox logo, a Celtics logo, a drum set, a pair of running shoes with untied laces, and a cupcake with sprinkles that could double as a dish of ice cream. Byron's suggestion to add "Amy" in italics above the five images perfected the design. I asked if the stone could be ready by July 20ᵗʰ, her half birthday. It was installed on July 26ᵗʰ, and it's beautiful. The front includes a small oval porcelain inlay of a hummingbird lighting on a sweet pea. Both images are symbolic. My husband's pet name for Amy was sweet pea. And her sister noted: "Amy was a social hummingbird. At least butterflies stop to light." An inground vase was later installed so we can leave cut flowers or a Christmas tree.

Memorial Service

By early March, I finalized details for Amy's memorial service in my hometown on Holy Saturday. It was important for me to hold such a ritual, since only eight relatives from there had been able to attend the funeral. Held at a small banquet facility, we began with some readings and a slideshow, followed by Amy's favorite dinner, Chicken Parmesan with Fettuccine Alfredo. It was comforting to be in the company of fifty-one family and friends. The next afternoon, I kept the Easter Sunday ritual of going to the botanical gardens, and made sure to have my picture taken with my first daughter in front of the giant Easter egg, as we have done almost every year. The picture I had taken a year earlier with Amy was featured on the memorial service program.

Thank-you Notes

It was important to me to send thank-you notes to those who had stepped up in our time of greatest need. I wrote them out at home, in airports, and libraries, sometimes writing as many as fifty a day. I hunted down addresses using sources including switchboard.com, Facebook messaging, phone books, and old school directories. Tears welled in my eyes when I bought LOVE stamps whose purple pansies were a perfect fit for Amy. In total, we sent more than one thousand, including one to each ACHS student, and I know we didn't reach everybody.

Investigations

Dealing with the medical and legal aftermath of Amy's death has been very difficult, because there is no "how-to" guide. Nobody cares more about these matters than I do, but I found it tough to gauge how much to push to be effective.

In February, I talked with a fellow parishioner, a pharmacist who became an attorney and worked for the Drug Enforcement Administration. We discussed his work decades ago, and he cautioned how involved I become in investigations, which made me realize that I really needed to be aligned with my family on what I was pursuing on Amy's behalf and why. Another parishioner told me that a relative who worked at the New England Organ Bank mentioned an apparent uptick in our state's heroin deaths in December. When I followed up, the Department of Public Health did not yet have numbers on heroin deaths in December, but the person with whom I spoke was very helpful referring me to resources. She encouraged me to provide any feedback to make their work more effective. I felt that my state tax dollars were supporting good work.

The state police called to follow up on their involvement; they planned to obtain Amy's laptop from the Geotown police and run forensics, and I faxed Amy's cell phone bill. In June, we learned that the state police were not going to do anything. It seems odd that their "hand-slapping" was to the Geotown Hospital for not notifying them or the Geotown police.

Mid-month, I spoke with the Geotown detective, who seemed to be actively pursuing Amy's case since I sent him the timeline on January 11th. In early June, I mailed Amy's journal and cell phone to Geotown after our town police returned them to me in late May, saying they never heard back from Geotown. While in a sealed evidence bag, I was able to manipulate her second rehab journal (brown leather) and transcribe it through the plastic. I entered her first rehab notebook (red cover, spiral bound) entries as well. Reading them was very intense and heartbreaking. I could tell that she had written letters on paper from the red notebook because I could see the imprint on remaining sheets. I asked around to no avail about a machine that could read from the impressions.

In early March, I faxed Amy's final phone bill to the various law enforcement officers. It was tough for me to open the envelope, not knowing who would be the last people she called, coupled with the fact that her cell phone usage had always been such a source of tension. The police still had her cell phone, laptop, and journal. (I followed up *again* in April.) In July, I wrote to the county district attorney's office to see if they could help me navigate "the system." I didn't want to rush the police investigation, but the more time that elapsed, the more information we could lose, and Geotown had only one detective.

Mid-March, I stopped at the Broton police to meet with the detective assigned to Amy's case. I couldn't help but wonder why law enforcement didn't have more teeth in dealing with Oliver's family over many years. The detective encouraged me to keep making phone calls.

The medical examiner's report arrived about eight weeks after Amy died. I reviewed it with my nurse friend George in mid-March. The autopsy looked pretty ordinary, but I really wanted help interpreting the numbers in the toxicology report. I have yet to find anyone who can provide a conclusive interpretation on the levels of heroin and cocaine, which has been frustrating. On March 13th, I received a box from the medical examiner containing the four rings that Amy had been wearing when she died, including one belly button ring and her BVMP ring. I mailed the medical examiner my follow-up toxicology questions and received a call back without a whole lot of answers. The doctor almost discouraged me from pursuing my questions and told me instead to simply "love your daughter." He lamented how our society is losing a generation to drugs.

In June, we received her medical records from Triangle. We now had in one place her self-reported history of drug use. The records said virtually nothing about what happened on December 26th, so I also requested the Emergency Medical Technician (EMT) records. The fire department needed the request notarized, and wanted a copy of the paper appointing me as administrator and of my driver's license. The report arrived in July. I reviewed it with George, and it appeared to him that the EMTs did everything right: They were at Amy's side within nine minutes of receiving the call, administered nasal Narcan (that is Naloxone, a narcotic antagonist, the equivalent of an epi-pen for opiate overdoses) and then gave it to her intravenously. An MD also rode in the ambulance.

The most critical report was the one from the DPH, the state agency which licensed Triangle. Throughout 2010, I kept sending questions to the investigator as they arose. For example, I'd heard that the director of the Triangle detox unit was apparently no longer there a week or two after Amy died. The mother of a former student urged me to ask whether the facility had had an AED (cardiac defibrillator) on the premises. In April, the DPH said they were only waiting for one more piece of information before they issued their report. In July, I sent my estate administrator's certification to the DPH so they would send me the investigation report, which was supposed to be soon. It arrived on December 14th.

My husband, daughter, and I initially met with attorneys a few weeks after Amy died to make sure we were not overlooking any concerns from a legal standpoint, especially time-critical matters. Mid-year, I obtained second opinions from two other attorneys who were very discouraging about filing any type of suit. While the final determination would be made based on the DPH report, they concurred with the first attorney that wrongful death and malpractice cases were extremely difficult to win, contrary to popular opinion. Most do not settle out of court, so they go to a jury trial. In the case of an overdose or suicide, jurors tend to blame the victim, citing their choice in the matter. One attorney also said that most families who pursue such cases regret it for the way families are raked over the coals in the process. Plus, the cases are very expensive, and the attorneys need to feel there's a reasonable chance of winning to take on the work on a contingency basis. According to a friend in another state with a large recovery community, the laws there are very different and a "standard of care" is assumed. On July 26th, 2011, upon review of the DPH report and other analysis, the attorneys told us they did not believe we had a viable case. My hope is that this book will ultimately help individuals and organizations, and inspire change in ways that lawsuits could not.

Twelve
Closing Reflections

From losing many people close to me, I knew to follow the advice that I'd given to others: Grief can be so unpredictable and you have to ride the wave. You have to give yourself the time and space to grieve the way you need to, follow your gut, and not be held hostage to other peoples' "shoulds." Try and be with the people, in the places, and doing the things that comfort you. When my close relative died, sometimes diving into work was the best thing I could do. At other times, it was the most absurd.

The most helpful nugget came from our friend, Giuliana, who forewarned that every family member's grieving style was different, and you had to respect that. She and her husband, Meyer, claimed that they had no idea what they were doing when Tommy died, yet their role-modeling was the candle in front of me as I tried to find a path in the darkness of my family's grief. From knowing I could drive to the hospital once I knew Amy was dead, to being able to kiss her forehead one last time, to writing and delivering her eulogy, their example paved a way for me. Also, having seen Meyer full-time at work after Tommy died helped me decide, at a time when it was technically too early to make major decisions, that I had to cut back to half-time at ACHS.

About six weeks after Amy died, I heard a National Public Radio clip featuring a Haitian-born structural engineer from New Jersey who described how many buildings looked fine after the 2010 earthquake, but had hairline eggshell fractures that would make them vulnerable over time. I couldn't help but make the analogy to those who grieve. Those who may not have suffered visible damage (like many buildings) may look okay, but can carry the "invisible" damage to the psyche. Resilience varies.

When people say they can't imagine what I'm going through, or they can't imagine what it's like to lose a child, I encourage them to ask. It's also okay to simply ask "how's it going," which leaves the door open to talk as much

The minister Gerald Lawson Sittser lost his wife, mother, and youngest daughter when their car was hit by a drunk driver; he and his three older children survived. I found very helpful his passage from page 38 of his book, *A Grace Disguised*.

Catastrophic loss of whatever kind is always bad, only bad in different ways. It is impossible to quantify and to compare. The very attempt we often make in quantifying losses only exacerbates the loss by driving us to two unhealthy extremes. One the one hand, those coming out on the losing end of the comparison are deprived of the validation they need to identify and experience the loss for the bad thing it is. They sometimes feel like the little boy who just scratched his finger but cried too hard to receive much sympathy. Their loss is dismissed as unworthy of attention and recognition. On the other hand, those coming out on the winning end convince themselves that no one has suffered as much as they have, that no one will ever understand them, and that no one can offer lasting help. They are the ultimate victims. So they indulge themselves with their pain and gain a strange kind of pleasure in their misery.

Whose loss is worse? The question begs the point. Each experience of loss is unique, each painful in its own way, each as bad as everyone else's but also different. No one will ever know the pain I have experienced because it is my own, just as I will never know the pain you may have experienced. What good is quantifying loss? What good is comparing? The right question to ask is not, "Whose is worse?" It is to ask "What meaning can be gained from suffering, and how can we grow through suffering?"

or little as you see fit. Not to minimize what happened to Amy, but I realize that her fate could have been a lot worse, Sittser's caution notwithstanding. Given her risky behaviors, she could have been murdered, violently hurt and left to suffer, enslaved, or simply disappeared. We know people whose loved one's overdose left them brain-dead, leaving the family to make a pull-the-plug decision, which seems worse. Even if Amy had survived the overdose, she still faced overwhelming odds in her disease.

I deeply miss the good Amy, and shudder to think how the diseased Amy's behavior could have harmed others going forward; for example, if someone else had been injured or died while under her care as a result of her use. It is a blessing that all of her car accidents were minor. And not to be crass, but I learned how you probably don't want your addict on your insurance driving your car, because in the event of an accident, you will be the one sued.

I've been asked whether I felt stigmatized as a result of how Amy died. Never. If others were disparaging, it was never to my face. I believe that when people heard how she died while receiving the shocking news that she had died, there was little room for stigma to tinge their reactions. Had I waited to disclose, rumor and stigma could have bred. I would encourage families to be forthcoming about overdose deaths to keep underscoring the enormity of this public health epidemic.

When one professional asserted that I was addicted to Amy's issues, my take was that I was doing my job as a caring and responsible mother. While an enormous amount of my energy did go into dealing with Amy's illness, it was not my sole focus. I enjoyed a fulfilling professional life, stayed fit, and had my running group with its poet laureate creative outlet. I maintained friendships over the decades and around the world. I kept writing my monthly letters. I adopted a dog. My years at BVMP resulted in meaningful connections with so many students, including Amy's friends. Taking care of my emotional health in these ways remains important as I grieve.

Perhaps the saddest, but ultimately most comforting, words came from my husband, who offered that maybe nobody could have helped Amy. The 3 Cs of Al-Anon reassure us that "we didn't cause the disease, we couldn't control it, we couldn't cure it." Psychiatrist Dr. Herowitz spoke in retrospect of Amy having a "malignant addiction." He noted how in his meetings with her she seemed to have a fascination with the world of drugs that exhibited in her eyes, and he suspected that he was not getting through to her. And as tough as it is to confront, some diseases, for some people, are fatal, including addiction. Psychiatrist Dr. Buprine said that ten percent of heroin addicts die every year. So if you do the math, after six and a half years, half of a given group of addicts is dead.

I asked my former colleague and good friend Lois, who grew up very street-smart, for her reflections. She said, "You trusted your daughter." For all my formal education, I lacked the smarts to know I was being lied to. Despite all my seeking help through professional sources, I didn't reach out to some close friends. Maybe I was embarrassed, expecting that the professionals would come through, or hoping that Amy would "outgrow" some of her behaviors, especially with education. I think back to my grandmother, who had to leave school after eighth grade to work as a domestic, but she made sure her children all graduated from college. She would remind them, "You may have the education, but I have the experience." She could spot a "no good rotten dirty stinker" from a mile away. I couldn't from across the table.

I also grew up with the eighth commandment, "Thou shalt not lie," and the fourth commandment, "Honor thy father and thy mother." I did not grow up being lied to, at least consciously, and I couldn't tell a lie to save my life. So I was totally out of my league with a daughter who wrapped me around her finger. When I was teaching, it was heartbreaking to see immigrant parents in pain about the decreasing influence they seemed to have on their children. I also lament how many parents of my generation are professionals who make decisions about the technologies and media messages in pop culture that can make parenting even more challenging.

The fact that I presented as a highly accomplished professional may have kept others from imagining I was struggling so much in parenting Amy. For example, my attempts at cell phone control never worked. Neither did meeting all her "friends." There had to be a better way, or was Amy going to see who Amy was going to see? Her adolescence had me incessantly deciding between "the lesser of two evils." I could prohibit her from using the car, but she was a good driver, and I preferred her driving than being a passenger of someone who might endanger her. She always complained that we lived in a "shack," didn't have a big-screen TV, and our house smelled like our three cats. Would remedying any of those have kept her home more? And would she simply have done more on our watch, as we discovered she had at least twice?

As Donna Latson Gittens wrote on July 5th, 2010, in a Boston Globe op-ed about life in an urban neighborhood, "Like any parents, we wanted to do well by our children. We set clear expectations and rules and enforced them because that's how families create the structured environment children need. Our rules included meeting our children's friends and their friends' parents—we were hovering before there were helicopter parents. Would we have behaved any differently if we lived in [a fancy suburb]? I doubt it. The parents I know in those communities act the same way." I thought my husband and I set clear expectations, but we proved inept at enforcing them. The rule about meeting friends and their parents was fraught with deception.

I'm most grateful to, and helped by, those who have been willing to share with me what we've learned, whether personally or professionally. But it still feels so unfair that we tried to get help but kept missing the mark. David Treadway, in his book, *Before It's Too Late*, asks, "When does therapy become potentially part of the enabling and denial system rather than part of the solution?" He adds, "Obviously, if slips continue to happen, there is something seriously flawed with the therapy. . . . The therapy itself may have become part of the problem." It's not clear how many of our practitioners had expertise working with families in a drug-abuse crisis, and I still question whether some should have recused themselves. Conversely, we seemed to get little from the sessions with the licensed alcohol and drug abuse counselor. It seems that the best chances of reaching someone with a drug problem may be a professional who is a recovering addict. In retrospect, I wish I had known to ask this qualifying question, "Are you in recovery?"

Much like a cancer patient sees an oncologist, someone with substance abuse issues should see an addiction medicine specialist. The progress in this field, coupled with neuroscience, is rapidly accelerating. I hope that within a few years, Amy's story will seem like it's from the "dark ages," much like cancer treatment only a few decades ago. I've also learned that treating adolescents is very different from treating adults, and urge readers seeking help for a child to tap the proceedings of the Joint Meeting on Adolescent Treatment Effectiveness (JMATE).

Addicts and their families need support. I remain aghast that only one of the numerous health professionals we worked with prior to Amy admitting she was an addict ever recommended A.A. or N.A. for her, or Al-Anon or Nar-Anon for us, not even the licensed alcohol and drug abuse counselor. The one who recommended twelve-step meetings for Amy was the social worker at the psychiatric hospital. As much as the facility made us uncomfortable overall, I may have underestimated their wisdom at the time.

While early intervention is important, there is the confidentiality balance: You want your kid to confide in the professional, yet if the kid thinks there's too much contact with the parents, they might not talk. After age eighteen with HIPAA privacy laws, parents are essentially relegated to being wallets, though releases can be signed. Before Amy's last pediatrician appointment in September 2009, I called the nurse and said I knew I couldn't talk with her due to HIPAA, but I was concerned that my daughter was injecting heroin and to please check for needle marks. One of Amy's providers now will not treat young adults unless they provide a release to involve their family, staying true to the diagnosis that addiction is a family disease. Kudos to him. I'll applaud any steps forward like this one as "progress, not perfection," an important concept of recovery often heard at twelve-step meetings.

As my husband noted after reading this manuscript, "With addiction you don't have the option of stepping back and saying, 'Teenagers will be teenagers and it will all work out.' This disease can end up taking your child's life, and you must fight it with all your power." Fighting it doesn't mean we can cure it or control it, much like cancer or diabetes, but just like with those diseases, you want the best care for your child. Yet I think back to when I spoke with the father of Amy's best friend, Audrey, and despite his assertion that "this is a battle we have to win," my family lost.

I've learned from Nar-Anon that we are ultimately powerless over the addict, which goes against our natural instinct as parents. I've never blamed myself for Amy's death, though it's human nature for "if onlys" to cross the mind. However, I was taken aback when a BVMP student asked me, "Do you regret bringing Amy home for Christmas?" I do wish that Circle Center had insisted that we visit her there instead.

Amy's psychology professor showed me the piece "Success" by Ralph Waldo Emerson. The next-to-last line reads "to know even one life has breathed easier because you have lived." We decided Amy's life was a success by paraphrasing "to know even one life still breathes because you have lived and died." One of my former students, who was a year ahead of Amy, commented that while Amy influenced so many people when she was alive, she may ultimately have more influence now, so please keep telling her story! I know Amy would want you to learn from what happened. If someone else had written a book like this a few years ago, I might not have had to write this one now—with, or without, my beloved Amy.

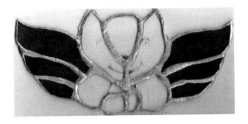

"Mom, I'm dead, stop worrying, relax."

Melissa
February 16, 2010

*Words that were in my head upon waking, **not** part of a dream*

Here is a talk I gave in Amy's memory at a candlelight vigil. It was held on a city common. Two of us who lost a child spoke, names of people who had died were read, and a small band played music. The weather was beautiful, albeit a bit windy for the candles. Close to two hundred people of all ages attended, sitting on rows of park benches in front of the gazebo.

One year ago today, August 6th, 2009, my twenty-year-old daughter, Amy, was at the Paul McCartney concert at Fenway Park with her dad. She had begged me to join them, but I felt too busy at work. A year ago tonight, she was making her dad a fifty-sixth birthday dessert: three layers of chocolate cake, with chocolate mousse in between, slathered in mocha mascarpone frosting. She had just finished a three-week microbiology course at BC, part of her nursing curriculum. She earned an A, scoring 108 on the first test, and "only" a 104 on the second.

But she was also scoring drugs. Big time. We knew she was on Suboxone, but she told us it was because of OxyContin. On November 16th, she brought me to meet her drug counselor, where she admitted that she was a heroin addict, needed to go to treatment, and would not be able to finish her semester. She entered detox the Saturday before Thanksgiving, rehab six days later, and a residential treatment house the Monday before Christmas.

We picked her up for a twelve-hour pass on Christmas Day, took her to the required A.A. meeting, retrieved her 90 minutes later, and after dinner her brother drove her back to her residential treatment house. We had had a picture-perfect Christmas. The next day, Geotown Hospital pronounced her dead at 6:00 p.m. from an overdose at her treatment facility. The ER had worked on her almost two hours and couldn't bring her back from her final speedball. She had allegedly scored drugs during the time of the A.A. meeting.

Nobody expected this outcome. She was young, had entered treatment voluntarily, had the support of her family, career goals, and so many wonderful friends. She wrote in her journal the day before Thanksgiving "I know the real Amy is inside me somewhere and I need to get her back...I'm sick of leading a double life." Further into treatment, she journalled, "I feel like the drugs have taken over my soul. What happened to the strong, motivated young woman I was last spring? The impending doom sets in as I realize my disease has never been this bad. I stand today as heroin's puppet. But just like they say, you can't scare an addict."

As our family followed Amy's coffin into church for her funeral, it struck me: what an awful way for her father to walk our daughter down the aisle. Amy's childhood friend had said, "I'll always remember Amy as a smart, beautiful, caring young lady and I'll always be proud to be her friend, and know that whether she knew anyone for five minutes or five years that she most definitely touched their heart."

As we took her serenity prayer card to the stores she frequented near her apartment, people remembered "Oh yeah, the tall skinny girl with the blue eyes who was always smiling."

My dear daughter Amy was my Red Sox fan, Celtics fan, runner, drummer, baker, and soul mate. I've learned that addiction doesn't care where you live. It doesn't care

... if your skin is dark naturally, or from tanning.
... if your eyes are earthy brown, or sky blue.
... if you mother has a GED, or a Harvard MBA.
... or if you're flipping burgers at Burger King, or studying nursing at BC.

Addiction is an equal opportunity disease. Every day, opiates kill two people a day in Massachusetts, and nationally more people now die of drug overdoses than from automobile accidents. As tragic as Amy's death is, I take comfort in knowing that she is now forever safe with her Creator, and her excruciating pain is over. But we miss her like crazy. And we have to make sure her death was not in vain. There is help out there we didn't know about, and there is hope. So I hope you will help anyone with a loved one in trouble to get the treatment they need. We cannot lose any more!

Resources

Resources are constantly changing. Here is a partial list that I have found helpful:

Support Groups for Families

http://www.al-anon.alateen.org is the national site, includes listings by state.

http://grasphelp.org/ Grief Recovery After a Substance Passing.

http://learn2cope.org/ Massachusetts group.

http://www.nar-anon.org/Nar-Anon/Nar-Anon_Home.html is the national site, includes listing by state. Some narateen groups are forming, such as http://naranonfl.org/wordpress/wp-content/uploads/2012/01/S-330-12-01-13-SponsoringaNarateenGroup.pdf.

http://www.parents4achange.net/ Connecticut group.

Sources of Referrals/Information—Government

http://archives.lib.state.ma.us/bitstream/handle/2452/46748/ocn466141823.pdf?sequence=1 The 2009 report of the Massachusetts OxyContin and Heroin Commission.

http://www.mass.gov/dph/bsas Massachusetts Bureau of Substance Abuse Services. Includes the 24-hour toll-free helpline http://www.helpline-online.com/index.html 800-327-5050.

http://www.drugabuse.gov/ National Institute on Drug Abuse (NIDA).

http://www.samhsa.gov/ Substance Abuse and Mental Health Services Administration.

http://teens.drugabuse.gov/ National Institute on Drug Abuse (NIDA) for teens.

http://www.whitehousedrugpolicy.gov/ Tabs include a long list of street drug names.

Sources of Referrals/Information—Nongovernment

http://www.casacolumbia.org/ National Center for Addiction and Substance Abuse. Many good resources and practical tips.

http://www.nbprograms.com/default2.asp New Beginnings. They include "Warning Signs" and "Responding" bullet points for teachers and parents.

http://www.drugfree.org/ This website was recently updated with sections on prevention, intervention, treatment, and recovery. You can subscribe to a weekly newsfeed at http://www.drugfree.org/join-together.

http://www.momstell.com/ Includes information on the National Family Dialogue.

http://www.moar-recovery.org/ Massachusetts Organizations for Addiction Recovery.

http://power-recovery.com/ Pennsylvania Organization for Women in Early Recovery.

http://jmate.org Joint Meeting on Adolescent Treatment Effectiveness. Conference presentations are archived.

Medical References

http://asam.org/ American Society of Addiction Medicine.

http://www.ceasar-boston.org/ Center for Adolescent Substance Abuse Research at Children's. Tells about the programs they offer.

http://www.mcleanhospital.org/patient/child/landing.php New program at McLean Hospital.

http://www.teen-safe.org/ Children's Hospital video clips of how parents can talk with children.

http://www.webmd.com/mental-health/alcohol-abuse/tc/teen-alcohol-and-drug-abuse-topic-overview.

Books and Articles

Benton, Sarah Allen. *Understanding the High-Functioning Alcoholic: Professional Views and Personal Insights*. Santa Barbara: Praeger, 2009. http://www.high-functioningalcoholic.com/.

Cataldi, Libby. *Stay Close: A Mother's Story of Her Son's Addiction*. New York: Martin's Press, 2009.

Clark, Diana. http://www.familyhealingstrategies.com/resources/ Includes an audiobook "What Love Looks Like" for parents of adult children struggling with addiction.

Mnookin, Seth. "Harvard and Heroin," Salon.com, Aug. 27, 1999.

Mnookin, Wendy. "My Son the Heroin Addict." Salon.com, Aug. 27, 1999.

Sheff, David. *Beautiful Boy: A Father's Journey Through His Son's Addiction*. New York: First Mariner, 2009. http://davidsheff.com/Home_Page.html.

Sheff, Nic. *Tweak*. New York: Ginee Seo Books/Atheneum, 2007.

http://www.hazelden.org This site also has a bookstore tab.

Questions to Ask a Facility Treating a Loved One Who Is Addicted

1) Before someone goes out on pass, do you have a document signed by the patient, facility, and family/significant other detailing expectations (for example, not seeing old friends, use of electronics)?

2) Do you drug test someone upon return from pass? If they claim they cannot produce a sample, do you give them fluids until they can?

3) If someone has relapsed, do you search their room for contraband? Do you notify the family? Do you have the patient sign medical orders or a healthcare proxy in the event of a relapse or overdose?

4) Do you hold the relapsee in detox or in another safe place for at least twenty-four hours of observation? Are "checks" by staff done at least every fifteen minutes?

5) Do you have Narcan available and staff trained to administer it? Do you have AEDs on site? Are staff trained to the latest cardiopulmonary resuscitation standards (such as if no mouthpiece is available, they still perform manual compressions)?

6) Do you have a minimum stay time in the facility before someone can go out on pass? Have you eliminated the sentimental lure of the holidays, birthdays, etc. when issuing passes, realizing these are just another day for someone trying to recover, especially in early recovery?

7) On what model, or on whose research, is your treatment model based and evaluated? (If they can't cite any research, that is probably not a good sign.)

8) Under whose auspices are you licensed or regulated?

Acknowledgements

The ultimate thanks go to Amy for writing her journals. I'm grateful for her high school teachers who helped her develop the confidence and skills to express herself as well as she did. They all bore their share of the late assignments that Amy tried to convince them to accept with that inimitable twinkle in her eye and those crumbs around her mouth. Her science and health teachers grounded and inspired her toward a promising nursing career. I thank her college professors who took her to the next level.

Dr. Boyd gently yet without hesitation urged me to publish Amy's journals upon first glancing at them less than three days after she died. My high school principal kept me in prayer and introduced me to author Nancy Kehoe, who shared wise guidance early in the project. Several other authors provided critical support at key junctures. Martha Fields generously consulted with ideas to jump-start the project, and Roberta Taylor helped me anticipate the work once the book was written. Sarah Allen Benton helped me better focus my messages, and David Sheff encouraged my efforts. Susan Schapiro, my high school teacher and friend, also urged me to write, and I am deeply sad that she did not live to see the published work.

I had to transform this manuscript from the book I needed to write into a book that others could read. I thank everyone who offered to review the drafts, including those who tried but found the task too difficult to complete. I'm most grateful for feedback from, and conversations with, reviewers including Meyer and Giuliana, Gino, Corinne, Isabel, Lily's mom, Audrey, my student informants, Amy's psychology professor, my first brother, and my husband; others not named in the book include my friends Cindy S., Ali M., Sandy H., Bill N., my student informant's mom, Byron's sister, Michael K., and relatives Joe N. and David C. I appreciate the efforts of my son and daughter, relatives O. and B., and friends George, Brad H., and Joanna H.

My b-school colleague and friend Barrie A. served as my "accountability buddy" through much of this project, and pushed me toward the final title for the book. She also facilitated the connection to attorney Eric Rayman, whose insight and expertise was exactly what I needed. School librarian Kathy A. was an invaluable sounding board and sanity-checker for many ideas.

I thank the clinicians who helped Amy along the way, and helped me better understand her story after she died. I am especially grateful for the nourishing conversations with Amy's friends who keep her memory alive and kicking, including Byron, Sherryl, Audrey, Tanisha, Lily, Ramona, and Claire. I hope that Patrick will reconnect.

The audiobook was made possible by the generosity and professionalism of Pam and Kevin McCluskey of Long Sought For Sound. Pam and I worked at the start-up in the early 1990s, and twenty years later she and her husband provide a recording environment that is technologically state-of-the-art, and I can't thank them enough for making it emotionally comfortable, as well. I'm also deeply grateful to my start-up colleague Steve for writing the music for "Amy's Song." Caroline Evans and Julianne Lowell provided prompt and professional copyediting, and Melissa and Jessika at Troy Bookmakers patiently guided me through publication.

Finally, I am indebted to my editor Laurel Lloyd, who has been a true companion on this journey. Our roots also go back to working at the high-tech start-up when Amy was a baby, and before her daughter (coincidentally, also Amelia) was born. Her conviction, adept editing, and brilliant ideas for design have produced a work that surpassed my dreams. I believe that even Amy is smiling with approval.

Amy's Signature Cake Recipe

Cake

Ingredients
1 package Devil's Food Cake Mix, preferably with pudding
1 cup sour cream OR Greek yogurt (to reduce calories)
3/4 cup water
1/3 cup oil
3 eggs

Directions
Heat oven to 350 degrees. Grease and flour three nine-inch round cake pans. In large bowl, combine all cake ingredients at low speed until moistened. Beat two minutes at highest speed. Pour into pans, bake approximately 20 to 25 min or until toothpick inserted comes out clean. Cool 15 minutes, remove from pans, cool completely.

Filling

Ingredients
1t unflavored gelatin
2T water
1 cup whipping cream
1/3 cup chocolate flavored syrup, or powdered cocoa for a less-sweet filling

Directions
In a small saucepan, soften gelatin in cold water. Stir over low heat until dissolved, set aside. In a small bowl, beat whipping cream at highest speed just until it begins to thicken. Gradually add gelatin and chocolate syrup or cocoa. Refrigerate about 30 minutes or until slightly thickened, stirring occasionally.

To assemble the cake, place one layer on a serving plate. Spread with half of the filling, top with second cake layer and spread with remaining filling. Top with remaining cake layer.

Frosting

Ingredients
1/4 cup cocoa
2-1/4t espresso powder
1-1/2 cup heavy cream
3/4 cup sugar (can use less to make it less sweet)
3/4t vanilla
6oz mascarpone

Directions
Combine all ingredients and whip; it takes a while to "set up" (don't lose faith!). Once it does, it's a matter of seconds until it's ready to spread. Keep refrigerated until serving time.

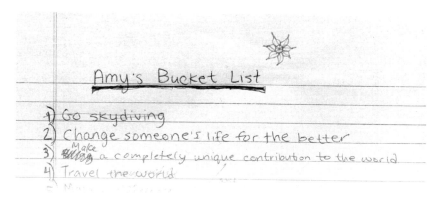

1) ~~Go skydiving~~

2) Change someone's life for the better

3) ~~Bring~~ Make a completely unique contribution to the world

4) Travel ~~the world~~

5) Make a difference

6) Touch someone's heart

7) Run a marathon

8) Find my spiritual awakening

9) Learn to play all sorts of instruments

10) Finish college and fulfill my potential

11) Try something new every day

12) Reconnect w/ friends + family and have meaningful relationships

13) See the sunrise from every state

14) Become and stay sober

15) Find pleasure in the simple things => The pleasure of what we enjoy is lost by wanting more